WHAT THE
BIBLE SAYS
ABOUT
THE HOLY
SPIRIT

WHAT THE
BIBLE SAYS
ABOUT
THE HOLY
SPIRIT

Russell Boatman

College Press Publishing Company, Joplin, Missouri

Library of Congress Catalog Card Number: 88-63252
International Standard Book Number: 0-89900-262-5

Table of Contents

DEDICATION

It seems particularly appropriate that this volume should be dedicated to my wife, Lutie. We are well into the golden years of our marriage, having reached that plateau as far back as August, 1985.

Jesus spoke of the Holy Spirit as "the Comforter" (*parakletos*). The term is derived from the preposition, *para*, (alongside) and the verb, *kaleo* (to call), hence (literally), one "called alongside." The word is translated "advocate" in I John 2:1. On the human plane, a good wife is a "paraclete" indeed — one called alongside to be both one's comforter and advocate.

Lutie is a daughter of the late Charles I. Kenney, a Christian preacher educated under the tutelage of such notables as John W. McGarvey, and Charles Louis Loos. To our union has been born three sons and a daughter, twelve grandchildren and two great grandchildren. Our marriage has thus been fruitful, genetically speaking, and with Lutie at my side throughout my ministry, now going on fifty-five years, our marriage has been fruitful for Christ and his church.

A Biblical proverb states it well, "Houses and wealth are an inheritance from fathers, but a prudent (Heb. *sakal* — understanding) wife is from Jehovah" Prov. 19:14. To that I say a hearty amen. As a pleasant surprise this dedication is hopefully being kept a secret, to be divulged the day the first copy of this publication is duly autographed and deservedly presented to Lutie, my "paraclete" — my comforter, my advocate (among my fellow mortals), my understanding wife from the Lord.

7

PERSPECTIVE: HAS THE HOLY SPIRIT UPSTAGED CHRIST?

We are living in a unique time frame in the history of the Christian faith. Were we to accept uncritically all that is being claimed by those professing to be leading the vanguard of spiritual renewal, one would have cause to wonder if the Holy Spirit has upstaged Christ. He seems to be the "in" person of the Godhead in this latter half of the present century.

This is not to say the Holy Spirit is personally responsible. He has not staged a coup. He has not usurped a place in heaven out of keeping with his role of subserviency to the Father and to the Son. Neither has he incited a demonstration on earth to capture for himself the praise and adoration heretofore accorded to Jehovah God and Jesus Christ.

However, the Holy Spirit, long relegated in Christian

literature and the thinking of the average churchman to a role of relative ambiguity, is today the subject of a plethora of literature, conclaves, seminars and seances unparalleled in Christian history. Except perhaps for the church at Corinth, not even the first century exhibits such a preoccupation with the person and gifts of the Holy Spirit as has come to characterize the burgeoning "charismatic renewal" of our time.

Undoubtedly, the general ignorance and wanton neglect of the Biblical teaching concerning the person and work of the Holy Spirit has contributed to the overemphasis of recent years. There is a saying that "nature abhors a vacuum and will rush in with something to fill the void wherever one is found." But an overemphasis can be as misleading, and as defective and destructive in terms of faith and practice as the de-emphasis of yesteryear. Let us note some specifics.

Prayer Addressed to the Holy Spirit

It is becoming increasingly popular to address prayers to the Holy Spirit. To do so is completely devoid of Biblical precept and precedent. No patriarch, no prophet, no priest, no apostle, in fact no one of record (of the Biblical record, that is) ever did.

We need not labor the point that it is proper to address prayer to Jehovah God, the father of our Lord Jesus Christ (and "our father who is in heaven" — to use an expression Jesus commended to us in the model prayer found in the sermon on the mount, Matt. 6:9ff).

It is also proper, though not common, to address prayer directly to Jesus. In the days of his flesh this was done often, and openly. Of that fact the four gospels bear witness. It is still proper to do so. At least Stephen did. In the throes of his martyrdom Stephen prayed, "Lord Jesus, receive my spirit." And again, "Lord Jesus, lay not this sin to their charge," (Acts 7:59,60).

It has been conjectured that this was a highly unusual thing, at best but a transitional stage employed perhaps while followers of Christ were not yet accustomed to his being away. But let it be noted that some three score years later the New Testament revelation virtually closes with a prayer addressed directly to Jesus: "Amen, come, Lord Jesus," (Rev. 22:20).

Of course the more common mode of prayer is "in Jesus' name." That is, by his authority. The phrase is not to be understood as a form of magical incantation, which when added to what we have said, spirit our prayers heavenward. But the point stands. No one of record (again we refer of course to the Biblical record) ever prayed to the Holy Spirit, nor did they pray "in the name of the Holy Spirit." But today there are those who do. Many do so unwittingly as they find themselves caught up in the catchy lyrics and tunes of our day.

Many prayer songs are addressed to the Holy Spirit. This has been true for many years. But upon being questioned it turns out that few were really aware of the implications of the lyrics and had no intention of actually invoking the Holy Spirit to answer "the prayers" verbalized in the hymns and choruses of which we speak. Consider the following examples. Who has not heard (and sung) this one:

> Spirit of the living God, fall afresh on me.
> Melt me, mold me, fill me, use me.
> Spirit of the living God, fall afresh on me.

Or this:

> Sweet Holy Spirit, sweet heavenly dove,
> Stay right here with us, filling us with your love.
> And for these blessings we lift our hearts in praise.
> Without a doubt we'll know that we have been revived
> When we have left this place.

Or this:

> Come, Holy Spirit, heavenly dove, with all thy quickening powers

11

Kindle a flame of sacred love in these cold hearts of ours.
In vain we tune our formal songs, in vain we strive to rise,
Hosannas languish on our tongues, and our devotion dies.
Come, Holy Spirit. Heavenly dove, with all thy quickening
  powers
Come shed abroad a Saviour's love that shall kindle ours.

Or this:

Holy Spirit, faithful guide, ever near the Christian's side,
Gently lead us by thy hand, pilgrims in a weary land.
Ever present, truest friend, ever near thine aid to lend,
Leave us not to doubt and fear, groping on in darkness drear.
Weary souls forever rejoice while they hear thy welcome voice,
Whispering softly, "Wanderer come, *follow me. I'll lead* thee
  home."

And this:

Holy Ghost with light Divine, shine upon this heart of mine.
Chase the shades of night away. Turn my darkness into day.
Holy Spirit, all Divine, dwell within this heart of mine.
Cast down every idol throne, *reign supreme, and thou alone.*

Need more be cited? Further examples are certainly not lacking.

Verily if this trend continues unchecked, particularly in view of the implications of the latter citation, it could be that the symbol of a dove may supplant that of the cross for a large segment of the church. It has well been said that were we to preach from the pulpit many of the things sung from the pews "the firing squad" would have their work cut out for them.

Worship Now Addressed to the Holy Spirit

The foregoing quotations make it evident that the Holy Spirit is now the recipient of worship. Again, there is neither Biblical command nor precedent. To worship Jehovah is a sacred duty incumbent upon every intelligent being. Even nature declares its maker's praise.

> The heavens declare the glory of God
> And the firmament showeth his handiwork
> (Psa. 19:1).

To worship Jesus, God's son, is likewise befitting, and due. He was worshipped openly and with Divine approval in the days of his flesh. Jesus never cautioned against it except when he perceived some were approaching him with unctuous flattery borne of ulterior motives. He is still a proper object of worship, adoration, devotion and heart-felt praise — even as God, the father. Consider these verses from the book of Revelation:

> Worthy art thou, our Lord and our God, to receive the glory and the honor and the power. For thou didst create all things, and because of thy will they were, and were created (Rev. 4:11).

Now hear this as the heavenly chorus turns its attention to the one sitting at the right hand of the majesty on high.

> Worthy is the Lamb that hath been slain to receive the riches, and wisdom, and might, and honor, and glory and blessing (Rev. 5:13).

And (according to the next verse) every created thing which is in heaven, and on the earth and under the earth, and on the sea, and all things that are in them, was heard saying:

> Unto him that sitteth on the throne, *and unto the lamb*, be the blessing, and the honor, and the glory, and the dominion, for ever and ever (Rev. 5:14).

There is more, but this should suffice to prove the point. Jehovah

13

and Jesus are objects of adoration and devotion in heaven and on earth.

But what about the one sitting at the left hand of God? (the Holy Spirit). Ah, where is it said that is where he is, or was, or ever shall be? It is a plausible conjecture that that is where he was before he was sent forth from the Father when Christ returned, (John 14:26; 15:26). But nowhere do the Scriptures say this, nor even imply it. Since the formulation of the doctrine of the trinity by the Council of Nicea, 325 A.D., this has been a common conjecture. "But what saith the oracles of God?" (Rom. 11:4).

I am inclined to view the Godhead in the general context of the trinitarian formula. But I am constrained to agree with the dictum of Thomas Campbell, as expressed in the sixth of the thirteen propositions which are at the heart of his famed 1809 *Declaration and Address*.

> Although inferences and deductions from Scripture premises, when fairly inferred, may be called the doctrine of God's holy Word, yet are they not formally binding upon the conscience of Christians farther than they perceive the connection, and evidently see they are so; for their faith must not stand in the wisdom of men but in the power and veracity of God — therefore no such deduction can be made terms of communion, but do properly belong to the after and progressive edification of the church. Hence it is evident that no such deduction or inferential truths ought to have any place in the church's confession. (*Declaration and Address*, Bethany Press, p. 46.)

To return to the point at hand, it deserves to be noted that John, in his first epistle, branded as "the antichrists" the Ebionite gnostics who denied the essential deity of Jesus as the Son of God, eternal with the Father (I John 2:18-27. Note particularly, v. 22). But though the gnostics denied also the Holy Spirit's eternal and essential oneness with the Father, John does not scourge them on that count. No one could accuse John of a low view of the Holy Spirit, but nowhere does John accord to the Holy Spirit the place of honor and worship and unity with the Father which he attributes to Christ.

When John was given a revelation of "the things which are (i.e. the things that then were) and the things which shall come to pass hereafter," he was instructed to "write the things which thou sawest," (Rev. 1:19). He really tried. Surprisingly, at least it was to me, he made no mention of seeing the Holy Spirit, per se. In fact the name(?) (or expression) "the Holy Spirit" does not even appear in the whole of the book of Revelation.

Revelation contains fourteen (14) references to "the spirit" in that somewhat ambiguous form of reference — beginning with 1:10 where he says, "I was in the Spirit on the Lord's day" and closing with 22:17: "And the Spirit and the bride say come." (Note: the capitalizing of the letter "s," in our familiar English versions is a translator's choice. The Greek text does not do so.) Between 1:10 and 22:17 ambiguous references to the spirit appear eleven times. Three texts (4:2; 17:3; 21:10) are akin to 1:10. John speaks of himself as being carried here and there "in the spirit." Seven of the eight remaining references are akin to 22:17. Each of the letters to the seven churches closes with the expression, "He that hath ears to hear, let him hear what the Spirit saith to the churches" (2:7,11,17,29; 3:6,13,22). Revelation 14:13 also makes mention of the Spirit speaking.

In nine (9) other texts the word *pneuma* appears. In 11:11 John speaks of the "spirit" of life. In 13:15 *pneuma* is translated "life." Three texts make reference to "unclean" spirits, spirits "of devils" and "foul" spirits, (16:13,14; 18:2). In 19:10 the "testimony of Jesus" is equated with "the spirit of prophecy."

Four texts remain to be noted: 1:4; 3:1; 4:5; 5:6. These contain the phrase: "the seven spirits of God." This expression is commonly viewed as denoting the personhood of the Holy Spirit. That could be. But, historically speaking, such an identification is a post-Nicene Council interpretation.

Revelation 1:4 can be readily assimilated into the trinitarian concept of the Godhead. However, in 3:1 Christ is described as the one "having the seven spirits of God." That muddies the waters, so to speak, but is not wholly irreconcilable. In 4:5 the seven spirits of God are identified as the seven lamps burning "*before* the throne," hence at least it can be said that the Holy Spirit is not enthroned at the left hand of the Father, opposite Christ, the Lamb of God.

The fourth passage, 5:6, speaks of Christ in the figure of "a lamb that had been slain, having seven horns, and seven eyes which are the *seven spirits of God* sent forth into all the earth." The latter phrase mitigates against the interpretation which equates the seven spirits with the seven angels sent to the seven churches of Asia. Only by lifting the latter out of their historical setting, leaving the first part of John's assignment (the writing of "the things which *are*") unattended can that identification be made.

The overriding point in the foregoing review is that even if the seven spirits of God are identified with the person of the Holy Spirit the fact remains that nowhere in the book of Revelation, nor elsewhere in the Scripture, is the Holy Spirit said to be worshipped by anyone at any time. And nowhere is it intimated that any one has, or should, pray to the Holy Spirit, as though there are *two* "mediators between God and man," (Cp. I Tim. 2:5). But today that is coming to be commonplace, and to challenge either practice is to be castigated as unspiritual, or having a low view of the Holy Spirit, or both!

The Role of the Holy Spirit

This brings us to the fundamental question. What is the role of the Holy Spirit? Any answer this early in our study must be, necessarily, provisional. For the purpose of this prefatory statement we do well to limit our answer to the reference data Jesus shared with his disciples on the eve of his crucifixion. John, chapters 14-16, constitute Jesus' only discourse of record on the person and work of the Holy Spirit. If the information he shared with them was sufficient to meet their need that early in the mission to which Christ had called them, surely the same information should suffice for a prefatory inquiry as to the role of the Holy Spirit, according to Christ our Lord.

In John, chapters 14-16, Jesus apparently was responding to questions arising in the minds of the disciples. There should be no gainsaying what he had to say. He was not being coy, nor evasive. He said some very specific things. The "voice of majestic glory" which Peter, speaking on behalf of his fellow apostles, declared: "we ourselves heard when we were with him on the mount" (See II Pet. 1:16-21) is a voice that echoes down the corridors of time and should be heard to this day. The substance of that "voice" (the fact that Jesus is in truth the very Son of God, beloved of the father) constitutes the authority whereupon it was commanded: "Hear ye him." That solemn command has in no sense been rescinded. Let us then hear what Jesus shared with his disciples that fateful night in the upper room. Several verses are especially pertinent:

> I will pray the Father and he shall give you another Comforter, that he may be with you for ever, even the Spirit of truth, whom the world can not receive: for it beholdeth him not, neither knoweth him; for he abideth with you, and shall be in you (John 14:16,17).

At first glance this passage seems a bit contradictory. Was the promised "Comforter" (Gr. *parakleton* — lit., "one called alongside") already "abiding" (Gr. *menei*) with them? The verb tense used here is the present indicative. The key, though not all that obvious, is in the next phrase: "he shall be (Gr. *estai*) with you." Jesus' ministry was inaugurated with a visible descent of the Holy Spirit upon him, (Luke 3:22) and ensued "in the power of the Spirit" (Luke 4:14, cp. 4:16-21). As surely as the disciples were "with" Jesus throughout his Spirit-filled and Spirit-led ministry, and he "remained" (*menei*) with them, in a sense the Holy Spirit was with them. But in the passage before us Jesus is

17

promising much more. The Holy Spirit is to be (*estai*) with them personally, and indeed came so to be.

At the very least Jesus is saying that they will come to know the Holy Spirit experientially, not just from observation. And that they did, beginning with the Holy Spirit's descent upon them on the day of Pentecost. Consider also another verse:

> But the Comforter, even the Holy Spirit, whom the Father will send in my name, He shall bring to your remembrance all that I said unto you (John 14:26).

From this we may conclude that at least one of the promised roles (functions) of the Holy Spirit would be that of a "memory-jogger." The disciples did not carry notebooks and most certainly were without benefit of modern recording devices. The rabbinical method of rote memorization would suffice to a degree, but not to the degree provided by the inspiration of the Holy Spirit, (cp. II Pet. 1:19,20). Consider also another key from Jesus' farewell discourse:

> But when the Comforter is come, whom I will send unto you from the Father, (even) the Spirit of truth, which proceedeth from the Father, he shall bear witness of me (John 15:26).

Note the unity that is implied between the Father and the Son. The first passage noted (14:16) says that the Father would give the Holy Spirit. The second (14:26) states he (the Father) would send the Holy Spirit "in Jesus' name." Here, (15:26) Jesus states that he himself will send the Holy Spirit, but will send him "from the Father" (who will be the one "giving" the Holy Spirit who is to be sent). Note also the purpose for which the Holy Spirit is sent: He is sent "to bear witness" of Christ, not of himself. This is even more clearly stated in the next text to be noted:

> I have yet many things to say unto you; but you cannot bear them now. Howbeit when he, the Spirit of truth, is come, he shall guide

you into all the truth: for he shall not speak from himself; but what things soever he shall hear, (these) shall he speak: and he shall declare unto you the things that are to come (John 16:12,13).

From these words of Christ we may conclude that the Holy Spirit was not sent to be either an innovator or an originator, no, not even an imitator. He most certainly was not to upstage Christ. He was not to bring glory, or even attention, to himself. His role *testify* was to call attention to Christ, to Christ's words and to his person. He was not sent into the world to be a "free spirit," so to speak — that is, to say whatsoever he might be of a mind to say. He was sent into the world to declare what he was directed to speak. At no point in the Biblical record can it be demonstrated, or even so much as intimated, that the Holy Spirit found that role too restrictive, or demeaning.

CONCLUSION

Our chief point, or intent, in what we have said is not to discount the validity of an in-depth study of the Holy Spirit, else this book would not have been painstakingly researched nor submitted for publication. After some two score years and ten of wrestling with the issues addressed in this publication, the greater part of it in the crucible of the college classroom, where students are not only priviliged but encouraged to exercise that brand of nobility for which the Bereans were commended (Acts 17:11), I am persuaded that truth is seldom found at either extreme. This is certainly so concerning many of the issues which will be set forth in the pages which follow.

I would greatly regret if the cold staid theology of the Holy Spirit in which I was indoctrinated should become the accepted norm. But it would be equally tragic were the subjectivism of the neo-Corinthian movement to emerge as the normative doctrine of the Holy Spirit. In saying this I have unveiled myself, showed my hand, betrayed my position, so to speak. Perhaps so, but not absolutely. I am still open to new insights. As for the candor which shall be expressed throughout may I simply say that I have not tried to be cagey. I am not comfortable with diversionary tactics in the discussion of Biblical doctrine.

On many topics that will be treated I will likely present views that may offend extremists on both sides, but not by intent. My purpose is to be neither contentious nor conciliatory, menacing nor mediatorial. To communicate what the Bible says about the Holy Spirit is my overriding objective. Readers, you are invited, as you read, to "search the Scriptures daily to see whether these things are so" (cp. Acts 17:11).

EXCURSUS: WINDS OF CHANGE

On the day of Pentecost there came a sound from heaven as of a rushing mighty wind and a new era in the drama of redemption swept in. Today, winds of change are again sweeping in. But the question arises: is the sound thereof "from heaven"? If so, the winds we "hear about" but do not hear, are indeed "winds of change."

On Pentecost there was but one gospel proclaimed. Those who were pricked in the heart by what they heard inquired what they should do. All received the same answer. And all who "gladly received the word" obeyed the same command. And they were all added that day to the same fellowship of the redeemed. And so it was also with those who continued to be saved thereafter (Acts 2:41,47).

If the current spate of "neo-Pentecostalism" is indeed what its proponents claim it to be — Pentecost Renewed — it is assuredly a "new" pentecost, not the original restored, nor anything quite like it. For whereas once all who heard the Word heard alike, and readily recognized the dialect in which they heard it, today bedlam has broken loose. The "tower of Babel" has replaced the church that Jesus promised to build, and apparently neither he nor God could care less what one believes or practices, as long as one "credits" what is said and done to the "overwhelming and/or infilling" (baptism) of the Holy Spirit.

Witness. Some two decades ago my wife and I received complimentary tickets to a banquet and program sponsored by the Full Gospel Christian Business Men's Fellowship International (FGCBMFI). The place was Miss Hulling's Cafeteria, downtown St. Louis, Missouri. We were assured we would not be asked to sign or buy anything, only to come and hear their testimony. That we did, and to their credit the FGCBMFI kept their promise. The food was excellent, the program entertaining.

The Master of Ceremonies was a handsome, charming young Presbyterian. Early on in the program he gave his personal testimony. It served as a prototype of those to follow. 1) His ministry had become routine, unproductive. 2) At a point when he was about to resign he had been invited to a meeting much like the one to which we had come, and "experienced" a spiritual renewal. 3) The "charismatic revival" was the "new and true ecumenical movement." The latter phrase became a recurring refrain as the program progressed.

A Methodist youth minister from the Haight Asbury sector of San Francisco was the next to testify. He too was once "caught up in a dreary routine." But he too had experienced the renewing of the Holy Spirit and was now a part of the "new and true ecumenical movement."

He was followed by a Southern Baptist evangelist from Texas. He had the physique of a lineman of the Dallas Cowboys. His "spirited" testimony followed the same pattern and echoed the same key phrases. The diversity of practice and doctrine of Southern Baptists as compared to Presbyterians and Methodists came to my mind as I heard him avow that he had received the same confirming sign and was now a part of the same "fellowship of the Spirit" — though still a Southern Baptist.

The next to testify was an older man dressed in the clerical garb of an Anglican priest. He stated he was a Vicar, no less. He explained the title signified he had charge of his "own cathedral." His testimony followed the same pattern and played on the same key phrases.

Then came a papist. Though yet gowned as such his testimony was to the effect he was now a member of a movement more "universal" than Roman "catholicism." Nonetheless, from his dress and sphere of employment it was obvious he was continuing his role in the "not so new and not so true," and not so encompassingly "catholic" movement.

The keynote speaker of the evening was a venerable liberal of the Disciples of Christ, a man whom I had not seen since my seminary days. My first thought was that he was about the last person I would have expected to see that night. As he picked up on the introductory line used by those whose testimony preceded his I could readily see why he would be a candidate for some kind of spiritual renewal. At that two questions were raised in my mind. Ponder them, and their spin-offs.

1. Why was there no one on the program who had enjoyed the privilege of a long-term Spirit-led ministry of the Word? Why are those who have never given a serious thought to denying, or turning aside from the faith, those who have never been minded to quit the ministry, who have never second guessed their high calling, those whose hearts cry out in the words of Paul, "Woe is me, if I preach not the Gospel" — all such as they and the multitudes of "laymen" who have lived lives unplagued by hidden sin and doubt, who come down to the hour of death with a faith radiant, triumphant and expectant — why are such as these excluded from the so-called new and true ecumenical movement? Have they been deceiving themselves, and others? Is that the reason they have been denied the gift of tongues (the "litmus test" of the baptism of the Holy Spirit, according to the parlayers of the cultist dogma)?

2. How is it that persons whose doctrines and practices are at odds with one another — not to mention being at odds with the Scriptures — how are they "one in the Spirit"? Note the conglomerate represented by the claimants of spiritual renewal — immersionists contending for believer's baptism versus pedobaptist effusionists, a champion of salvation by faith only and a bead-counting papist, an Augustinian, a Calvinist, a Wesleyan, and a man professing to eschew creedal systems that Christ may be the center of one's faith. Yet one in the Spirit?

From the beginning it was not so. From the dawn of the Christian era committed Christians have reckoned that what the New Covenant Scriptures teach and command, Christians are to believe and obey. They have not always agreed as to what is taught therein, else there would not be so many denominations. But the fact there are bears witness to the fact concerned believers have been persuaded that those professing to follow Christ are obligated to propose truth and oppose error. Were they right about that? Or are doctrine and practice but an expendable option? "What saith the oracles of God?" (Rom. 11:4).

Jesus, in his sermon on the mount, raised the question, "Why call ye me, Lord, Lord, and do not the things I say?" (Luke 6:46). Matthew has reported him as saying (7:21-23),

> Not everyone that sayeth unto me, Lord, Lord, shall enter into the kingdom of heaven, but he that doeth the will of my father who is in heaven. Many will say unto me in that day. Lord, Lord, did we not prophesy by thy name, and by thy name cast out demons, and by thy name do many mighty works? Then will I profess unto them, I never knew you. Depart from me, ye that work iniquity.

Not the Gospels only, but every New Testament document underscores Jesus' warning. The following list is representive, but by no means exhaustive:

> Acts 2:38-42; 5:32; 7:51; 18:5,6; 20:18-21,26-31; Romans 1:5; 6:16-18; 16:26; 16:17,18; I Corinthians 1:10-13; II Corinthians 6:14-18; Galatians 1:6-9; 5:4; Ephesians 4:4-7; Philippians 3:1-3; Colossians 2:8,16-20; I Thessalonians 4:7,8; II Thessalonians 1:7-10; 3:14; I Timothy 4:1-7; II Timothy 4:1-5; Titus 1:10,11; 3:1-10; Hebrews 2:1-4; 10:26-31; James 1:22; 2:14-25; I Peter 4:17-20; II Peter 2; I John 2:18-23; 4:1-6; II John 7-9; III John 9-11; Jude 3-7,17-23; Revelation 22:18,19.

The words of the apostle John, written in a time of confrontation with the gnostic heretics is equally appropriate today, whatever form heresy may take. Writing on behalf of the apostolic witness he wrote:

> Beloved, believe not every spirit, but prove the spirits, whether they are of God: because many false prophets are gone out into the world . . . . He that is of God, heareth us. He that is not of God heareth us not. By this we know the spirit of truth and the spirit of error (I John 4:1-6,7).

That rule has not been rescinded. It is still the ultimate test of truth. To this day it remains true: "By this (the New Testament witness to the teaching of the apostles) we know the spirit of truth and the spirit of error."

SECTION ONE
BASIC
BIBLICAL
DATA

1

PREVAILING PROBLEMS AND ETYMOLOGY

ANALYSIS OF THE PREVAILING PROBLEM

One scarcely needs to be told that the study of the Holy Spirit is commonly viewed as confusing, and an understanding of the subject nigh impossible. It is of little wonder that this is so. The subject is shrouded in mystery. This is due in part to:

1. *The awesomeness of the terms — holy, spirit* and *ghost.*
a) Holy is a word that communicates a kind of "stand-offish" aura. Moses was drawn as a moth to a flame by the wonder of the burning bush that was not consumed by the flame which enshrouded it. He is recorded as saying: "I will turn aside now, and see this great sight, why the bush is not burned" (Exod. 3:3). But when God said, "Draw not hither. Put off thy shoes from off thy feet, for the place whereon you stand is holy ground" (v. 5) Moses likely felt as though he were walking on eggs. Both the Hebrew *kadosh* and its Greek counterpart *hagios* communicate

the idea of something "set apart" for God's use. When Isaiah heard the seraphim crying one to another, "Holy, holy, holy is Jehovah of hosts" (Isa. 6:3), Isaiah cried out in consternation, "Woe is me, I am undone" (Hebrew *danah*, "cut off," v. 5). In the lingo of our day Isaiah was saying, "Oh no, I've had it!"

b) *Spirit* is a term that is not quite so threatening for it has a variety of meanings, some of which are rather mundane. But when it is used as a noun and then capitalized it takes on an other-worldly aura suggesting intangible beings with whom we are not sure we can cope.

c) *Ghost* presents a more serious communication problem. Even those somewhat inured by its frequent usage in the KJV find the term commonly suggests the imagery of Halloween — hobgolins and sheet-enshrouded spooks at midnight. Of these things we will say more when we note the history and development of the key words involved in this study.

2. *The vagueness of the basic vocabulary as to specific reference*, that is, the variety of meanings common to the word spirit also contributes to the problems inherent in this study. The problem roots in all three classical languages which have contributed to the vocabulary of our English translation. The Anglo-Saxon root of our NT vocabulary also becomes involved when the term "ghost" is added to the admixture.

a) The adjective "holy" does not present a serious problem. As used in the Scriptures with reference to things Divine its basic meaning — separate, or set apart (cp. sanctified) has a dual application. It is used in contrast to: 1) God's "good" spirit, as opposed to evil spirits, (Neh. 9:20, vs. Sam. 16:23), and 2) of things "set apart: for sacred use, as opposed to that which is common, ordinary, vulgar."

b) The nouns "spirit, Spirit," confront us with a serious problem of identification. Our English word is derived from the Latin *spiritus* and is used to translate the Hebrew *ruah* (and *neshamah*) and the Greek *pneuma*. Each of the three languages uses a single word for wind, breath, and spirit (the life principle of man and

30

beast alike, and of God). So, too, of the Anglo-Saxon *gast* ("ghost" of the KJV).

What we have just affirmed probably needs a bit of clarification. The tri-fold application of the Hebrew, Greek and Latin words of which we speak likely developed somewhat as follows:

1) *Wind.* Whatever one's race or culture, men become aware early on of a vast invisible reality — an entity or force which surrounds us but cannot be seen or grasped. Only the effects of its presence can be discerned. Trees bend and sway. Objects are picked up, without hands, and are hurtled through space or sent tumbling across the landscape. One can feel the unseen force pressing against one's body to a degree comparable to the observed effect upon various objects being moved about. But the entity itself seems to be without substance. In the language of the OT literature (Hebrew) it is called *ruah*. In the language of the NT documents (Greek) it is called *pneuma*. In Latin the word for it is *spiritus*. We speak of it as the wind.

2) *Breath.* Mankind everywhere is likewise conscious of a somewhat similar entity within our bodies. Our chests rhythmically rise and fall. When we are "winded" from over-exertion or have had "the wind knocked out of us," our lungs struggle to regain an ample supply of the unseen substance which surrounds us. We call the process breathing, hence speak of being out of breath when we are winded. In Hebrew, Greek and Latin alike the same word which is used with reference to the wind is used also to speak of the "breath" of breathing creatures.

3) *Spirit.* The words which are used primarily to speak of the wind and secondarily of breath are used in both Testaments to speak also of a metaphysical entity. They are used in a theological sense with reference to supernatural beings of all kinds, and of the intrinsic nature of the supreme Being of the universe — Jehovah God, no less.

Since the translators of the King James Version leaned heavily upon the Latin Vulgate, many words of Latin derivation, particularly theological terms, were carried over into what is still

31

called (despite repeated and somewhat extensive revisions) the Authorized Version. Theological language therefore to this day is rooted deeply in the King James verbage. Our word spirit is a shortened form of the Latin *spiritus* which the Vulgate translators used to translate the Hebrew *ruah* and the Greek *pneuma* when they were persuaded those words had reference to the innate essence of supernatural beings, whether of God, angels, devils or demons. Two hundred and thirty-two (232) times *ruah* is so translated and *pneuma* is so translated one hundred and seventy (170) times.

When prefixed by *hagios* (holy) the King James translators reverted to a word stemming from the old Anglo-Saxon word *gast*. It is thus that the Holy Spirit is called the Holy Ghost in the KJV. Incidentally, the word ghost (even when capitalized and prefixed by the word Holy) is not as hallowed a term as some have been led to believe. Like *ruah*, *pneuma* and *spiritus*, the Anglo-Saxon *gast* (ghost) also was used to speak of the wind, of breath, and of spirits of all kinds — of man, beasts, angels, demons, devils and deity.

We do well to bear in mind the variety of meanings of our word "spirit," and the equally varied meanings of the several words in the Hebrew, Greek and Latin MSS which are translated by the English word spirit (and Spirit). Only from the context can it be determined when *ruah* and *pneuma* should be translated spirit, and when the same should be capitalized.

3. *Were all this not enough the sheer volume of Biblical references contributes to the complexity and perplexity of the subject at hand.* Over seven hundred and eighty times our word spirit appears — sometimes capitalized, sometimes not so. In the OT it is prefixed three times by the Hebrew word *kadosh* (translated by our English word "holy"). In each case "holy" is uncapitalized (even in the KJV) in that the word is an adjective, and is a part of a descriptive phrase used with reference to an attribute of God rather than as a name or title. In our English NT the phrase *tou hagiou pneumatos* is routinely rendered "the Holy

32

Spirit," being reckoned as the title of a Divine personage.

While we are noting the sheer volume of references that need to be considered, let us note their distribution. The Hebrew word *ruah* appears in the text of the OT three hundred and eighty-three (383) times. Two hundred and thirty-two (232) times it is translated "spirit." In the remaining one hundred and fifty-one (151) usages it is translated "wind" ninety (90) times, "breath" twenty-eight (28) times, and by such words as air, anger, blast, cool, courage, mind, quarters, tempest, vain, and windy in the other thirty-three verses in which the word *ruah* appears.

The Greek word *pneuma* appears in the NT some three-hundred and eighty-three plus (383 +) times. MS variations account for the differences in the count. The King James version, heavily dependent upon the Western text (Textus Receptus) which in turn was heavily dependent upon the Latin Vulgate, accepts the validity even of such a passage as I John 5:7 (KJV, cp. ASV, RSV, NIV, *et al*). With some seven hundred and sixty-six references to be considered our work is cut out for us.

And as though that were not enough, the Hebrew word *neshemah*, which is also translated "spirit" (twice, Job 26:4; Prov. 20:27) appears twenty-one times in the OT, and like the word *ruah* it is also translated breath, and blast, and soul. That raises the count to some seven hundred and eighty (780) texts which need to be read in context for a complete analysis of our subject.

Were we to add to the admixture the Hebrew word *nephesh*, which is commonly translated "soul" — four hundred and twenty-eight (428) times to be exact, and translated "life" an additional one hundred and nineteen (119) times — along with a miscellany of one hundred and forty-two (142) other usages, for a total of six hundred and eighty-eight (688) texts altogether, we would raise the count of possible relevant references to a number well in excess of one thousand, five hundred, (1,554 if I have counted aright). It bears repeating, the sheer volume of textual data contributes to the complexity of the subject before us.

By way of summary, the word spirit appears in all but nine (9) of the OT books and in all but two (2) of the NT documents. The exceptions are: (OT), Leviticus, Ruth, Esther, Song of Solomon, Amos, Obadiah, Jonah, Nahum and Habbakuk; (NT), II, III John.

4. *Whenever a subject is ignored, or reputed to be too deep for a common mortal to understand, an opening is made for charlatans and sensationalists to step in.* The doctrine of the Holy Spirit has not just been ignored. The Holy Spirit has often been belittled. Even among those professing to "speak where the Bible speaks" some have been so blatant as to say, "one can buy all the Holy Spirit available to us from off the Bible shelf of the nearest bookstore."

The tragedy is that reactionary movements generally go to the other extreme. Such has been the case with the modern "spiritual renewal" or "charismatic" movement. Again take note of the prologue to this volume: "*Has the Holy Spirit Upstaged Christ?*" and the appended Excursus: "Winds of Change." Truth is rarely found at the extremes to which reactionary movements would have us go.

Is one minded to ask, "Why were not the writers of the Scriptures not more specific? Why did they use words from the common vocabulary of their times which had so many different meanings?" One might as well ask, "Were they writing today in the more extensive and often more technical language of our time, would they (could they) have done differently?" Is not what we have noted as true in our tongue as it was in the language of the people to whom the Scriptures were originally addressed?

WE HAVE THIS TREASURE IN EARTHEN VESSELS

It is ever true, even in the best of our modern translations, "we have this treasure in earthen vessels" (II Cor. 4:7). Whenever God addressed men, whether through angels or

34

through the direct inspiration of the Holy Spirit, he spoke in the contemporary mode of the recipient(s) addressed. The multitudes on Pentecost who heard the apostles "speaking in other tongues as the Spirit gave them utterance" (Acts 2:4) asked in wonderment: "Are not all these that speak Galileans? How hear we every man in our own *language* (Gr. *dialectos*) the mighty works of God?" (2:6). Of what avail were it otherwise?

Most of the words of our language have many shades of meaning, and often even diverse meanings. We have to take in context what is said or written today to determine precisely what was, or is, communicated.

It is significant that Jesus in his discourse on the regenerating work of the Spirit (John 3:3-12) risked leaving the impression that the operation of the Spirit is as vagrant as the winds. Whether he spoke to Nicodemus in his native tongue, Aramaic Hebrew, (the most likely possibility) or in Koine Greek, (the prevailing language of the Mediterranean world, or in Latin (the least likely choice) the word he would have been obliged to use with reference to what we call "the Spirit" would have had the varieties of meanings we have noted earlier. Nonetheless, Jesus even compared the Spirit to the winds which blow, increasing the risk to which we have alluded. But he credited Nicodemus (and us) with the common sense to see where the analogy ceases.

As we have taken pains to note, mankind from of old has sensed that beyond our own spirits there are other spirits — and a greater spirit above all. As our spirits control a myriad of actions which reflect our nature, and purpose — some good, some bad, some helpful to others, some hurtful and even destructive — so there must be spirits, even a Great Spirit, at work in the world which surrounds us. Even in this "age of enlightenment" mankind still so reasons. Thus storms, floods, earthquakes, volcano eruptions and the like are called "acts of God." Paradoxically the beneficent forces at work in our sphere are ascribed to "Mother Nature."

The Scriptures provide no basis for a pantheistic view of

nature. God is not merely "in all, and through all, but *over* (Gr. *epi*, above) all" (Eph. 4:6). In the following chapter, "The Teaching of the Old Testament Concerning the (Holy) Spirit," we will take note of those Scriptures which provide the basis for the New Testament disclosure of the person and work of the Holy Spirit.

We perhaps would do well to note forthrightly the manner in which the word "spirit" and "ghost" came to replace the Hebrew *ruah* and the Greek *pneuma* in the King James Version of the Scriptures. *Pneuma* has been carried into our language via such words as pneumonia (wind disease) and pneumatic (of, or pertaining to, wind). Hence drills driven by air pressure are called pneumatic drills. In the early days of the "horseless carriage" inflatible rubber tires were called pneumatic tires. This was in keeping with one of the primary meanings of the term *pneuma*, and its Hebrew counterpart, *ruah*.

The term "spirit" entered into the vocabulary of the church via the Latin Vulgate. As previously noted, *spiritus* is the Latin equivalent of the Hebrew *ruah* and the Greek *pneuma*. At the time the KJV was "authorized" (i.e., made the authoritative text of the Anglican church by King James), England was barely two generations removed from papal control. The break had very little to do with doctrinal matters. It was almost totally politically motivated. Thus the Latinized theological terms, familiar to the populace via their long term use of the Latin Vulgate, were carried over into the King James version with but few exceptions. Thus spirit supplanted *ruah* and *pneuma* almost everywhere those terms appear in the original text of the Scriptures.

The most notable exceptions are those texts in which a colloquial expression for dying supplanted the simple statement that the person expired. "Ghost" first crept into the Scriptures via the adoption of an Anglo-Saxon idiom for dying — "gave up the ghost" (A.S. *gast*). The pattern was set when the KJV translators saw fit to say of Abraham (Gen. 25:8), Ishmael (v. 17), Isaac (35:29), and Jacob (49:33) that they "gave up the ghost."

The translators again resorted to the idiom when they came to the book of Job. (See Job 3:11; 10:18; 11:20; 13:19; 14:10; cp. Jer. 15:9 and Lam. 1:19). Thus it is that the death of Jesus is depicted in the KJV in the same idiomatic language. (See Matt. 27:50; Mark 15:37,39; Luke 23:46; John 19:30.) So also with the death of Ananias and of Sapphira, Acts 5:5,10, and of Herod, Acts 12:23.

An exception was made in the case of Stephen who asked the Lord Jesus to "receive his spirit" (*pneuma*), and added, "Lord Jesus, lay not this sin to their charge," and thereupon "fell asleep," (Gr. *ekoimethe*, Acts 7:59,60).

The ASV, from which one can normally expect a more literal rendition, has perpetuated the error except for two of the four gospel accounts of the death of Jesus. (See Matt. 27:50 and John 19:30).

Whether the expression in question gave rise to the notion there are disembodied spirits (or ghosts) wandering about that have been "given up" but never received into the nether world, or whether that notion gave rise to the translation is a moot question. In either case the phrase needs to be deleted from our vocabulary as unwarranted and misleading. It is to the credit of the translators of the New American Standard Version (NASV) and the New King James Version (NKJ) and the New International Version (NIV) that they have uniformly expunged the "halloween" phraseology in favor of a more literal translation. Even the hallowed phrase, "the Holy Ghost" has been deleted from the NKJ in the interests of a more accurate rendering of the inspired text.

Aside from a dwindling array of intransigent holdouts and the singing of the classical "Doxology," the Holy Spirit may at long last be called by a term more compatible with the inspired text.

2

THE TEACHING OF THE OLD TESTAMENT CONCERNING THE HOLY SPIRIT

The scholastic term for the study in which we are engaged is pneumatology. The word is coined from the Greek words *pneuma* (spirit) and *logos*. The latter, when added as a suffix to a noun, denotes "the doctrine (or study) of." Thus theology is the doctrine, study, of *theos* (God). Christology is the doctrine (study) of *christos* (Christ, "the anointed one"). Hence pneumatology, technically, is the study of pneumata (spiritual beings, or spiritual phenomena — particularly the doctrine concerning spirits intermediate between God and man, including the spirit of God and of Christ, and/or of the Holy Spirit).

In its common usage, pneumatology focuses on the study of the Holy Spirit. But were we to so limit the term in a study of the teaching of the Old Testament concerning the Holy Spirit there would be little to say, except by way of inference. Surprisingly, at least it was to me, the term *Holy Spirit* is found nowhere in the Old Testament. Even the adjectival phrase (his, thy) *Holy Spirit* is found but three times in the whole of the OT.

In David's penitential psalm (Psa. 51) the phrase "thy *holy* Spirit" is used in a parallellistic context as a synonym for God's presence:

Cast me not away from thy presence, and take not thy *holy* Spirit from me (v. 11).

Twice (Isa. 63:10,11) we find the phrase, "his (God's) *holy* Spirit":

But they rebelled and grieved his *holy* Spirit; therefore he was turned to be their enemy. Then he remembered the days of old, Moses and his people, saying . . . where is he that put his *holy* Spirit in the midst of them?

The next closest expression is found in a public prayer of Nehemiah:

Thou gavest thy *good* spirit to them (Neh. 9:20).

This expression stands in contradistinction to an expression we find in such passages as Judges 9:23, I Samuel 16:14,15,23, 18:10, 19:9, wherein it is said that "evil spirits from God" were sent in punishment for disobedience. From this we are not to suppose that God has a corps of evil spirits standing by whom he calls upon from time to time to do his "dirty work" for him. God's beneficence visited good upon Israel. His righteous judgments brought punishment. The resulting effect of God's actions provided the basis for the appraisal in each case.

Such manner of speaking illustrates a point of view that has been called "Hebrew verticalism." Since God is omnipotent, omniscient and omnipresent, nothing happens of which he is not aware, nor beyond his control. His blessings are the working of his innate spirit of goodness and lovingkindness (mercy), Psa.

40

23:6. His judgments are the working of subordinate elements of his spirit — moods, so to speak, evoked by intransigent evil, which, under provocation, God ultimately answers in kind.

The teaching of the Old Testament concerning the Holy Spirit is inferential, at best. We have grown accustomed to the reading of the New Testament doctrine of the Holy Spirit back into the sundry references to the spirit of God, the spirit of Jehovah, his Spirit, etc., which are found in the Old Testament. By the same token we have grown accustomed to reading back into the New Testament the Nicene formula which was given creedal status at the Council of Nicea, 325 A.D. That practice, at both levels, deserves at least to be re-evaluated. This will be done in a subsequent chapter: "The Doctrine of the Trinity."

RELATIONSHIP OF THE SPIRIT TO GOD

Old Testament pneumatology is generally summarized under four headings: A. The relationship of the Spirit to God. B. The relationship of the Spirit of God to the external world, C. The relationship of the Spirit of God to man, and D. Special problems.

The relationship of the Spirit to God involves texts which seem in some cases to suggest an identification and in others to suggest a distinction. A classic example is a text which we have previously mentioned: Isaiah 63:10,11, (cp. v. 14).

> (v. 10) But they rebelled, and grieved his *holy* Spirit: therefore he was turned to be their enemy, and himself fought against them. (v. 11) Then he remembered the days of old, Moses, and his people, saying, Where is he that brought them out of the sea with the shepherds of his flock? where is he that put his *holy* Spirit in the midst of them? . . . (v. 14) As the cattle that go down into the valley, the Spirit of Jehovah causeth them to rest: so didst thou lead thy people, to make thyself a glorious name.

Committed trinitarians, while allowing that verse 10 would

seem to refer to God's personal umbrage at Israel's rebellion and his personal retribution against them, yet see in verse 11 a distinction between God and "his holy Spirit" which (earlier) he had "put in the midst of them." Verse 14 seems to again suggest an identification of "the Spirit of Jehovah" ("his holy Spirit"?, v. 10, v. 11) and God himself. At no point did the Hebrew people make a distinction. It remained for the post-Nicene theologians to do so. Again we remind the reader that this facet of the study will receive more extended consideration in a subsequent chapter, "The Doctrine of the Trinity."

1. Psalm 139:7-10 definitely suggests an *identification* of the Spirit of God with God himself. The passage is a classic example of a poetic style called parallelism. It is so called because the second line paraphrases, or contrasts, or completes, or in some other manner relates to the thought expressed in the first. The form exhibited by Psalm 139 is called synonymous parallelism in that the second line of each couplet repeats the thought of the first line but uses different words. The writing style is an aid to interpretation by virtue of the fact that if the sense of one line is not clear the other may be readily discernible. In verse 7 of Psalm 139, for example, "thy (God's) Spirit" is readily seen as a synonym for God's "presence":

(7) Whither shall I go from thy Spirit? Or whither shall I flee from thy presence?

(8) If I ascend up into heaven, thou art there: If I make my bed in Sheol, behold, thou art there.

(9) If I take the wings of the morning and dwell in the uttermost parts of the sea:

(10) Even there shall thy hand lead me and thy right hand shall hold me.

Psalm 51:11, noted earlier, likewise identifies God's "holy Spirit" with his very "presence." But in such a passage as Gen. 6:3 ("And Jehovah said, My Spirit shall not strive with man for ever") we do not have a parallelistic couplet to aid us. Thus interpreters differ as to whether God is speaking of Himself or of another "person" within the sphere of Deity whom NT writers speak of as "the Holy Spirit." The Hebrew people were not so minded. But since the canonizing of the Trinitarian doctrine by the Nicene council Genesis 6:3 has more often than not been read in the light of Paul's exhortation in Ephesians 4:30: "Grieve not the Holy Spirit of promise." Thus a distinction between God himself and his Spirit is often read into the passage.

2. However, there are texts which seem to suggest a *distinction* between God and the Spirit. Genesis 1:2 states concerning the primordial earth that it was "waste and void, and darkness was upon the face of the deep, and the Spirit of God moved upon the face of the waters." In a public prayer of Nehemiah, previously mentioned, Nehemiah paid tribute to God's goodness, saying, "Thou gavest also thy *good* Spirit to instruct them, and withheld not thy manna from their mouth, and gave them water for their thirst." As previously noted, this text is capable of other interpretation in the context of Hebrew verticalism, but it can also be reconciled with the implications of such a passage as II Peter 1:19-21.

Psalm 104:29,30 can readily be linked with Genesis 1:1,2 and interpreted as suggesting a distinction between God and his Spirit.

Thou hidest thy face, they are troubled.
Thou takest away their breath (*ruah*), they die.
Thou sendest forth thy Spirit (*ruah*), they are created.
And thou renewest the face of the ground.

The classic words of Zechariah 4:6 are worthy of note. Jehovah is recorded as communicating with Zechariah, and the prophet writes concerning the message received: "This is the word of Jehovah unto Zerubbabel, saying: Not by power, nor by might, but by my Spirit, saith Jehovah of hosts."

43

Time and space do not permit a review of the scores of OT passages in which the Hebrew word *ruah* is used in a context in which God's relationship to man and the world about us is spoken of. Nor is it likely that any significant gain would accrue from the effort. The texts we have cited are those generally selected by champions on both sides of the question before us. None are so clear as to settle the inquiry beyond any shadow of doubt.

RELATIONSHIP OF THE SPIRIT OF GOD TO THE EXTERNAL WORLD

Many texts speak of the operation or presence of the Spirit of God in connection with the external world — the created order of the heavens and the earth.

1. Early on in the creation account, Genesis 1:2 states that "the Spirit of God moved (that is, was hovering) upon the face of the deep." The Hebrew *merachepheth* expresses the agitative spirit exhibited by a mother hen while either incubating her eggs or fostering her young. Its use here likely suggests a vital force exerted upon the primordial sea wherein the Genesis record states the first terrestrial life forms appeared.

2. Psalm 104:30 offers to Jehovah this word of praise: Thou sendest forth thy Spirit, they (God's created order, both the mundane creation and man) are created: thou renewest the face of the ground." From this we learn he is both the creator and sustainer of the created order. Paul personalized this fact when he informed the Athenian philosophers that God not only "made the worlds and all things therein" but "in him we live, and move, and have our being" (Acts 17:24,28). In Colossians 1:16-18 we are told that Christ shared in the work of creation and now shares in sustaining the created order. "In him all things consist" (Gr. *sunistemi* — cohere, hold together). Thus we have a foundation stone for a trinitarian concept of the Godhead (Col. 2:9; Rom.

1:20).

3. The Spirit of God is said to make the earth fruitful. The Old Testament makes many allusions to the fruitfulness of the earth. Isaiah 32:15 associates at least the restoration of the earth's fruitfulness to the renewing or pouring forth of the Spirit of God. Isaiah 35, one of the many beautiful psalms of praise in the book of Isaiah, amplifies what is said in Isaiah 32:15. Psalm 107:33-43 notes that the reverse is equally true. When God's Spirit ceases to "strive with men" (Gen. 6:3), that is to say, when he abandons them to walk in their own chosen ways, their fruitful fields may be ridden with pestilence and drouth, and become barren wastelands, and the people reduced to hunger and want. These observations lead to the next facet of the work of the Spirit as seen in the Old Testament.

THE RELATIONSHIP OF THE SPIRIT OF GOD TO MAN

1. Preeminently, the Spirit of God was *the agent or medium of man's creation*. At least this was true at the point that the man whom God formed of the dust of the earth was imbued with the life principle — breath (Hebrew, *neshemah*, Gen. 2:7, cp. Job. 33:4). The passage in Job suggests this may have been true of the body also, or is true in the forming of our bodies in our mother's womb. The latter suggestion poses problems with respect to malformed fetuses and the stillborn and may well be pressing poetic language too far. Job 33:4 reads: "The Spirit (*ruah*) of God hath made me, and the breath (*neshemah*) of the Almighty giveth me life. Hebrew verticalism is apparent in this text.

Isaiah 42:5 attributes the breath (*neshemah*) of our bodies, and our spirit (*ruah*) to God, the creator. Moses and Aaron, (Num. 16:22) in an intercessory prayer addressed God as "the God of the spirits (*ruah*) of all flesh," beasts as well as man. They too have (are) "living souls" (*nephesh chaiyah*, Gen. 1:30; 7:15,22). Zechariah addressed God as the one "who formeth the spirit (*ruah*) of man within him" (Zech. 12:1).

2. *The agent for man's restoration and redemption.* Genesis 6:3, a text we have already had cause to consider, informs us that God's Spirit serves as an agent for man's restoration. But even the Spirit of God "will not strive with men for ever." Peter speaks of the time frame to which Genesis 6:3 has reference (one hundred and twenty years) as "the long suffering of God" in which we "waited in the days of Noah while the ark was a preparing" (I Pet. 3:20). The verb translated "strive" (*dun*) appears only twice in the OT. Job (19:29) warns that "wrathful ire brings the punishment of the swords, that you may know there is a *judgment.*" In the days of Noah it brought the awesome judgment of the flood.

David's penitent psalm (51) focuses on the redemptive aspect of God's holy Spirit, as he prayed (vv. 10,11):

> Create in me a clean heart, O God: and renew a right spirit within me. Cast me not away from thy presence and take not thy *holy* Spirit from me. Restore unto me the joy of thy salvation and uphold me with a willing spirit.

Cp. Psalms 143:10,11.

> Teach me to do thy will, for thou art my God: thy spirit is good. Lead me in the land of uprightness. Quicken me, O Jehovah, for thy name's sake: in thy righteousness bring my soul out of trouble.

Several of the messianic prophecies of Isaiah focus on the role of the Spirit in the redemptive work of Christ. See Isaiah 11:1-5; 42:1-8; 44:1-4; 48:12-16; 59:15b-21; 61:1-4; 63:10-14. The first and the last of the series of predictions reads as follows:

> (1) There shall come forth a shoot out of the stock of Jesse, and a branch out of his roots shall bear fruit: (2) and the Spirit of Jehovah shall rest upon him, the spirit of wisdom and understanding, the spirit of counsel and might, the spirit of knowledge and of the fear of Jehovah: (3) and his delight shall be in the fear

of Jehovah; and he shall not judge after the sight of his eyes, neither decide after the hearing of his ears; (4) but with righteousness shall he judge the poor, and decide with equity for the meek of the earth; and he shall smite the earth with the rod of his mouth, and with the breath of his lips shall he slay the wicked. (5) And righteousness shall be the girdle of his waist, and faithfulness the girdle of his loins (Isa. 11:1-5).

(1) The Spirit of the Lord Jehovah is upon me; because he hath anointed me to preach good tidings unto the meek; he hath sent me to bind up the broken hearted, to proclaim liberty to the captives, and the opening of the prison to them that are bound; (2) to proclaim the year of Jehovah's favor, the day of vengeance of our God . . . (Isa. 61:1,2, cp. Luke 4:17-19).

Among Ezekiel's messianic prophecies we find these familiar words predicting the role of the Spirit in the messianic age:

(26) A new heart will I give you, and a new spirit will I put within you: and I will take away the stony heart of your flesh, and will give you a heart of flesh. (27) And I will put my Spirit within you, and cause you to walk by my statutes, and ye shall keep my ordinances, to do them (Ezek. 36:26,27).

Thus it is written: "Not by power, nor by might, but by my Spirit, saith Jehovah of hosts" (Zech. 4:6).

3. *The impartation of skills and wisdom for God's service* is also ascribed to the Spirit of God. The Old Testament is replete with examples of this function of the Spirit.

a) In the construction of the tabernacle and the vestments of the priests, and later in the building of the temple, endowed workers were assigned to the tasks for which they were thus prepared. In Exodus 28:3 Moses was instructed:

Thou shalt speak unto all that are wise-hearted, whom I have filled with the spirit of wisdom, and they shall make Aaron's garments, to sanctify him, that he may minister unto me in the priest's office.

In Exodus 31:3-5 God informed Moses concerning Bezalel,

47

the son of Uri, of the tribe of Judah:

> I have filled him with the Spirit of God, in wisdom and in
> understanding, and in knowledge, and in all manner of workman-
> ship, to devise skillful works, to work in gold, and in silver, and in
> brass, and in cutting of stones for setting, and in carving of wood,
> to work in all manner of craftsmanship.

We may conclude that the Spirit of God equipped and qualified Bezalel for the office of construction foreman. From the verses which follow (6,7) we learn that Ohaliab of the tribe of Dan, was to be his chief assistant, and that a number of "wise-hearted men" in whom God "put wisdom" were likewise qualified for service. The fact is repeated in Exodus 35:30-35, with the additional information that the work force included skillful textile workmen also — the embroiderer, workers in blue, in purple, in scarlet, in fine linen, and weavers. Chapters 36-39 detail the various facets of the project. Note the closing words: "And Moses saw all the work, and behold, they had done it as Jehovah had commanded, even so had they done it: and Moses blessed them."

In the building of the temple the same phenomenon is again cited, but not so extensively. In I Kings 7:13,14 we learn that Hiram, "a man filled with wisdom and understanding and skill," was brought from Tyre to head up the temple project. From II Chronicles 2:13,14 it may be inferred that Hiram came by his skills as an apprentice to his father. Hiram's father is described as a man "skillful to work in gold, silver, brass, iron, stone, timber, as well as in textiles of blue, purple, crimson, and fine linen, and also to grave any manner of engraving, and to devise any device." This would suggest he inherited his abilities. But are not even inherited talents gifts of God?

b) Powers were also conferred by the Spirit of God upon the judges and certain kings of Israel, especially those who served as defenders of the nation militarily. An oft repeated phrase in the

book of Judges reads: "the Spirit of Jehovah came upon . . . ."
See Judges 3:10 (Othniel), 6:34 (Gideon), 11:29 (Jephthah),
13:25; 14:6,19; 15:14 (Samson).

The same phrase appears three times in the story of King
Saul. See I Samuel 10:6,10; 11:6. In I Samuel 16:13 the phrase
again appears in the account of the anointing of King David.
Significantly the next verse (v. 14) states that "the Spirit of
Jehovah departed from Saul and an evil spirit from Jehovah
troubled him."

The expression, "an evil spirit from Jehovah" occurs eight
times in the OT, once in Judges (9:23) where such is said to have
been visited upon Abimelek. Seven times in I Samuel the affliction is reported as visited upon or lifted from Saul
(16:14,15,16,23a,b; 18:10; 19:9). (Cp. II Kgs. 22:22,23 where
God is said to send forth "lying spirits.") This problem area has
been touched upon and will be addressed later.

c) The power to prophesy was also mediated through the
Spirit. Abraham is the first person to be specifically designated in
the OT as a prophet, (Gen. 20:7). However, Jude states that
"Enoch, the seventh from Adam, prophesied" (Jude 1:14).
Noah, whom Peter describes as "a preacher of righteousness" (II
Pet. 2:5), was a prophet in the classical sense of the term in that
he predicted both the time and extent of the flood that was to
wreak God's judgment upon his generation.

A prophet, whether called *nabi* (Heb.) or *prophetes* (Gr.), is
primarily a spokesman. That the Hebrew term may be so defined
is illustrated by the context of Exodus 7:1,2. When Moses tried to
beg off from his assignment, insisting it was beyond his capability,
God told him to relate to his brother Aaron what he had just been
told and have Aaron tell Pharaoh, noting: "Aaron shall be thy
prophet" (Exod. 7:11).

The Greek words transliterated prophet, prophecy, prophesy
are derived from the preposition "pro" (for) and the verb
"pheteo" (to speak). Since the ability to predict the future is more
striking than speaking ability per se, the prophetic office is

popularly conceived as being primarily predictive — not merely foretelling. However, most of the Divine revelation that has come down to us via the Scriptures is primarily a resume of their preaching and historical reporting. Moses, for example, wrote the Pentateuch, comprising one fourth of the OT, but consisting generally of historical narative interspersed with legal sections. Predictive sections are few and rare. Yet Moses is designated by none less than Jehovah as a prophet exemplar (Deut. 18:15-18).

One readily calls to mind Isaiah and Jeremiah when the prophets of Israel are mentioned. But the extensive documents which bear their names are primarily historical narrative and proclamation. Neither inspiration nor the prophetic office are limited to the prediction of future events.

d) The prediction of the future operation of the Spirit is an important factor of the OT teaching concerning the Spirit. Two facets of that revelation deserve special mention. 1) The Spirit of God would be particularly manifested through the Messiah. This has already been noted but bears repeating. Isaiah, the great messianic prophet, was the most eloquent spokesman. Such passages as Isaiah 11:1-5; 42:1-4, and 61:1-3 bear rereading. 2) Also noteworthy is the prediction that in the Messianic age the Spirit, in keeping with the universality of the Messiah's mission, would be "poured out upon all flesh," i.e., without respect to race, or gender, and upon both old and young. Note the eloquent statement to that effect in the passage Peter cited on Pentecost.

It shall come to pass in the latter days that I will pour out my Spirit upon all flesh; and your sons and your daughters shall prophesy, your old men shall dream dreams, your young men shall see visions: and also upon the servants and upon the handmaidens in those days I will pour out my Spirit . . . . And it shall come to pass that whosoever shall call upon the name of Jehovah shall be delivered (Joel 2:28,29,32a).

Under the old covenant the Holy Spirit was not "poured out."

50

It was dispensed in careful "measure." (The common expression was, "The Spirit of Jehovah came upon . . . ." (See Jdgs. 3:10; 6:34; 11:29; 14:6,19; 15:14; I Sam. 10:10; 11:6,13). While the Holy Spirit was "upon them" they were empowered to perform mighty deeds. Under the New Covenant the Holy Spirit is "poured out" and is promised to indwell and abide with all who call upon the Lord in the obedience of faith. Note again the promise as stated by Joel, and interpreted by Peter, Acts 2:38,39. Cp. Eph. 1:13,14; 3:14-19; Mark 1:8; I Cor. 12:13, etc.

For additional reference data see the Appendix: *Spirit in the Old Testament: Instrument of God's Action*, by Dr. James D. Strauss, Lincoln Christian Seminary, Lincoln, Illinois.

3

THE TEACHING OF THE NEW TESTAMENT CONCERNING THE HOLY SPIRIT

The New Testament writers, like their Old Testament counterparts, made no effort to set forth a theology of the (Holy) Spirit. They did not attempt to define, describe or precisely identify the Holy Spirit. At best, pneumatology is that branch of theology which arises out of an attempt to search out, classify and systematize the Biblical references to various happenings attributed to the agency of the (Holy) Spirit.

Such happenings are sometimes attributed to God himself, via such expressions as 1) "the spirit of God" (Gen. 1:2; Ezek. 11:24b; Matt. 3:16; I John 4:13, etc; used 13 times in the OT, 15 times in the NT) or "the spirit of Jehovah" ("the Lord": KJV, NIV) — used 20 times in the OT, (e.g. Jdgs. 3:10). Cp. NT., Luke 4:18, Acts 5:9; 8:39; II Cor. 3:17,18. 2) "the Spirit of Christ" (Rom. 8:9; I Pet. 1:11; of Jesus, Phil. 1:19) and "the spirit of his Son" (Gal. 4:6). 3) "the Holy Spirit" (85 times in the NT, 89 times in the KJV). 4) Ambiguously — "the Spirit," used scores of times in both testaments, from Gen. 1:2 to Rev. 22:17.

Throughout, the focus of such references is upon the action, the thing accomplished, the purpose served. As noted in chapter two, if the resultant effect brought unpleasant consequences the visitation was viewed as "an evil spirit from Jehovah." Note: The small case "s" is used in each instance, and the spirit is said to have been "from," not "of" Jehovah. We read of "his good Spirit," and "his holy Spirit," but never "his evil Spirit," or "the evil spirit of Jehovah," or "of God."

References to the Holy Spirit are proportionately more numerous in the New Testament than in the Old Testament. Of the seven hundred and eighty times the word "spirit" appears in our common English translations, approximately one half of the references are found in the much smaller confines of the New Testament. And when the references are narrowed down to the usage of the term, "the Holy Spirit" and its nearest Old Testament equivalents, "his (God's) holy Spirit" (Isa. 63:10,11) and "thy (God's) holy Spirit" (Psa. 51:11), the ratio becomes almost thirty to one in favor of the New Testament.

It is then from the New Testament one should expect to learn more fully of the office and work of the Holy Spirit, particularly the role of the Holy Spirit in the Christian era. The role of the Holy Spirit as set forth in the New Testament may be summed up under two heads: a) as it relates to Christ, and b) as it relates to the church.

THE ROLE OF THE HOLY SPIRIT AS IT RELATES TO CHRIST

1. The birth of Christ is attributed to the instrumentality of the Holy Spirit. Matthew states succinctly: "Now the birth of Jesus Christ was on this wise: When his mother Mary had been betrothed to Joseph she was found with child of the Holy Spirit" (Matt. 1:18, cp. 1:25). That, Matthew proceeds to explain, came

to pass in fulfillment of a prophecy spoken by the Lord through Isaiah. The prophecy alluded to, (Isa. 7:14) makes no mention of the role of the Holy Spirit, or the Spirit of God, or of Jehovah, but a supernatural birth calls for a supernatural progenitor. New Testament writers, with the advantage of hind sight, as well further revelation via the inspiration of the Holy Spirit, often see more in Old Testament happenings and predictions than the data specifically stated therein. Luke 1:26-38, particularly v. 35, supplements Matthew's account, providing the oft specified second (or more) witness. (See Num. 35:30; Deut. 17:6; II Cor. 13:1; etc.)

In Luke's account of Mary's sojourn to the house of Elizabeth, her kinswoman, the wife of Zachariah, (Luke 1:39-56) the role of the Holy Spirit in the birth of Christ again receives mention. Elizabeth, who had been barren, was in the sixth month of a long-awaited pregnancy. At Mary's salutation "the babe leaped in her womb" and Elizabeth was "filled with the Holy Spirit" (v. 41). Moreover, Zacharias her husband is also said to have been "filled with the Holy Spirit" (v. 67). This revelation often comes as a surprise to those who have been taught that phenomenon began with the descent of the Holy Spirit at the birth of the church (Acts 2), and was generally restricted to Christ and the twelve apostles. Thus some are surprised to learn that it was prophesied of John the baptist that he would be "filled with the Holy Spirit, even from his mother's womb" (Luke 1:15).

If John the baptist was filled with the Holy Spirit from his mother's womb it might be reasonable to assume such was true of Jesus also. Surprisingly, however, this is nowhere said of him. Aside from his conception, the next mention of the Holy Spirit's direct role in the life of Christ is at his baptism (of which we shall speak later). For the present, be it noted that Christ's holiness is nowhere attributed to Mary. Jesus' holiness, wherever mentioned, is attributed rather to the agency of the Holy Spirit (Luke 1:35; 3:22; etc).

2. The presentation of Christ in the temple is the next inci-

dent in the life of Christ in which the Holy Spirit is recorded as being at least indirectly involved. It is said of Simeon, a devout man looking for the consolation of Israel, that "the Holy Spirit was upon him" (Luke 2:25) and that "it had been revealed unto him by the Holy Spirit" that "he should see not death before he had seen the Lord's Christ" (v. 26).

In the wake of Simeon's prediction concerning the child (vv. 29-32), Anna, a venerable prophetess, "gave thanks unto God, and spake of him (Jesus) unto them that were looking for the redemption of Jerusalem" (vv. 36-38). The role of the Holy Spirit is not mentioned but in the context it would seem to be implied.

3. The boyhood of Jesus receives scant mention in the Gospel narratives. In fact, of the whole of Christ's life prior to his baptism and the onset of his ministry at age thirty, only about seven events or days of Christ's life are as much as mentioned. a) We have mention, of course, of his birth and the visit of the shepherds to whom the angel of the annunciation appeared (Luke 2:8-20). b) On the eighth day of his life he was circumcised according to the requirements of the law (Luke 2:21), and c) on his fortieth day he was presented in the temple, as required by the law (Luke 2:22ff). d) Mention is made also of the visit of the wisemen, likely some time after his birth and the events we have just noted. Contrary to our Christmas pageantry they did not come to the manger-stable but "to the house where the young child (not the babe) lay" (Matt. 2:1-11). In view of several incidental facts mentioned in the account it could be conjectured their visit was weeks removed from the night of his birth. e) Following the visit of the wise men Joseph was divinely warned to "take the young child and his mother and flee to Egypt" (Matt. 2:13). f) Later, Joseph, upon learning of Herod's death, was divinely directed (Gr. *chrematistheis*) to return (Matt. 2:22,23). Divine communication is implicit in each of the six events in Jesus' life that have been chronicled thus far. g) At age twelve we have recorded the temple episode (Luke 2:41-52). The role of the Holy Spirit might be inferred from the report of the boy Jesus'

sagacity, but no such mention is found in the narrative.

4. The next eighteen years are years of silence. Thus, out of the first thirty years of his life only seven distinctly identifiable days of Jesus' life are mentioned. We have no hint as to how, or if, his life was influenced by the Holy Spirit during those maturing years. Not until he reached the age of thirty (Luke 3:23), at which point of time he came of age according to the culture of his time, did Jesus begin his public ministry.

5. Jesus' baptism marked his entry into the work for which He was sent. Immediately the role of the Holy Spirit surfaces, dramatically. All four gospels record his baptism and the descent of the Holy Spirit upon him (Matt. 3:16,17; Mark 1:9-11; Luke 3:21-23; John 1:31-34; Cp. Acts 10:38). Several aspects of the event deserve special notice:

a) The descent of the Holy Spirit upon Jesus is reported in the language of similitude. It was the Holy Spirit, not a dove, that descended upon him and abode with him. The form of the descent was as the descent of a dove. Moreover, for the sake of realism and identification of the person of whom the voice from heaven was speaking, the Holy Spirit, for that special occasion, took dove-like "bodily form." John says the Holy Spirit thereafter "abode with him" (John 1:31-34). But there is no intimation that Jesus went about thereafter with an apparition resembling a pigeon nesting in his hair or nestled upon his shoulder.

b) In that John the baptist, up to that time, was the central figure in the spiritual renewal that was ensuing, the audience might have assumed the voice from heaven was speaking of John himself, had not the descent of the Holy Spirit, synchronized with the voice from heaven, taken a bodily form and descended upon Jesus. Otherwise, John's disclaimer, (Luke 3:16,17) might have been brushed aside as a modesty on his part.

c) The Gospels' account of the baptism of Christ introduces a new element in the New Testament doctrine of the Holy Spirit and of baptism. Though John is said to have been "full of the Holy Spirit from his mother's womb" (Luke 1:15), the baptisms he performed carried no promise of the Holy Spirit as an accessory, accompaniment or an accrual thereto. But he announced it would be quite the opposite with the baptism that would be inaugurated by Jesus. He would baptize in the Holy Spirit (Matt. 3:11,12; Mark 1:8; Luke 3:16,17; John 1:33).

Following the baptism Jesus received at the hands of John, Jesus was soon reported to be "making and baptizing more disciples than John," but with the explanatory note that "Jesus himself baptized not, but his disciples" (did so), John 4:2,3. It was not, however, at this time that John's prediction was fulfilled. That awaited the birth of the church and the inauguration of the gospel of the death, burial and resurrection of Christ.

In Christ's commission to his disciples, as he was about to be taken into the heavens, he commanded them to "go into all the world and preach the gospel to all the nations, baptizing them into the name of the Father and of the Son and of the Holy Spirit" (Matt. 28:19). Is this not worthy of notice? 1) At the baptism of Jesus we have the only instance in recorded (Biblical) history that the Father, Son and Holy Spirit were manifested simultaneously. 2) The only commandment in all the Scripture that is ordained to be performed into (Gr. *eis*) the name of the Father, Son and Holy Spirit is the baptism ordained by Christ, (Matt. 28:19) and 3) the only commandment which carries the direct promise of "the gift of the Holy Spirit" (Acts 2:38,39) is the baptism which is enjoined upon us in the great commission of Christ. Jesus, though sinless, was baptized to "fulfill all righteousness" and received in that very hour the Father's most overt approbation.

d) The bestowal of the Holy Spirit constituted a public and formal sign of Christ's Messianic office. The Jews should have understood that right readily. 1) Their priests were anointed with oil, a generally recognized symbol of the Holy Spirit (Exod. 28:41; 29:2; 40:13-15; Lev. 4:3,5,16; 6:20,22). 2) The kings were anointed when set in their office (I Sam. 9:16; cp. 10:1; 16:13; I Kgs. 1:39; cp. Psa. 2:2; 23:2). 3) The prophets were anointed for their office (I Kgs. 19:16; Ezek. 16:9). Jesus, who is at once our prophet, priest and king was anointed for his high office (Isa. 61:1-3). In fact the title, messiah, literally means, "the anointed one."

6. Jesus' temptation is said to have ensued upon having been led of the Spirit into the wilderness for the express purpose of being tempted of the devil (Matt. 4:1,2). Note that neither God nor the Holy Spirit is said to have tempted him, (see James 1:13), but he could scarcely be our kinsmen, after the flesh, unless he were "tempted in all points like as we are" (Heb. 2:14-18; 5:9). But neither could he be our saviour, were he not "yet without sin" (Heb. 4:15).

7. Jesus' miracles were accomplished through the power of the Holy Spirit. Luke's narrative is the gospel of the working of the Holy Spirit in and through the life of Christ. a) In Luke 2:25-35 Luke relates in some detail the presentation of Christ in the temple for the rite of purification. Therein it is written: "And behold, there was a man whose name was Simeon: and this man was a devout man, looking for the consolation of Israel: and the Holy Spirit was upon him. And it had been revealed (Gr. *kechrematismenon*) unto him by the Holy Spirit that he should not see death until he had seen the Lord's Christ" (vv. 25,26). The narrative goes on to say that Simeon "came in the Spirit into the temple" (v. 27) and when Jesus' parents brought him in, Simeon "received him into his arms" (v. 28), and blessed God, and prophesied concerning Jesus.

b) In describing the onset of Jesus' ministry Luke reports, "And Jesus, full of the Holy Spirit, returned from the Jordan" (4:1). Luke then states that he was "led in the Spirit in the wilderness" (v. 3) where he was then tempted by the devil, as noted above. Luke then states that following the temptation episodes "Jesus returned in the power of the Spirit into Galilee: and a fame went out concerning him throughout all the region round about" (4:14).

Luke 4:16-30 describes Jesus' return to Nazareth, where he

had been brought up. He is said to have entered "as his custom was" into the synagogue on the Sabbath day (v. 16) and that he stood up to read. There was delivered unto him the book of the prophet Isaiah and he opened it to the place where it is written:

> The Spirit of the Lord is upon me, because he anointed me to preach good tidings to the poor; He hath sent me to proclaim release to the captives, and recovering of the sight to the blind, to set at liberty them that are bruised, to proclaim the acceptable year of the Lord (Luke 4:18,19).

When he had thus read and returned the book to the attendant he startled them by announcing: "This day hath this Scripture been fulfilled in your ears" (v. 21).

d) In the latter half of the chapter we have reported a series of encounters with the spirits of unclean demons. The same are said to have come out of many, saying, "Thou art the Son of God" (v. 41). Luke 7:18-23 relates John's imprisonment and plaintive inquiry: "Art thou he that cometh, or must we look for another?" (v. 20). In that hour he cured many of diseases, plagues, evil spirits and bestowed sight on many blind. He then answered the delegation from John by telling them to go back and tell them what they had seen and heard.

g) Upon the jubilant return of the seventy, rejoicing that even the demons were subject to them in Jesus' name, Jesus replied, "Rejoice not that the spirits of demons are subject unto you, but rejoice that your names are written in heaven" (Luke 10:20). Luke then states, "In that same hour he rejoiced in the Holy Spirit" and prayed a prayer of thanksgiving to his "Father, Lord of heaven and earth" (v. 21).

h) Luke 11:13 records a variant of one of Christ's teachings concerning prayer: "If ye then, being evil, know how to give good things to your children, how much more shall your heavenly Father give the Holy Spirit to them that ask him."

8. Let it also be noted that Jesus' resurrection is said to have

been accomplished by the power of the Spirit. First Peter 3:18 speaks of Jesus as having been "put to death in the flesh, but made alive in the Spirit." Thus we are promised that: "if the Spirit of him that raised up Jesus from the dead dwelleth in you, he that raised up Christ Jesus from the dead shall give life also to your mortal bodies, through his Spirit that dwelleth in you" (Rom. 8:9). 11.

From the foregoing we see that Christ's entire earthly life, from conception to birth, and from the manger cradle to the empty tomb, was lived in the power of the Spirit. Scarce wonder then that the apostle Paul should express the confidence that his own imprisonment should "turn out to (his) salvation, through the supply of the Spirit of Jesus Christ" (Phil. 1:19). Let us be of the same confidence, ever.

9. Finally, Jesus informed the twelve in the upper room the night he was betrayed that he would be directly involved in the sending of the Holy Spirit upon them. For one thing he said: "I will pray the Father and he will send another Comforter that he may be with you for ever, even the Spirit of truth" (John 14:16,17). Moreover, the Holy Spirit would be sent in Jesus' name (14:26). (Cp. 15:26 and 16:13-17).

THE ROLE OF THE HOLY SPIRIT
AS IT RELATES TO THE CHURCH

The role of the Holy Spirit in the founding and early history of the church was necessarily extensive. The infant church, as with any other infant, required special attention and assistance. Jesus, the founder of the church, certainly knew that would be true. He had already spent some three years of his life recruiting and training the twelve apostles for their role in founding the church. The fact that the apostleship was not intended to be a permanent office, nor could it be, is at the least suggestive. To qualify as an apostle required two credentials that by their very nature put an

61

early terminus on the qualifications for that special office. Peter
stated it succinctly:

> Of the men that (1) have companied with us all the time the Lord
> Jesus went in and out among us, beginning from the baptism of
> John unto the day that he was received up from us, of these (2)
> must one become a witness with us of his resurrection (Acts
> 1:21,22).

Christ's commission to his eleven disciples is variously stated
in an abridged form in each of the synoptic gospels. There is no
contradiction in the three statements. None of the writers had any
intention of correcting the others. Jesus likely said much more
than can be gleaned even from a composite of the three
statements. Each writer was simply supplying his readers the gist
of Christ's final instructions. It is noteworthy that Luke, whose
gospel we have already seen to provide a fuller account of the
role of the Holy Spirit in the life of Christ, is the writer who saw fit
to record Jesus' Holy Spirit oriented promise and command:
"Behold, I send forth the promise of my Father upon you: but
tarry ye in the city, until ye be clothed with power from on high"
(Luke 24:49).

The great commission gives to the church its charter, con-
stituting the church a teaching institution whose field is the world,
and whose commission is to the end of time. To insure that the
church would be adequately equipped for its world-wide, age-
long task, Jesus did three things. (We have already touched upon
two of them.) a) He spent three years training an apostleship, b)
in conjunction with his Father he endued them with power from
on high, c) through the inspiration of the Holy Spirit he made
provision for the writing of the New Testament Scriptures,
calculated to "furnish us thoroughly unto every good work" (II
Tim. 3:16,17). The second of those three provisions now claims
our attention. As relates to the church:

1. *The Holy Spirit prepared for the coming of the church.*

The descent of the Holy Spirit on Pentecost heralded the beginning of the gospel age. Acts 1:8 states it succinctly: "Ye shall receive power when the Holy Spirit is come upon you, and ye shall be my witnesses both in Jerusalem and in all Judea, and Samaria, and unto the uttermost parts of the earth." Incidentally, this verse provides the outline for the narrative which follows: Chapters 1-7 relate the beginnings of the church in Jerusalem and Judea. Chapters 8-12 relate the beginnings of the church in Samaria. Chapters 13ff relate the beginnings of the world-wide expansion of the church into the uttermost parts of the earth.

Acts 2:1-4 describes the descent of the Holy Spirit on Pentecost, the awaited signal for the apostles to begin the task enjoined upon them in the Great Commission. In verses 14-22 Peter explains to the multitude that history was then in the making. The signs which caught their attention, a) the sound "as of a rushing mighty wind," b) the apparition of "tongues like as of fire" and c) the miracle of divergent tongues, heard by the sojourners as though they were being addressed in their "back home" dialect — these were harbingers of the new age.

As proof of his thesis that the messianic age was now come upon them Peter said of those signs, "This is that which was spoken of by the prophet Joel." Whereupon he quoted Joel's prophecy concerning the "pouring forth" of the Holy Spirit as the sign of "the latter days." The prophecy, as cited and interpreted by Peter, while "speaking as the Spirit gave him utterance," opens with the announcement: "It shall come to pass in the last days, saith God, I will pour forth of my Spirit upon all flesh . . . and thy (sons, daughters, young men and old, servants and handmaidens) shall prophesy." The prediction closes with the announcement: "And it shall be that whosoever shall call upon the Lord shall be saved" (Acts 2:17-21; cp. Joel 2:28-32).

Thus the descent of the Holy Spirit on Pentecost heralded the closing of "the former days," the Mosaic dispensation and the favored and almost exclusive role of fleshly Israel. And it marked the onset of "the latter days" in which "whosoever calls upon the name of the Lord shall be saved." A grace period of forty years, the span of a generation, appears to have been extended the Jews, but their exclusive role as "an elect race" was for ever ended. (Cp. Heb. 8:7-13, particularly v. 13). Today, the church is that "elect race, a chosen generation, a royal priesthood" (I Pet. 2:9) over whom Christ presides as "the prophet like unto Moses" (Acts 3:22, cp. Deut. 18:15-18), "the high priest (for ever) of our confession" (Heb. 3:1; 7:17), and King, occupying the throne of David, fulfilling David's own prediction (Acts 2:33-36; cp. Psa. 110:1).

2. *The Holy Spirit supplied the message to be proclaimed.* This was predicted by Christ aforehand. See John 14:16,17,26; 15:26,27; 16:7-14. Despite the fact the apostles had three years plus of intensive schooling under the master teacher, the apostles from the outset functioned in their important role under the guidance of the promised Holy Spirit, (Acts 2:5; 15:28; I Cor. 2:13; II Pet. 1:16-21; I John 4:6).

3. *The Holy Spirit was recognized as the discloser of the Old Testament prophecies being fulfilled.* This has already been touched upon in part, as the course of events which took place on Pentecost was noted. Acts 2:4 is a pertinent text in that it informs us that what Peter declared to be taking place was not of his own private interpretation (cp. II Pet. 1:20,21). Peter was speaking as the Spirit gave utterance when he quoted Joel 2:18-23, and gave to the prophecy a "this is that" application. Peter was not speaking of himself. Were that so he would not have said some of the things he said on that occasion. For example, when Peter answered the question of the guilt-stricken multitude, telling them to "repent and be baptized for the remission of their sins" and declaring that in so doing they would "receive the gift of the Holy Spirit" (Acts 2:38), he went on to declare that the promise was not to them only, "but to them also that are afar off (the gentiles, no less) even to as many as the Lord our God shall call unto him" (v. 39). In that he was most certainly "speaking as the Spirit gave utterance."

In Acts 4:8-12 Peter, said to be "filled with the Holy Spirit," addressed the rulers of the people, (Annas, the high priest, Caiaphas, John, and Alexander, "as many as were kindred of the high priest." He declared that in crucifying Jesus, whom God raised up, they had unwittingly fulfilled the enigmatic prophecy in a proverb, Psalm 118:22.

In Acts 4:23-31 we are told that when Peter and John were released they returned to their own company. The opening verses of Psalm 2 were called to mind. The authorship was attributed to the Holy Spirit via the mouth of David, and said to be fulfilled in Jesus' crucifixion. The scene closes as follows: "And when they had prayed the place was shaken where they were gathered together, and they were all filled with the Holy Spirit, and spake the word of God with boldness," v. 31.

The book of Acts (see 28:25-28) draws to a close with an account in which Paul expresses the same confidence in the leading of the Holy Spirit. To the unbelieving Jews who visited him in his Roman imprisonment, Paul spoke this final word of warning: "Well spake the Holy Spirit through Isaiah the prophet, saying . . ." (at which point he quoted a familiar passage from the text recording the call of Isaiah to the prophetic ministry. The quotation includes the familiar words which Jesus had occasion. to recall:

This people's heart is waxed gross, and their ears are dull of hearing, and their eyes they have closed: Lest haply they should see with their eyes, and hear with their ears, and understand with their hearts, and should turn again (convert) and I should heal them (Isa. 6:9,10; cp. Matt. 13:15; Mark 4:12).

4. *The Holy Spirit was present in, and working with, the church.* This is to be seen from the following: a) The Holy Spirit was identified with the church. 1) For example, when Ananias and Sapphira lied to the church at Jerusalem concerning the price received from the land they sold, Peter rebuked Ananias,

saying: "Why has Satan filled your heart to lie to the Holy Spirit? . . . You have not (just) lied to men, but unto God" (Acts 5:3,4). The immediate consequences underscored what Peter said. When Sapphira repeated her husband's folly Peter asked her: "How is it that you have agreed together to try the Spirit of the Lord?" Again the deadly consequences underscored what Peter charged. 2) The story of Stephen (Acts 7) is another example. Being "full of the Holy Spirit" (v. 55) he rebuked the intransigent Jews, saying: You stiffnecked and uncircumcised in heart and ears, you do always resist the Holy Spirit: as your father did, so do you" (v. 51). At that they gnashed on him with their teeth and stoned him to death (vv. 54,59).

b) The Holy Spirit was (is) given to all who obey Christ (Acts 2:38,39; 5:32). The gift of the Holy Spirit is not "a second work of grace," given to meritorious saints some time posterior to their salvation. Acts 2:38,39 records the promise that those who repent and are baptized "in the name of Jesus Christ" (i.e. by the authority of Christ, the baptism he authorized on the terms he authorized) shall receive the gift of the Holy Spirit. In a day when "the obedience of faith" (Rom. 1:5; 6:17,18; 16:26) is being down-graded "that grace may abound" Acts 5:32 needs to be shouted from the tallest transmitters towering over our housetops: "God gives the Holy Spirit unto all them that obey him."

c) The Holy Spirit was deemed an essential for leadership and service in the church. 1) Some one, by way of paying tribute to the legendary Mark Hopkins as a teacher par excellent, defined the ideal college as a school with Mark Hopkins on one end of a log and a student on the other. The apostles enjoyed a higher privilege than that. They had experienced in excess of three years (no summer vacation interrupting) in the school of Christ. Yet, that notwithstanding, they were instructed to wait until they were endued with power from on high before taking the leadership in the founding of the church. 2) Even "the seven" chosen to "serve the tables" of the widows in the Jerusalem church, hence regarded as the prototype of the diaconnate, were chosen from among men "full of the Holy Spirit" (Acts 6:3). While that requirement is not specifically stated in the listings of the qualifications for elders (bishops/stewards/pastors, teachers) and deacons in I Timothy 3 and Titus 1, the lifestyle described would at least suggest that being full of the Holy Spirit would be essential to the attainment thereof. So, too, with the office of the evangelist as set forth in I and II Timothy and Titus.

d) The Holy Spirit accentuated the effectiveness of the witness. In Acts 6:8 it is said of Stephen that he, "full of grace and power, wrought great signs and wonders among the people." But Stephen had to contend with opposing forces, even as the prophets before him, including John the Baptist, Christ and his apostles. Stephen's opposition came primarily from a synagogue known as "the synagogue of the Libertines" (of the "liberals" in our modern vernacular and setting). Does that not sound familiar? But it is noted: "They were not able to withstand the wisdom and the Spirit by which he spoke" (v. 10). So they stooped to treachery, suborning (bribing) men to lie about him. Long ago I observed that "liberals" are not all that liberal — not with their own agenda, goals, money, ideas, etc., they are not!

e) The Holy Spirit provided confirming signs to support the preaching of the word in the founding days of the church, much as forms and scaffolding are used in the early stages of the building of physical structures. Note these were not distributed indiscriminately. 1) The gift of the Holy Spirit which provides the power to produce "the fruit of the Spirit" (the moral manifestation of the Spirit) was, and is, given to all obedient believers (Acts 2:38,39) but v. 43 of the same chapter notes that "many signs and wonders were done through the apostles." 2) The first healing miracle is reported in 3:1-10, but it was Peter who healed the cripple at the gate of the temple. 3) Chapter 4 reports phenomenal growth, numerically, but v. 33 notes it was the apostles who "with great power gave their witness of the resurrection." 4) A prime qualification in the choosing of "the seven" was that they be "full of the Holy Spirit," but only after the apostles laid hands upon them are any of them reported as performing signs. See Acts 6:8 (Stephen); 8:6,7,13 (Philip). And only after the apostles laid hands on the Samaritans did the Holy Spirit "fall upon" any of them, (8:17). Cf. Judges 6:34 (Gideon); 11:29 (Jephthah); 14:6 (Samson); etc.

f) The Holy Spirit "comforted" the church in a time of persecution. Acts 9 describes the conversion of Saul of Tarsus, the arch persecutor of the church. Verse 31 reports: "So the church throughout all Judea and Galilee and Samaria had peace, being edified; and walking in the fear of the Lord was comforted and multiplied." The word translated "was comforted" is the verb form of the word Jesus used in his farewell address to designate and describe the Holy Spirit. *Paraklesei* is formed from a verb meaning "to call" (*kalein*) and the preposition *para* (alongside), hence the Comforter (Holy Spirit) is one Christians are priviliged to "call alongside" of us in life's journey.

g) The Holy Spirit guided in the settling of controversy. The Jerusalem conference of the apostles and elders narrowly avoided a schism over the issue of the circumcision of gentile converts, and a few lesser but related items. The cyclical letter that was sent forth to report the decision reached contains this significant phrase: "It seemed good to the Holy Spirit and us" (Acts 15:28; Cp. I John 4:1-6).

5. *The Holy Spirit prepared the way for the extension of the Gospel to the Gentiles.* Despite the plain implications of the great commission it would seem that the apostles were quite content to remain in Jerusalem and wait for the annual festivals to bring to them "Jews, devout men from every nation under heaven" (Acts 2:5). Surely these could carry the Gospel back to their several locales. But the growing persecution soon brought an end to that.

The persecution that ensued upon the stoning of Stephen now appears to have been providential. The church was scattered abroad. But that did not kill the church. One can no more destroy a church whose members are on fire for God by scattering the members than one can put out a fire in the fireplace by scattering the embers. "They that were scattered abroad went everywhere preaching the word" (8:5).

Though most of the scattered saints likely confined their witness to their "own kind of people," some of them "preached to the gentiles also" (Acts 11:19,20). Philip was one of the first to cross the line. Philip went to Samaria and preached Christ to them. The Holy Spirit credentialized his message by the signs which he did (Acts 8:6), insomuch that Simon, the resident fakester, was amazed and at least provisionally converted. When word of this reached the apostles in Jerusalem, Peter and John were sent to look into it. They did so, and demonstrated endorsement by laying their hands on the Samaritans, imparting to them confirming signs of acceptance (v. 17).

Acts 10 describes the episode which opened the doors even wider, admitting to baptism a household of full gentiles. The sequel, Acts 11, relates the founding of the church at Antioch where for the first time Jews and Gentiles came together in one body, and the name "Christian" was first divinely called (Gr. *chrematisai*) upon the disciples. Significantly, it was also there, at the first fully integrated, interracial church that the Holy Spirit formally initiated the world-wide mission for which Paul had been called to the apostleship.

6. *The Holy Spirit was, and is, present within obedient believers.* The indwelling of the Holy Spirit provides four important ministries. a) He bears witness to our filial relationship to God. Romans 8:16 affirms: "The Spirit bears witness with our spirits that we are children of God." Through the Scriptures the Holy Spirit communicates to us the conditions whereby we may attain "the spirit of adoption as sons whereby we cry, Abba Father" (Rom. 8:15). Our spirits communicate to us whether or not we have met those conditions. When our spirits agree with the Word of God given by the inspiration of the Holy Spirit our sonship with the Father is certified and made sure.

b) The Holy Spirit is said to be "the earnest of our inheritance" (Eph. 1:13,14). Paul states that "we are sealed with the Holy Spirit of promise which is the earnest of our inheritance, unto the redemption of God's own possession, unto the praise of his glory." Earnest money is money advanced to bind a contract, demonstrating the one making the payment is serious, and committed to follow through with the agreement.

c) The Holy Spirit is given to "strengthen our inward man" (Eph. 3:16). So Paul prayed for the saints in his beautiful intercessory prayer (Eph. 3:14-21). Each of us experience a warfare between the flesh and the spirit. "The flesh lusteth against the spirit" (Gal. 5:17). But it is our privilege as Christians to "call alongside" of us, and even to have dwell within us, the Comforter (*paraclete*). Thus we gain the victory over the flesh, the world and the devil. With the Holy Spirit within us the lusts of the flesh, the lust of the eyes, and the vain glory of this life" (I John 2:16) can be overcome.

d) The Holy Spirit enables us to weed out the works of the flesh and produce the fruit of the Spirit. Note the use of the generic term, fruit, a singular noun. This is in harmony with the singular verb used in Galatians 5:22,23. We do not bear a variety of fruits, but fruit with many virtues — in keeping with the nature of the Spirit that dwells within us. As a prize specimen apple is round, red, mellow, yet crisp, juicy, sweet, yet tangy, a delight to the eyes and delicious to the taste, so the fruit of the Spirit *is* describable by many virtuous qualities which constitute desired attributes of the Christian life — love, joy, peace, longsuffering, goodness, faithfulness, meekness, self-control, and such like. Note that phrase. Paul did not exhaust the list of qualities which make for godliness (Biblical shorthand for God-likeness). What joy it is to be filled with the Spirit, and thus be "filled unto all the fullness of God" (Eph. 3:16).

4

NATURE AND IDENTITY OF THE HOLY SPIRIT

The nature and identity of the Holy Spirit, along with the doctrine of the essence and form of the pre-existence of Christ, was presumably settled once and for all by the Council of Nicea some sixteen and one-half centuries ago. The Nicene Creed, which was first hammered out in approximately its present form in 324 A.D., was refined and made the official dogma of "the church" in 325 A.D. However, it has come down to us as reshaped at Constantinople in the year 381 A.D.

The main difference between the original form and the Council of Constantinople revision relates to the role of the Scriptures as the basis of authority. Such a phrase as "according to the Scriptures" appears nowhere. The inspiration of the Scriptures as such is but obliquely intimated at best. While extolling the Holy Spirit, the phrase "who spake by the prophets," is tacked on as though an afterthought.

Circa 385 A.D., Priscillian, a Spaniard, added a "verse of

Scripture"(?) to his copy of I John 5. Between John's affirmation: "It is the Spirit that beareth witness, because the Spirit is the truth" (v. 7, in most versions) and verse 8 (in all versions): "For there are three who bear witness, the Spirit and the water and the blood." Priscillian inserted the words: "For there are three that bear witness in heaven, the Father, the Word and the Holy Spirit (KJV, Holy Ghost): and the three agree in one." From there the spurious text found its way into later Latin copies of the NT (e.g. revised Vulgate), as compatible with the theology developing within the Western church, and from there into the KJV. In addition to being lacking in any Greek MS of antiquity it is lacking in all ancient language versions of the New Testament — Syriac, Arabic, Ethiopic, Coptic, Armenian, Slavonian, etc.

Some two hundred years after the Spaniard Priscillian's revision of I John 5:7,8 became the official dogma of the Western church, a provincial synod in Toledo, Spain (589 A.D.) added the famous "filioque" ("and the Son") nuance to the phrasing of the Nicene Creed. With this revision the creed now affirmed that the Holy Spirit not only "proceeded from the Father," but "from the Father *and the Son*." Thus the creed that tens of millions of devout and not so devout church goers recite as their "confession of faith" now reads:

> I believe in one God, the Father Almighty, Maker of heaven and earth, and all things visible and invisible.
>
> And in one Lord Jesus Christ, the only-begotten Son of God: Begotten of his Father before all worlds, God of God, Light of light, very God of very God: Begotten, not made; Being of one substance with the Father; by Whom all things were made; Who for us men, and for our salvation, came down from heaven, and was incarnate by the Holy Ghost of the Virgin Mary, and was made man: And was crucified also for us under Pontius Pilate. He suffered and was buried: And the third day he arose again according to the Scriptures: And ascended into heaven, and sitteth on the right hand of the Father: And he shall come again with glory, to judge both the quick and the dead; whose kingdom shall have no end.

> And I believe in the Holy Ghost, the Lord and Giver of Life, Who proceedeth from the Father *and the Son*: Who with the Father and the Son together is worshipped and glorified; Who spake by the Prophets: And I believe in one holy Catholic and Apostolic Church: I acknowledge one Baptism for the remission of sins: And I look for the Resurrection of the dead: And the Life of the world to come. Amen.

Is that what the Scriptures actually teach? and in so many words? It is not within the perimeters of this study to discuss the Christology of the Nicene Creed, but we are obliged to evaluate the pneumatology expressed. We noted in the preface to this study, under the title "Has the Holy Spirit Upstaged Christ?" that there is neither Scripture precedent nor command for the Holy (Ghost) Spirit to be "worshipped and glorified." No patriarch, prophet, priest, apostle, evangelist, nor any angel, seraphim, or other heavenly being of record (that is, of the Biblical record) is reported as doing so, nor is it intimated that it is God's intent that any one ever should, or shall.

The concept of the Holy Spirit as a person, to be distinguished from Jehovah God and Jesus as a third person in a triune Godhead, was long in the making. At best it is a theological deduction hammered out in the wake of the Monarchian controversy which arose toward the end of the second century A.D., and raged for over a hundred years. The Nicene Conference attempted to lay to rest the questions which had been raised and debated throughout Christendom.

The issue began as a Christological question: How can belief in an actual incarnation be reconciled with the fundamental doctrine of the Old Testament revelation, as expressed in what is called "The Shema" (Deut. 6:4,5):

> Jehovah our God is one Jehovah: and thou shalt love Jehovah thy God with all thy heart, and with all thy soul, and with all thy might.

The Shema was one of the stumbling blocks to the orthodox

73

Jew when called upon to accept the Christian doctrine of the incarnation of Jesus. His credentials as the Messiah demanded their consideration and might have gained greater acceptance except for the fact he did not seem to be concerned about the one thing the Jews wanted most for him to do. He showed no disposition to head up a rebellion against Rome, with a view to ending the Roman occupation and restoring the Davidic kingdom to Israel in a physical, political sense. (That is still a stumbling block, not just to the Jews but also to current "Israeli watchers." Their concept of at least the initial facet of Christ's second coming calls for him to do the same thing in the context of the Arab occupation and presence in "the holy land"). His failure to meet the Jews' Messianic expectations was added to the fact he "also called God his Father, making himself equal with God" (John 5:18). This put his claim to be their messiah in conflict with their understanding of the Shema.

When the Holy Spirit is introduced into the picture as yet a third person in the Godhead (co-existent, co-equal and co-eternal with the Father) the issue is heightened. No Jew of record, throughout the whole course of the OT dispensation, can be shown to have believed that the promised Messiah would be a heavenly being. He might be a second Moses, or a re-incarnation of Elijah, but a second person in a dual or triune Godhead was unthinkable. Not even the virgin birth Immanuel prediction (Isa. 7:14) was so interpreted. We are so accustomed to reading the OT writings in the light of the NT that it rarely occurs to us how we might interpret the OT without the NT to help us. And, we might add, without centuries of theological and creedal reconstruction to aid(?) us. The aid received therefrom is indeed at times subject to question.

THE RELATION OF THE HOLY SPIRIT
TO THE FATHER AND THE SON

This brings us to the point at issue. What is the relation of the

Holy Spirit to the Father and to the Son? 1) Does the term simply denote in anthropomorphic language the presence or influence of God at work in a given situation? Is the term just a form of reference to a supernatural influence sensed or observed? Or 2) Is the term a form of reference describing the innate essence of a Divine person who performs his mission in a context in which his personhood is purposefully obscured lest he receive the honor that is due to the One sending and directing him in his mission? In short, is the Holy Spirit but a mode of Divine influence (whether of the Father or the Son, or both), or a person who for some undisclosed reason is not to be known to us (in this life at least) by name? Obviously the Biblical mode of reference "the Holy Spirit" or "the Spirit" is not a name. At best it is but a form of reference. Usage of such address as "Come, Holy Spirit" or "Holy Spirit, light Divine" is without Biblical precedent.

Arguments Against the Personhood
of the Holy Spirit. Stated and Met

Seven arguments are commonly advanced in denial of the personhood (personality) of the Holy Spirit by those who believe the term refers only to the benevolent influence which emanates from God and/or from Christ, primarily in the form of Divine providence. Those who consider the Holy Spirit to be a person, a Divine being in a triune Godhead, are not cowed by the array of opposition.

1. The Greek noun *pneuma* is neuter, and neuter pronouns are used (at times at least) with reference to the Holy Spirit. The texts most often cited are the KJV rendering of Romans 8:16 and 26, "The Spirit itself beareth witness with our spirits" (v. 16) and "the Spirit itself maketh intercession for the saints" (v. 26).

a) It is true that the term *pneuma* is a neuter noun. As was noted early on in this study (Chapter 1) the Hebrew word *ruah*, the Greek *pneuma*, the Latin *spiritus*, are words which, in each language, were 1) originally used to designate the wind, 2) then expanded to include the breath of breathing creatures, 3) further expanded to designate the "life principle" of all sentient living creatures, and 4) ultimately used even of God the increate one, and of the myriad hosts of heaven.

b) God, while addressed as Father, and wherever referred to in the scriptures is spoken of in the masculine gender, is nonetheless said to send forth his "Spirit" (*pneuma*) upon all flesh (Acts 2:17,18). Jesus said of Him: "God is a Spirit" (*pneuma*, John 4:24). Does such usage of the neuter noun strip God of his masculinity?

c) Moreover in Galatians 4:6 Paul speaks of "the Spirit (*pneuma*) of his (God's) Son." And in the same chapter and context in which Romans 8:16, and 26 appear Paul speaks of both the Spirit (*pneuma*) of God and the Spiri (*pneuma*) of Christ "in the same breath (*pneuma*)," so to speak. We need not labor the point. Paul depicts the Holy Spirit in personal terms.

The other side of the coin is that for generations tropical storms and hurricanes have uniformly been given feminine names. But that seems not to change the nature of the storms. Ships (warships generally excluded) are commonly given feminine names, and schools are referred to nostalgically as "alma mater." This hardly feminizes either of them.

The Holy Spirit performs no functions analogous to characteristic sex distinctions. It is pressing the reference data too far to suggest the Holy Spirit actually fathered Mary's firstborn child. While Mary is said to have been with child of (Gr. *ek*) the Holy Spirit, the Holy Spirit was in no wise considered to be Jesus' father. He was the Son of God. Jesus was born of a virgin, by the power of God mediated through the Holy Spirit. Heavenly beings are either increate or created. They do not procreate (cp. Luke 20:35).

2. The term, the Holy Spirit, is not a name — its nearest OT equivalent simply described God's moral character and essence. This is a half-truth. The term "*his holy Spirit*" *is* twice used in the

76

OT, (Isa. 63:10,11), and David implored of God, "take not *thy holy* Spirit from me," (Psa. 51:11).

As for the want of a name, even Jehovah God was not known by his distinctive name (at least not generally) prior to the call of Moses (Exod. 6:3). Jesus, though he existed from the beginning with God, was not so named, nor so known, prior to his birth. He was designated aforehand by the title which speaks of his messianic office, and the descriptive designation "immanuel" is mentioned in the prediction of his virgin birth, but his name "Jesus" (Saviour) awaited his birth.

3. The Holy Spirit cannot be fitted into the "family" (Father, Son and ?) model. Granted. But Jesus' role as the Son of God become incarnate cannot be demonstrated prior to his birth in Bethlehem. Not in all the recorded Messianic hopes and expectations of Israel was it ever conceived that the Messiah would be a person within the Divine family, who would "empty himself of the form of God" and become incarnate among men.

We have no way of establishing whether or not Jesus occupied a role equivalent to a "son" in his pre-existent state. Certainly he did not exist as a "procreated son" nor even as an "adopted son" prior to his earth experience. However, such scriptures as Hebrews 1:5,6 give us pause:

> For unto which of the angels said he at any time, Thou art my Son, This day have I begotten thee? and again, I will be (future) to him a Father, and he shall be (future) to me a son? And when he again bringeth the firstborn into the world he saith, and let all the angels of God worship him.

John speaks of his pre-existent state in terms of "the logos" (the word). To press "sonship" as we know it in the family context of this life, calling for an act of procreation, a gestation period of some duration, then a birth and a gradual awakening to self-consciousness and filial relationship, is to tamper with Christ's increateness.

77

To insist on conforming the Godhead to the family analogy in the form in which we experience it is nothing new. The church of the early post-apostolic era did that, but in a different fashion. *Magna mater* (great mother) cults were found flourishing throughout the Graeco-Roman world. The exaltation of Mary as "the Mother of God" was an adaptation of cultist fantasy. The NT writers made no such concession to paganism, with a view to making the Christian faith conformable to a concept human reason deemed necessary in the Divine sphere also.

4. The Holy Spirit has never been manifested as a distinguishable personal being. This is true. But Jesus, the Son of God, was not manifested as a distinguishable personal being prior to his earth life as Jesus of Nazareth. Moreover, that manifestation was limited to a tiny province and to the brief span of one generation. Did He then not have personhood before that? Was he relatively a non-entity, a mere concept in the mind of God?

Did the "logos" who became flesh and dwelt among men in the person of Jesus only become a person when he was in human flesh? Are spirit beings faceless non-persons? Do we become non-persons twixt death and the resurrection? Some arguments which challenge the personhood of the Holy Spirit create more problems than they would hopefully solve.

5. The Holy Spirit has never been physically manifested, not even anthropomorphically speaking. Yet Jesus has been manifested in the flesh and Jehovah has been manifested anthropomorphically. In addition to spiritual attributes which we to some degree share with God, mention is made of his face (Psa. 143:7), mouth (Deut. 8:3), eyes (II Chron. 16:9), ears (Psa. 31:2), right hand (Exod. 33:23). But not so with the Holy Spirit.

All this is true. But again, except for a brief interlude in a tiny province the same is also true of Jesus. As for the anthropomorphic manifestations of God these are figures of speech (except perhaps for God's unique revelation of himself to Moses, Exod. 33:17-23). Even in the Garden of Eden, Adam and Eve are said only to have heard his voice (Gen. 3:8). The reason is learned when Moses asked to see his glory: "You can not see my face; for no man shall see me and live" (Exod. 33:18,20). The manifestation of the Holy Spirit at Jesus' baptism was not anthropomorphic. But neither did he become a pigeon. The descent was "as a dove." The effect upon Jesus was personal.

6. The Holy Spirit is said to have been "poured out" on several occasions. This could not be said of a person. This argument is crass, to say the least. Consider these expressions: a) We are said to be "baptized into Christ" (Gal. 3:27), and into his death (Rom. 6:3). b) We are also said to "put on Christ" (Gr. *enedusasthe*, be enclothed with). c) On the other hand, Christ is said to dwell in us (Eph. 3:17). And Paul states that "Christ in you" is one's "hope of glory" (Col. 1:27).

Are these sayings contradictory? How can we be in Christ and at the same time Christ be in us? This is only a problem when the Scriptures are interpreted in a crassly literal fashion. We are living in America, but unless the "spirit" (the dreams, the ideals, the goals, and the personal dedication thereto) that has made America the country we love lives in us and abounds, the America we know and love will be no more.

Much of the trouble in the understanding of the Scriptures roots in the inability or unwillingness to accept the fact "we have this treasure in earthen vessels" (II Cor. 4:7). It takes many analogies, many figures of speech, to even begin to express and encompass those spiritual truths which constitute the Word of God.

To speak of the Holy Spirit being poured out upon us is a figurative expression somewhat akin to OT texts which speak of the Spirit of God having "come upon" certain chosen individuals (e.g. Gideon and Samson) who were thereby empowered to do extraordinary things. The difference is, under the old covenant the Holy Spirit was thereby superimposed upon those chosen. Under the new covenant the Holy Spirit works within us. The term "poured out" suggests a fullness necessary for a given circumstance or mission. But even that distinction is not absolute.

79

Titus 3:5,6 speaks of the Holy Spirit being "richly poured out" upon us in connection with baptism, "the washing of regeneration."

7. Mary was told by an angel, "The Holy Spirit shall come upon you, and the power of the Almighty shall overshadow you. Wherefore the holy thing which is begotten shall be called the Son of God" (Luke 1:35). From this classic example of Hebrew parallelistic language it may be inferred that the Holy Spirit and the power of the Almighty are one and the same thing, simply two different ways of speaking of God's own power. The contingent clause, "Wherefore the holy thing that is begotten in thee shall be called the Son of God," is said to settle the matter. The text clearly says that the resultant child shall be called the Son of God, not the son of the Holy Spirit.

By way of refutation we need to bear in mind that Mary continued to be a virgin for some time subsequent to the predicted conception. Suggestion of cohabitation of a Divine being with a woman is unwarranted. Cain is called "the son of the evil one" — Satan (I John 3:12). Jesus told the Pharisees, "You are of your father, the devil, and the lusts of your father it is your will to do" (John 8:44).

Lineage and character are often spoken of in the analogy of sonship. Adam is called "the son of God" (Luke 3:38). But this is not to suggest God cohabitated with mother nature or mother earth to bring him into being. God used Mary to "prepare a body" for Jesus (Heb. 10:5). He used the Holy Spirit not to "inseminate" Mary but to impart the Divine Spirit of the Son. The Holy Spirit is an agent God has employed from the dawn of creation, to "brood over, move upon" things he made, i.e. to fashion and renew what has been made. That observation does not divest the Holy Spirit of personhood or make him but a servant, not a part of the Godhead. In fact between the primordial creation in which the logos (the Son) fulfilled the primary role as God's agent of creation and the onset of Jesus' public ministry the Holy Spirit seems to have held that role, at least insofar as earth events were concerned.

The Case for the Personhood of the Holy Spirit

Seven arguments can be advanced for the view that the Holy Spirit is a personal being in the sphere of what Paul has called "the Godhead" (Acts 17:29; Rom. 1:20; Col. 2:9).

1. The first argument, in a sense, has already been stated. The refutation of the arguments against the personhood of the Holy Spirit is a compelling argument for its acceptance. But it is not enough to disprove what others would have us believe. We must have a reason (in fact two or more, at the least, Deut. 17:6; 2 Cor. 13:1) for what we believe and teach. Thus we are constrained to cite other reasons for believing the Holy Spirit is a person, though unnamed in the formal sense, and though his interrelationship with the Father and Son is not communicated to us within the framework of familial analogy.

2. Personal attributes are ascribed to the Holy Spirit. a) As we already have noted personal pronouns are almost invariably used with reference to the Holy Spirit. b) Jesus spoke of his coming in intimate "comforting" terms (no pun intended). The Holy Spirit would come in his place, though not in the flesh, but certainly in his stead — so much so that he would not speak from himself but rather call to their remembrance what Christ had taught them (see John 16:13-15). He is said to have a mind (Rom. 8:27) and a will (Heb. 2:4). He can be grieved (Eph. 4:30) and outraged (Heb. 10:29).

3. The activities ascribed to him throughout the book of Acts are personal. He supplied the message proclaimed on Pentecost (Acts 2:4). He was lied to and tested by Ananias and Sapphira (Acts 5:3,9). He guided Philip to the Ethiopian (Acts 8:26,29) and Peter to the house of Cornelius (Acts 10:19; 11:12). He initiated the missionary labors of Saul and Barnabas (Acts 13:2; 16:6,7; 20:23).

4. The blasphemy against the Holy Spirit is cited by Jesus as the ultimate, the one unpardonable sin (Matt. 12:31; Mark 3:29; Luke 12:10). It is beyond the scope of this chapter to discuss a matter as weighty and involved as the doctrine of the blasphemy against the Holy Spirit. That will be done later. For now, suffice it to ask, is it reasonable to believe that blasphemy against an influence emanating from a person shall be reckoned as more heinous than a calumnous verbal assault against one's own person? All three synoptic Gospels record the warning, and note that blasphemy against God and against his Son is forgivable (i.e. provision is made and conditions are cited in the Scriptures for the forgiveness of that sin), but blasphemy against the Holy Spirit "has never forgiveness," neither in this life nor the life to come. It is an "eternal" sin (Mark 3:29).

5. Jesus affirmed that the Holy Spirit would come to his disciples in his stead. In so doing he spoke of the Holy Spirit in the most personal terms. The term translated "comforter" is the Gr. *parakletos*, literally, "one called alongside." Such a designation is scarcely suited to a non-personal entity.

6. Matthew's phrasing of Jesus' final commission to the apostles, (Matt. 28:18-20) along with other primary "trinitarian" texts uniformly imply a distinction between the Father, the Son and the Holy Spirit. (See Matt. 3:16,17; Mark 1:10,11; Luke 3:21,22; John 14:16,26; 15:26; 16:13; I Cor. 12:4-6; II Cor. 13:14.)

7. Finally, the monadic, monolithic view of the Godhead is shattered by the biblical doctrine of the deity of Jesus, and is incongruous with the personhood of God. There is no sound reason — Biblical, philosophical, or otherwise — to deny the personhood of the Holy Spirit. To those who contend that such a doctrine is "unthinkable," one may reply: "That depends on who is doing the thinking."

Of such are the arguments for and against the Nicene doctrine of the trinity as it relates to the personhood of the Holy Spirit. Largely untouched is the corollary(?) thereto — the dogma that the Holy Spirit is "co-existent, co-eternal and *co-equal*" with the Father and with the Son. The latter does not necessarily follow. It is inferrential at best. It is certainly nowhere so stated in the Scriptures.

For additional reference data see the Appendix: *Theology of Holy Spirit in New Testament: Christ Jesus, Church, Community, Creation.* (Contributed by Dr. James D. Strauss, Lincoln Christian Seminary, Lincoln, Illinois).

5

HISTORY AND CRITIQUE OF THE DOCTRINE OF THE TRINITY

The doctrine of the trinity is a theological formulation that was long in the making. That does not mean that what is stated thereby is not Biblical. But it is to say that the doctrine in its classical form is the distillate of the reasoning of men of a bygone day. It is also to say that the doctrine is not plainly, manifestly, overtly set forth in the Scriptures.

The renowned Benjamin B. Warfield, himself a trinitarian of repute, in a discerning twenty-column article in the classical edition of *The International Standard Bible Encyclopedia* (Eerdman's) pp. 3012-3022, begins by noting:

> The term "Trinity" is not a Biblical term, and we are not using Biblical language when we define what is expressed by it as the doctrine that there is one only and true God, but in the unity of the Godhead there are three co-eternal and co-equal Persons, the same in substance but distinct in subsistence (Being), p. 3012.

In the fifth of twenty-two numbered and extensive sectors Warfield again displays remarkable honesty and candor. While continuing to build a case for the Trinitarian formula, he writes:

5. Not Clearly Revealed in the OT   So strongly is it felt in wide circles that a Trinitarian conception is essential to a worthy view of God, that there is abroad a deep-seated unwillingness to allow that God could ever have made Himself known otherwise than as a Trinity. From this point of view it is inconceivable that the OT revelation should know nothing of the Trinity . . . . Whether there really exists traces of the idea of the Trinity in the OT is a moot question . . . . It is a plain matter of fact that none who have depended alone upon the revelation embodied in the OT have attained to the doctrine of the Trinity (p. 3014).

Amid his candor, Warfield also exhibits his astuteness as a theologian by suggesting that the doctrine of the Trinity is carried in the Scriptures as minerals are carried in a stream — in solution. Only as waters cease to flow do the minerals precipitate and solidify. Thus he accounts for the Trinity dogma as a post-apostolic conception.

In further defense of a doctrine that depends on post-apostolic formulation, Warfield again expressed candor and resourcefulness in saying: "A doctrine so defined can be spoken of as Biblical only on the principle that the sense of Scripture is Scripture" (p. 3012). And again: "The definition of a Biblical doctrine in un-Biblical language can be justified only on the principle that it is better to preserve the truth of Scripture than the words of Scripture" (Ibid.). That, too, is a moot question. It was in that context that Warfield advanced his tantalizing rationale to the effect that when a doctrine (such as the Trinity) lies in the Scripture in solution; "when it is crystallized from its solvent state it does not cease to be Scripture" (Ibid.).

The foregoing is written to serve as a background for a review of the tortuous route over which the sub-apostolic theologians

86

(often called "the apostolic fathers") travelled to finally arrive at the doctrine of the Trinity as it came to be canonized in the Nicene creed. As mentioned previously, the issue began as a Christological issue, as men pondered the question: "How can belief in a real incarnation be reconciled with the fundamental affirmation of Scripture that God is one?" Basically, the way around the problem took two routes: adoptionism and Arianism, with some side roads explored along the way.

Adoptionism

In the adoptionist model it was suggested that Jesus became the Son of God and the Messiah in two stages: First, in the Divine arrangement for his virgin birth, via the agency of the Holy Spirit. No unchaste ramifications were suggested or entertained. Secondly, at his baptism, God formally, audibly and visually, adopted Jesus as his Son with his pronouncement from heaven and the bestowal of the Holy Spirit in a visible form — a "bodily form" initially, as a sign to those witnessing the event; but also internalized, to come to full power in his forthcoming ministry.

Arianism

Historically it was Arianism that gained the spotlight in the long drawn out ante-Nicene controversies over the essence and interrelationship, or distinctions (if such there be) within the Godhead. Arius, a presbyter of Alexandria, Egypt, (circa 256?-336 A.D.) took up a concept which had been formerly advocated by the Ebionite gnostics in the latter half of the first century. He proceeded to develop a thesis which has served as a prototype of various forms of unitarianism, including neo-gnosticism as taught by the self-styled Jehovah's Witnesses.

The classic postulate of Arius which triggered the controversy that soon gathered around him, was: "There was a time when Christ was not." Thus Christ did not exist before the beginning of creation. He was rather himself the beginning of creation, "the first born of creation," through whom all else — spirits and worlds, were created and made.

Athanasius, also of Alexandria, a deacon who was soon advanced to a bishop, took up the cudgel against Arius. He won the battle, at least in the eyes of his peers. Athanasius is generally credited for having laid the ground work for the trinitarian formula reflected in the Nicene creed, and purportedly preserved in a fifth century document that has come down to us as "the Athanasian creed."

Sabellian Modalism

Besides Adoptionism, Arianism, and Trinitarianism, Modalism entered the arena, advanced during the height of the controversy by one Sabellius who attempted to bridge the gap between the unitarian and trinitarian extremists. Sabellian Modalism advanced the novel theory that the Father, Son and Holy Spirit are not three persons in a Godhead, co-existent and eternal, but three separate modes of manifestation, temporary and successive.

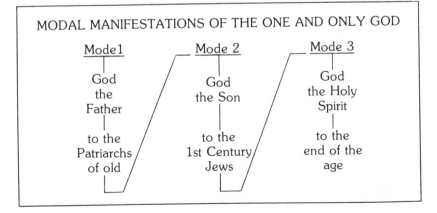

MODAL MANIFESTATIONS OF THE ONE AND ONLY GOD

Mode 1	Mode 2	Mode 3
God the Father	God the Son	God the Holy Spirit
to the Patriarchs of old	to the 1st Century Jews	to the end of the age

Simply stated, modalism teaches that God, the one and only God that is (or ever shall be) first manifested himself to the patriarchs as "the Father," a role they could readily comprehend, being compatible with their own role in the culture of their time. Secondly he manifested himself as a Son, via his incarnation in Jesus of Nazareth, the virgin-born child of Mary. In this brief interlude an eternal God compressed himself into the form of man, and lived as man (presumably from conception to the ascension). During this stage the person "God, the Father" no longer existed as such. He had emptied himself of that role and form of being. Thirdly, presumably at some point in the ascension, the man Christ Jesus ceased to exist as such and became purely a Spirit being, the Holy Spirit.

Modalism akin to the Sabellian model continues to surface from time to time. Active proponents today commonly go by the name, Church of God in Christ. They are also known as the "Jesus Only" or "Oneness" Pentecostals in that they baptize "in the name of Jesus only." Their rationale: though Jesus commanded baptism be done "in the name of the Father, and of the Son, and of the Holy Spirit" (Matt. 28:19), when the Holy Spirit descended on Pentecost to "guide (the apostles) in all the truth," Peter commanded the penitents to "be baptized in the name of Jesus (only)" (Acts 2:38, cp. 19:5). Hence their shibboleth: "Bless God, the name of Jesus is the name of the Father, and of the Son, and the Holy Spirit." The three, they say, are one in him — in "Jesus Only."

Such a hypothesis is fraught with grave problems which demand an answer. 1. Who was in charge of the universe when God, the Son (to be), was gestating in the womb of Mary? Or did the metamorphosis take place at Jesus birth? If then, was the fetus neither a human or Divine being, just so much tissue developing in human form? When does a fetus become a person? Are abortionists right after all?

2. To whom did men pray when God, the Father of Abraham and Isaac and Jacob, had ceased to exist as a person

and was beginning existence anew in the womb of a virgin?

3. To whom did Jesus pray during the days of his flesh, and who answered him when he prayed? For example, at his baptism (Matt. 3:17), and his transfiguration (Matt. 17:5), and when he prayed, "Father, glorify thy name" (John 12:28,29). Was Jesus a super ventriloquist? Could he bounce his voice off of clouds?

4. Was he schizophrenic? Did he go about talking to himself, often out loud? Someone has suggested it is not so bad when one starts talking to oneself, but when one starts answering oneself it is time to be concerned. If Jesus were the only God there was in the days of his flesh, just a temporary mode in a three-mode sequence, Jesus not only talked to himself, he answered himself — right out loud at that.

5. Was John mixed up concerning the identity of "the antichrist(s)"? Many are today. According to John we should speak of such in the language of pluralism. He did, and not in an eschatological context. He said, "even now have there arisen many antichrists" (I John 2:18,19, cp. 4:3). Moreover, he labeled by that name one branch of gnosticism then prevailing, and identified its insidious error: "This is the anti-christ, even he that denieth *the Father, and the son*" (I John 2:22).

BIBLICAL BASIS PROPOSED FOR THE DOCTRINE OF THE TRINITY

The Old Testament

It is an old saying that "what becomes patent in the NT was latent in the OT." Perhaps so. But some question whether the doctrine of the trinity is patent (open to perusal) in the NT. At best, it was well in excess of two hundred years following the penning of the final NT document that the doctrine of the trinity was cast into its classic form. Moreover, as previously noted, no sect of Judaism, no school of Rabbis, in fact no one (of record) having only the OT scriptures from which to work, conceived that the

God revealed in the OT was a triune God, or even a dual-person deity. Only as we read the OT in the light of the NT do we find what might be interpreted as hints that God was preparing our minds for a trinitarian view of a Godhead in which perfect unity exists despite a triplicity of persons.

That noted, in the light of the NT reference data that may be cited in support of the doctrine of the trinity, two items of reference data in the OT may be offered in support of the doctrine: a) The Hebrew word for God, *Elohim*, is a plural noun. Those of the unitarian persuasion are quick to point out that plural forms may be "hebraisms" denoting majesty and completeness. Such a premise is not supported by inequivocal evidence, but bears consideration.

b) Other plural forms of speech are found which do offer some support. In Genesis 1:26 God (*Elohim*) is cited as saying, "Let us make man in our image." In 3:22 we read that Jehovah God (*Yahweh Elohim*) said, "behold the man is become as one of us, to know good and evil." Isaiah 6:8 records concerning his call that he heard the seraphim cry one to another, "Holy, holy, holy (thrice holy) is Jehovah of hosts," and he heard the voice of the Lord (*Adonai*, pl., "lords") saying: "Whom shall I send, and who will go for *us?*" (v. 9).

Isaiah 48:16 seems to make a distinction between God and his Spirit. The plural construction (*Adonai*) of the Hebrew word for Lord (*Adon*) is used. Here Isaiah writes: "*Adonai* (the Lords) have sent me, and his Spirit." Again it is countered that *Adonai*, the plural form of *Adon* is a Hebraism denoting majesty, not plurality. That is said to conform to Hebrew thought before the coming of Christ, and the light of the NT sheds back upon the OT. But be that as it may, the text provides some basis of a distinction between the Lord and his Spirit.

The New Testament

The New Testament, taken together with the Old Testament,

provides the basis for nine propositions from which a trinitarian doctrine of the Godhead may be inferred. Basic data is as follows:

a) God is one. "Jehovah, he is god, there is none else besides him" (Deut. 4:35). "Hear, O Israel, Jehovah, our God is one god" (cp. Mark 12:29,32, citing Deut. 6:4). "No idol is anything in the world, there is no God but one" (I Cor. 8:4). Note, while on the surface these texts would seem to lay to rest any suggestion of plurality within the Godhead, both the NT passages were cited by Jews who accepted the full deity of Jesus.

b) Jehovah Elohim, the Father, is God. In addition to texts cited in proposition one, note John 8:54. Jesus affirms: "It is my Father that glorifies me: of whom you (Jews, monotheistic to the core) say, that he is your God." "Yet to us there is one God, the Father, of whom are all things, and we unto him; and one Lord, Jesus Christ, through whom are all things, and we through him" (I Cor. 8:6).

c) Jesus Christ the Son is God, even the Son of the Living God. (Matt. 16:16,17). According to verse 17, it was the Father himself who revealed to Peter that bedrock (*petra*) truth of the Christian faith. (See also John 1:1-14; 3:16; Phil. 2:5-11; Heb. 1:1-4; I John 2:22; etc.)

d) The Holy Spirit is God. "Know you not that your body is a temple of the Holy Spirit, which is in you, which you have from God?" (I Cor. 6:19). "Know you not that you are a temple of God? and that the Spirit of God dwelleth in you" (I Cor. 3:16). "Now the Lord is the Spirit" (II Cor. 3:17). Cp. Jesus' farewell discourse in which he stated that the Holy Spirit whom the Father would send in Jesus' name, would be "another Comforter" (*paraclete* — one called alongside) John 14:16,17,26; 15:26; 16:13.

e) The Father, Son and Holy Spirit are distinguishable from one another. Hear Jesus: "I (one person) will pray the Father (another person, unless Jesus meant he would be talking things out with himself, thinking out loud, so to speak), and He will send you another Comforter (a third person in the sphere of deity) that

He may abide with you for ever" (John 14:16). Note the circumstances of Jesus' baptism: Father, Son and Holy Spirit all manifested, but as three separate persons: one in heaven, one on earth, one transmitted from heaven to earth.

f) The Father is spoken of as personal. This hardly requires proof. What a distinction between the gods of the heathen and the God of Heaven! No dumb idol is Jehovah! He speaks, He acts. He holds the world in his hands. He sent his Son to be our Saviour.

g) The Son is most certainly a person. "He became flesh and dwelt among us, and (men) beheld his glory, glory as of the only begotten from the Father, full of grace and truth" (John 1:14). How human he was. "Touched with the feelings of our infirmities, yet without sin" (Heb. 4:15).

h) The Holy Spirit is spoken of as personal. While the noun *pneuma* is neuter, and occasionally neuter pronouns are used, the reason is grammatical, not propositional. We have previously noted the explanation for the phenomenon. That usage is counterbalanced by the repeated use of masculine pronouns, as in John 14:26; 15:26; 16:7-14.

In addition, personal characteristics are repeatedly attributed to the Holy Spirit. He has a mind (Rom. 8:27). He loves (Rom. 15:30). He wills (I Cor. 12:11; Heb. 2:4). He reveals truth (John 16:13). He was sent to call to the memory of the apostles things Jesus had taught. He can be lied to and grieved (Acts 5:32, cp. v. 9, Eph. 4:30). And he was sent as another Comforter, to be with the disciples in Jesus' stead.

i) The Father, Son and Holy Spirit are spoken of as one. Cp. proposition 5 (above). First Corinthians 12:4-6 closely links the three personages as sharing jointly in the bestowal of spiritual gifts:

> Now there are diversities of gifts, but the same Spirit. And there are diversities of ministrations, and the same Lord. And there are diversities of workings, but the same God, who worketh all things in all.

This is a provocative text. The nine "gifts, ministrations and workings" are mentioned in a context which seem to suggest the three classifications of *pneumatikon* (cp. v. 1) are related respectively to different manifestations of a divine trinity. But verse 11 then reads: "But all these worketh the one and the same Spirit, dividing unto each one severally even as he will" (Cp. Heb. 2:4).

At the least the passage suggests there is some distinction of persons and distinction of labor in "the Godhead." Jesus once said: "My Father worketh until now, and I work" (John 5:17). While closely related, their work was not identical. So, too, with the Holy Spirit. It is written: In the beginning God created the heavens and the earth . . . and the spirit of God moved upon the face of the waters" (Gen. 1:1,2).

Unlike many who express themselves on the topic before us I candidly confess that while my faith has been deeply rooted in the trinitarian model of the Godhead, I readily acknowlege the arguments advanced are inferential. They are creedal in their essential phraseology. But to varying degrees so are the alternatives.

AN ANALOGY FROM NATURE

When called upon to explain how three persons, the Father, Son and Holy Spirit, can be one in essence, and yet so diverse in manifestation they can be reckoned as three entities (persons), an analogy from nature comes to mind.

Throughout the high Sierras, Rockies and other lofty mountain ranges of our western states, there is to be seen a phenomenon present in the tourist season that is worthy of reflection. Atop the high mountains, and often for some distance down the slopes, are to be seen massive deposits of ice and snow. To be seen also are clouds of mist being drawn heavenward as the sun in the rarefied air melts the snowfield deposits. But not all the melt is vaporized by the action of the sun and wind. Much of it turns to water and flows down from the snow fields into the valley below.

All of that of which we speak is one in essence, the most widely distributed chemical compound on the face of the earth, H_2O. In its liquid state we call it water. As a vapor we call it mist, or steam, depending on the temperature thereof. In its solid form we call it ice or snow, depending on the state of crystallization in which it is observed. But whatever the form in which we observe or make use of it, liquid, solid or gaseous, hot or cold, or whatever degree thereof in between, its chemical makeup, its essential essence, remains the same — H_2O, two molecules of hydrogen and one of oxygen, per atom. Yet each form differs in appearance and serves a different purpose.

Fortunately for life forms upon the earth, for which it is essential for life itself, and particularly so for mankind, the three forms in which H_2O appear serve three different functions, and many sub-functions in each of its major forms. We use its solid form to cool, chill and freeze various commodities, to serve as slides for sledding and skiing, and as bridges across streams and bodies of water. We use its gaseous state for sterilizing and for other functions in which evaporation is essential to the process. We use water for bathing, for cleansing of items various and sundry, to float water craft carrying passengers and freight up and down rivers and across large bodies of earth's most plentiful resource.

An illustration actually proves nothing, but it often opens windows for our minds, that "the eyes of our hearts may be enlightened" (Eph. 1:18). To those who aver that the idea of three Gods being one God, yet three in manifestation and function is unthinkable, again we say, "What is thinkable depends on who is doing the thinking."

It is also fortunate for us that in our relationship to the Godhead we are never faced with the problem which is often latent in the heads of families. Husbands and wives are supposed to be one. But very early children learn that oneness can be broken and used to personal advantage. One can get away with some things by going through one channel (father) and gain other advantages by-passing father and working on the sympathies of mother, or vice versa. But not so with the Godhead. The same terms and/or conditions on which we make peace with God, or serve Christ or grieve not the Holy Spirit are the basis on which we establish the right relationship and serve one and all.

Again, let it be remembered, that analogies, illustrations and the like prove nothing. But they open the mind to possibilities that might not otherwise occur to us. However, dogmatic trinitarians will do well to bear in mind what we have briefly touched upon passing. If belief in the Nicene formulation of the doctrine of the trinity is essential to an orthodox view of the Godhead, then no school of Jewish thought, yea, not Jew *per se*, prior to the Christian era held an orthodox view of God — neither Moses, the lawgiver, nor the prophets, nor the poets. In fact until the onset of the Arian controversy which culminated in the Nicene council, this was true of the church also.

Despite the implications we now see in such texts as Isaiah 7:14 and 9:6 no one (of record) reading such texts in the pre-Christian era conceived that the Messiah would actually be a Divine personage, co-equal, co-existent and co-eternal with Jehovah, who would somehow empty himself of the form of God and be born in the guise of a man. Messianic prophecies were uniformly interpreted as referring to a fellow mortal whom God would call, as he did Moses and the prophets, and anoint with his spirit and power.

The manner in which even the most devout Jews understood the messianic prophecies underscores the fact that while rabbinical interpretations of such predictions were flawed, that was understandably so. If we had only their reference data and found in the Shema (Deut. 6:4,5) the touchstone of our faith, in much the same sense that John 3:16 serves us today, we would likely be no more trinitarian than they. The Divine demonstration chronicled for us in the Gospels was yet to come. And even then, even the apostles, though witnesses of that demonstration, and sitting at his feet as he taught them, were slow to comprehend it.

96

Recall John's words, written while reflecting upon Jesus' triumphal entry: "These things understood not his disciples at the first, but when Jesus was glorified, then remembered they that these things were written of him, and that they had done these things unto him" (John 12:16).

Theological reflection at the level of the apostolic witnesses may be reckoned as inspired of God. This is not necessarily true, if at all, of church councils. The latter is also true of current authors, the present writer included. Nonetheless, we venture a third and final argument, admittedly philosophical, supportive of a view that sees some distinction of persons within the sphere of deity philosophically tenable, if not essential.

A Philosophical Argument

All arguments in the area of our present inquiry are to some degree philosophical, some more so than others. The following is admittedly an exercise in speculation, but not without some basis in logic and reason. In the light of observation and experience it would seem that some being with whom God can inter-relate, existing eternally with God himself, is necessitated by the attributes assigned to God throughout the Scriptures.

For example, God is defined as love — love in its highest form of expression. For one to love demands both a subject (a lover) and an object (someone loved). If there were no one, even no thing for God to love prior to his work of creation, then he only became a lover somewhere in the process, or the aftermath, of creation. Or was God originally swallowed up in narcissistic self-adulation? Love can be a growing thing, but it requires an object for love to be substantive.

Likewise, the other attributes of a personal character attributed to God could have neither occasion nor meaning, and certainly no mode or avenue of expression if God once existed as a solitary monad.

The foregoing argument proves nothing, for it proceeds from the perspective of our limited human experience, but from all that our experience teaches us, it is so. And do not the Scriptures teach us that God made man in his own image, after his likeness? That is certainly not to be interpreted physically, but metaphysically. And it is in the realm of metaphysics we are now reasoning.

If God became a lover upon creating the Logos described in the prologue of John's gospel, as per the Arian hypothesis, then in one sense God changed. That change would lie at the very heart of the Divine nature. The Old Testament virtually closes with God himself declaring: "I am Jehovah (*Yahweh*) I change not" (Mal. 3:6). The affirmation is most significant in view of the meaning of the name by which God has seen fit to be known. Yahweh signifies the one who has intrinsic, self, underived existence. It is to be noted that the name is shared with Christ in Psalm 110:1. Jesus so understood the saying, and even the lawyers could not gainsay it. (See Matt. 22:44; Mark 12:36. The same was noted by Peter in Acts 2:34 and is further so noted in Heb. 1:3.)

The same equality with Jehovah is nowhere attributed to the Holy Spirit by the Biblical writers. That is of later ecclesiastical, creedal reconstruction. It may be true, but not uncontrovertibly so, according to the Scriptures. However once the door is opened to accept the essential and eternal Godness of the pre-incarnate Christ the Logos, the rigid monotheism of Judaism is broken. If an analogy can be drawn from the fact that man, a tripartite being, was created in God's image, the triunity of God is at least a viable hypothesis.

Section Two
SPIRITUAL GIFTS

6

THE BAPTISM OF THE HOLY SPIRIT

PART ONE

East is east, and west is west, and never the twain shall meet. So goes an old saying. The saying is both true and false. Were two travelers to set forth to follow the equator around the earth, but in opposite directions, the east bound traveler and his west bound counterpart would meet somewhere on the other side of the globe, unless one or the other should turn back or turn aside. The saying is therefore not absolutely true.

Those pursuing a study of the baptism of the Holy Spirit are often somewhat akin to the two globe trotters. Unless one or the other backs down, or turns aside from a headlong, headstrong pursuit they will clash head-on. And neither will get anywhere, neither in terms of arriving at the truth, nor with respect to convincing the party of the opposition.

There are two principal, but strongly opposing, views on the subject of the baptism of the Holy Spirit. Both views are championed as "restorationist" positions. 1) The self-styled "pentecostalist" position is that the baptism of the Holy Spirit, as credentialized by the speaking in tongues, was the normative experience of the church in the apostolic age. Hence the mark of the restoration of the apostolic order "in these latter days" will be the renewal of the Holy Spirit at the baptismal level, credentialized by speaking in tongues.

A verse (Joel 2:23), taken from the same chapter of Scripture that Peter cited on Pentecost as being fulfilled then and there, is commonly cited as proof of the Pentecostalist position. The text reads:

> Be glad then, ye children of Zion, and rejoice in Jehovah your God: for he giveth you the former rain in just measure (lit. "in righteousness"), and he causeth to come down for you the rain, the former rain and the latter rain.

The clause, "the former rain and the latter rain" is interpreted as promising that an outpouring of miraculous spiritual gifts would mark both the former and the latter days of the church age.

2) The position that has become traditional with our segment of Christendom, also set forth as a "back to Pentecost" and hence a "restoration" movement, strongly denies that the baptism of the Holy Spirit, as credentialized by tongue speaking (or otherwise) was ever the norm of the church. Therefore, much less will the baptism of the Holy Spirit, or tongues as a sign thereof, be a distinguishing mark of a restored church.

Christian churches/churches of Christ generally have agreed with the Pentecostalists (ill-advisedly so) that speaking in tongues was *the* credentializing mark, the proof positive, of the baptism of the Holy Spirit. The reasoning is as follows: a) Since tongue speaking (at least as it was manifested on Pentecost) was a limited phenomenon — limited in both time and distribution, and b) since such speaking is nowhere demonstrated today, c) therefore the baptism of the Holy Spirit (of which such tongue speaking was the credentializing sign on both occasions) nowhere occurs today. The argument that the baptism was fulfilled for all time "representatively" by two historic episodes: a) on Pentecost, (the apostles receiving the gift in representation of the Jews), and b) at Caesarea, (the house of Cornelius receiving the gift on behalf of the whole of the Gentile world), is seriously flawed. Those so persuaded are obliged to crack the door at least once to credentialize Saul of Tarsus for the apostleship. He both professed and demonstrated himself to be "no whit behind the very chiefest apostles" (II Cor. 11:5). Specifically, he declared he spoke with tongues, and apparently not just on a one-time basis (I Cor. 14:18).

Pentecostals are quick to point out a) that tongue speaking was most certainly not limited to two episodes. (See Acts Chs. 2 and 10, cp. Acts 19:1-6; I Cor. 12-14 and, by inference, Acts 8:14-18). And, b) neither was the baptism of the Holy Spirit. (See I Cor. 12:13, and by inference note the text from Joel cited by Peter on Pentecost, Acts 2:16-21, plus the context of John the baptist's prediction of the baptism of the Holy Spirit, particularly as recorded in Matthew 3:7-12, Luke 3:7-17.)

The "faith-only" revisionists of Christian doctrine agree with the Pentecostalists in universalizing the baptism of the Holy Spirit but for an altogether different reason. Their problem is to find an escape hatch from the NT linkage of baptism with the remission of sins and salvation. If the repeated NT references to the benefits which accrue from baptism can be interpreted as referring to Holy Spirit baptism versus water baptism their dogma of salvation by faith alone can be taught with less and less respect for what Paul has called "the obedience of faith" (Rom. 1:5; 16:26; cp. 6:17).

TERMINOLOGY: TRADITIONAL, AND OPEN-ENDED

Any attempt at a serious open-minded restudy of the Biblical doctrine of the baptism of the Holy Spirit calls for a reassessment of the traditional terminology that has become loaded and stereotyped. Even Biblical language itself sometimes falls into that category. Further study and new insights are often stifled thereby.

1. The vintage stereotyped terms which have been in common use for so long they are often equated with the Biblical data *per se* need to be laid aside if we are to enter upon an open-ended restudy of the baptism of the Holy Spirit. With a view to lessening the bias of both the author and perchance "the objector" of this study, we suggest some new forms of expressions that may not be as readily viewed controversially.

The discussion of spiritual gifts has long been categorized by many under such headings as: a) the baptismal gift (or simply, the "baptism") of the Holy Spirit, b) the "spiritual" gifts (plural) or the "miraculous" or "extra-ordinary" or "specialized" gifts of the Holy Spirit, and c) the gift (singular) of the Holy Spirit; and in that descending order. The latter has been often referred to as the "ordinary" gift of the Holy Spirit, or sometimes (somewhat less disparagingly) as "the indwelling presence" of the Holy Spirit.

Those of the non-Pentecostal persuasion have espoused the position that a) the twelve apostles (Matthias included, but none of the rest of "the 120 brethren") received on Pentecost the baptism of the Holy Spirit as a lifetime endowment. b) Cornelius and his household received the baptism of the Holy Spirit, but on a limited basis. For them it was but an affair more or less of the moment, and included nothing more than the power to speak in tongues on that lone occasion.

Such a paradigm is fraught with difficulties. If the baptismal gift the apostles received was a lifetime gift, and included the power to perform signs and wonders, and even to impart (through the laying on of their hands) miraculous gifts to others (Acts 8:18), how could the gift Cornelius and his household received as an affair of the moment be called by Peter, "the like gift" as that which he and his fellow apostles received "at the beginning"? (Acts 11:15-17).

Either the baptism of the Holy Spirit is not as stereotyped a gift as some would have us believe, or the gift Peter was referring to was not the baptism of the Holy Spirit, only the gift of tongues *per se*. The problem of the latter conjecture is two-fold. 1) Peter equated the miracle he witnessed at Caesarea with the miracle demonstrated via himself and his fellow apostles on Pentecost. 2) The only sure proof we have that the apostles were baptized in the Holy Spirit on the day of Pentecost is that Peter informs us that what he witnessed at the house of Cornelius caused him to "remember" the word of the Lord, how he said, "John indeed baptized with water, but you shall be baptized in the Holy Spirit" (Acts 11:16).

Luke did not see fit to tie the miracle of Pentecost with John's prediction that Christ would demonstrate his more exalted role by baptizing in the Holy Spirit. Perhaps Luke took it for granted that his readers would make the application on their own from what he recorded in Acts 2:1-4. Peter took nothing for granted when called upon to justify having extended the rite (and right) of water baptism to the gentiles. Since God gave unto them the like gift which He had poured upon the apostleship at "the beginning" of the church, even the baptism of the Holy Spirit, how could he (Peter, who witnessed the demonstration) refuse to baptize them in water?

2. But the real problem is yet to be faced. Peter had said to his hearers on Pentecost, concerning what they were seeing and hearing (cp. Acts 2:23): *"This is that"* which was spoken by Joel (2:28-32), to wit:

> And it shall come to pass in the last days, saith God, I will pour forth of my Spirit upon all flesh: and your sons and your daughters shall prophesy, and your young men shall see visions, and your old men shall dream dreams. Yea, upon my servants and on my handmaidens will I pour forth of my Spirit and they shall prophesy (Joel 2:28,29; Acts 2:17,18).

Note: (1) In the verses that immediately follow (see Joel 2:30,31; Acts 2:19-21). Joel switched to apocalyptic language, adopting the imagery of fearsome celestial phenomena commonly used by the prophets to predict the downfall of kings and nations, and/or the end of an era. See Isaiah's prediction of Babylon's downfall (Isa. 13:1,9,10, and of Edom (34:8-10), and Ezekiel's prediction of the downfall of Egypt and the then reigning Pharaoh (Ezek. 32:2,5-8). Compare Jesus' prediction of the destruction of Jerusalem and the downfall of the house of Herod and of Caiaphas, and their underlings: and (covenantly speaking) the end of the era, and the coming of the NT era with its universal gospel replacing Moses and the Law (Matt. 24:29-31).

Note: (2) More to the point is the fact that in the prosaic language of the verses printed above, Joel's prophecy indicated the outpouring of the Holy Spirit would be far more extensive than the initial outpouring on Pentecost and the Caesarean episode might indicate. Women as well as men, both the young and old, servants, handmaidens, yea "all flesh" (mankind) would receive the gift of the Holy Spirit which Peter unequivocally identified as the "baptism in the Holy Spirit" (Acts 11:15-18).

And that is not the end of the problem. How can the two-episode theory be reconciled with Jesus' prediction of the baptism of the Holy Spirit? If we had only Mark's account one might do so. But the account given by Matthew 3:7-12 and Luke 3:7-9 forbids such a restricted application. Both accounts set the promise of the baptism of the Holy Spirit in the context of a warning concerning the alternative thereto: the baptism of fire. The two baptisms, both of which are the province of Christ to administer, are (together) universal. Those who are not baptized by him in the Holy Spirit will be baptized in fire — the awesome destruction that awaits the unredeemed in the lake of fire. The two baptisms are plainly said to encompass the entire human race.

Note the context, and what is said. Except for the forced interpretation that the second facet of the prediction (the baptism in fire) was jointly fulfilled with the other (the baptism in the Holy Spirit), it is commonly recognized that the fiery baptism spoken of refers to the coming destruction of ungodly men in the time of the wrath to come (Cp. II Thess. 1:7-10; Rev. 20:12-15).

There was neither wind nor fire on the day of Pentecost. Those who "heard a sound *as* of a rushing mighty wind" behaved in a manner quite out of keeping with those who hear the awesome sound of an actual hurricane or tornado. They ran *toward* the sound thereof, not from it. Evidently when only a sound *as* of such a wind was heard, when the trees did not sway, bend, break or uproot, and when litter and the like did not come hurtling toward them, curiosity replaced anxiety. They ran to see what was happening. Upon arriving at the place from which the phenomena were emanating they saw not fire but an apparition described as "tongues *like as* of fire." The apostles were not busy beating out flames. They were speaking in the idiom of the "back home" language (Gr. *idia dialecto*) of all who heard.

Note the context in which John spoke of the baptism of fire. The word "fire" appears three times in the warning which he sounds forth.

He (Christ) shall baptize you in . . . (Matt. 3:10-12).

Elements	(✔)Check: Recipients
Fire (v. 10)	( )A few "corrupt" trees (✔)"Every tree not bearing fruit"
The Holy Spirit —— (v. 11) And Fire	( )Apostles & Cornelius' household only (?) ( )All "born of water and the Spirit" —— ( )A few impenitent persons (✔)All impenitent unregenerates
Fire (v. 12)	( )A fork full, or so, of "chaff" (✔)All "the chaff"

Two facts should be very obvious from the foregoing reference data. 1) John certainly was not suggesting only a few fruitless trees and a little chaff here and there is ordinarily burned, hence by analogy only a few of the wicked will be cast into hell, to be destroyed by unquenchable fire. By the same token it is equally plain: 2) John also most certainly was not suggesting that only a few fruit trees receive any special care, and only a bushel or so of wheat is ever harvested, hence by analogy only a token few of the human race, (twelve Jews and one household of Gentiles) were chosen to receive the baptism of the Holy Spirit.

From the context of the passage (Luke 3:16,17), it should be evident the two baptisms spoken of — in the Holy Spirit, and in fire (together) — are universal in their scope. If we do not receive the one from Christ in this life, we shall be sentenced to receive the other in the time to come. Thus it is written: "In one Spirit are we all baptized into one body, whether Jews or Greeks, whether bondman or free, and were all made to drink of the one Spirit" (I Cor. 12:13).

FRESH "OPEN-ENDED" TERMINOLOGY
SET FORTH AND ASSESSED

As an alternative to the traditional terminology we hereby suggest three descriptive terms which have been found helpful: a) The Apostolic (unique) gift of the Holy Spirit, b) the Assisting (utilitarian) gifts of the Holy Spirit, c) the Abiding (universal) gift of the Holy Spirit.

The Apostolic (Unique) Gift

That the apostles had a unique, unequaled, bestowal of the Holy Spirit is a fact few would care to challenge. How are we to account for their clearly demonstrated prerogatives and powers?

To say they were baptized in the Holy Spirit (which no one denies) is not enough. So was Cornelius and his household (Acts 11:15-17). But what prerogatives or what powers did they exercise beyond the day of their conversion? Upon whom did they lay hands and impart thereby the gift of tongues, or some other? What portion of the New Testament revelation was any of them called upon to write for posterity? Apart from receiving a credentializing sign, needed to attest to the fact that "to the Gentiles also God has granted repentance unto life" (Acts 11:18), what else accrued from the episode?

One thing of record resulted. No doubt it was the very reason God visited the baptism of the Holy Spirit upon them in a manner that was immediately manifest to all present. One thing needed to be signally demonstrated once for all: "To the gentiles also God has granted repentance unto life" (Acts 11:18). On the basis of what the six Jewish brethren that came with Peter had witnessed, he asked: "Can any man forbid the water that these should not be baptized who have received the Holy Spirit as well as we?" (Acts 10:47). Since the day of the "faith only" reconstructionists had not yet come, none rose to the challenge. The report silenced the questioners back home (Acts 11:18) and was convincing to the Jerusalem conference also (Acts 15:7-10).

Viewed in that light we can readily see why Peter commanded Cornelius and his household to be baptized in water. Water baptism dramatizes the manward side of the conversion process. Hence we have in the episode a clue as to why Paul speaks of the "one baptism" (Eph. 4:5) as one of the seven bonds of our unity in Christ — not water baptism only, nor Holy Spirit baptism only, but "of the water and of the Spirit" (John 3:5). They are two sides, the outward and inward facets, of the *one* baptism which unites us with our water and Spirit-baptized, *and baptizing*, Lord, (Matt. 3:11).

The question remains: If indeed "in one Spirit are we all baptized into one body" (the apostles included) how then is it the apostles manifested a unique endowment of the Holy Spirit? One possible explanation may be found in the intriguing implications of John 20:22,23. Following his resurrection Jesus is said to have breathed on them, and said: "Receive ye the Holy Spirit." This passage has but one parallel. At the first creation Jehovah breathed upon the body he had formed of the ground, and "man (Adam) became a living soul," the progenitor of the whole of the human race (Gen. 2:7). On the threshold of "the new creation" (II Cor. 5:17), the parent stock from which the church was to stem was breathed upon by its Creator. This may suggest that the apostles were thereby prepared for a greater receptivity of the Holy Spirit than has been the experience of any others.

Under the Old Covenant the Holy Spirit is said to have "come upon" certain chosen ones, and later "to have departed" (I Sam. 16:12). The expression "came upon him" speaks of special endowment. The phrase is used with reference to the apostles (Acts 1:8), but there is a difference. To them it was promised the Holy Spirit would be "in" them, and would "abide with them" even "for ever" (John 14:16,17).

At the risk of seeming to cloud the issue rather than clarify it, perhaps this is as good a time as any to call attention to the fact that the nominative phrase, "the baptism of (in) the Holy Spirit," is nowhere found in the Scriptures. The verbal phrase, "baptize in the Holy Spirit," is found seven times. In five of the seven usages the expression appears in the context of a promise of something yet to come. (Matt. 3:11; Mark 1:8; Luke 3:16; John 1:5; Acts 1:5.)

Of the two remaining references, one (Acts 11:16) appears in the context of an historical flashback. Peter, upon witnessing the descent of the Holy Spirit at Caesarea, "remembered the word of the Lord, how he said, John indeed baptized in water, but you shall be baptized in the Holy Spirit." Seeing that promise extended to the Gentiles also opened up a new world for Peter. He was slow to enter in upon that new world but he recognized it none the less as positive proof that "to the Gentiles also God had granted repentance unto life."

The remaining reference is I Corinthians 12:13, in which Paul, in a matter-of-fact manner of speaking, states categorically: "In one Spirit are we all baptized into one body, and were all made to drink of one Spirit." If there are baptizings in the Holy Spirit, then there is such a thing as the baptism of the Holy Spirit. According to Paul, in the text just cited, baptism in the Holy Spirit is one of the facets of our salvation which makes of us one body in Christ.

That raises a thorny question: "Why then do we not all speak in tongues? That was *the* sign of the baptism of the Holy Spirit in the instance of both historic episodes unequivocally identified as such in the Scriptures. Why the change, if indeed the situation has changed? The question demands an answer. We shall address the question extensively in a later chapter; here but briefly, in the context of I Corinthians 12:13.

The question raised is definitely answered in the context of I Corinthians 12:13. In the previous paragraph Paul lists nine different spiritual gifts (tongues and the interpretation of tongues being included among them). Throughout, he makes it clear that not a one of the gifts is given to everyone, if indeed everyone receives even one of the listed gifts. He closes the paragraph with this blanket statement: "But all these worketh the one and the same Spirit, dividing to each one severally even as he will" (v. 11).

That should settle the question as to why everyone does not speak in tongues, though "in one Spirit we are all baptized into one body" (v. 13). (Cp. Heb. 2:1-4, particularly the last clause of v. 4.)

Baptize, Baptism Defined: Metaphorically

This seems a good time to define the terms baptize and baptism. These are onomatopoetic words, i.e. words the sound of which suggests the sense or meaning. Words which are coined from the sound heard when certain things are done are so called. Splash, bang, rattle, hiss, roar, crackle, squish, dip, etc., are examples. Baptize is a classic example. Like our English word dip the Greek root *bapt* is a phonetic syllable in which the Greeks attempted to imitate (vocally) the sound heard when something was dropped or dipped into a liquid. Etymologically, baptize means: "the act of (ize) *bapting* (dipping).

Metaphorically, the meaning of a word moves from the *sound* of the action to the *result*. Whenever something is dipped, immediately it is overflowed, overwhelmed. Hence, metaphorically, to be baptized is to be overwhelmed. We can only speak of ourselves as baptized in the Holy Spirit if we are yielded to His control. The gifts He gives are "according to His own will," not by popular, or our personal, demand.

<h2 style="text-align:center">PART TWO</h2>

At this point in our study we do well to note that when the terms, baptize, baptism are used metaphorically the emphasis shifts from the action ordinarily implied by the verb to the effect of the action. This is to be noted not only in the case of the baptism of the Holy Spirit but also of the baptism of fire. It is also true of the inferential expression, the "baptism of suffering" (Matt. 20:22,23; Mark 10:38,39; Luke 12:50).

When something (or someone) is "dipped," whatever the substance the object of the verb is plunged into, the object is forthwith withdrawn. In the case of non-aquatic creatures the quick withdrawal is obviously necessary. But when one is baptized in the Holy Spirit, or in fire, or into the experience of "suffering for Christ," in the sense of being subjected to the extensive persecution of which Jesus was warning, one is not momentarily plunged into the Holy Spirit, or into the fiery judgment that awaits the wicked, nor into the throes of persecution, and forthwith withdrawn. In each of these metaphorical usages of the term under consideration the emphasis shifts from the action implied by the literal meaning of baptize and/or baptism to the state one enters thereby.

Since we are not "dipped" into the Holy Spirit and forthwith withdrawn therefrom we can only speak of being baptized in the Holy Spirit if one has placed oneself under the Spirit's control. Thus the powers (gifts) imparted by the Holy Spirit are "according to his own will," not by popular or personal demand. We need also to note there is another class of "spiritual gifts" which are grown, not bestowed. Those gifts are the abiding evidence that one's life has been voluntarily placed under the control of the Holy Spirit. That is baptism of the Holy Spirit in the sense in which Paul idealizes the phenonmenon in I Corinthians 12:13.

It never ceases to amaze me to learn of a "charismatic renewal" meeting in which the sponsors openly invite the public to come and "learn how to speak in tongues." Many a "seance" devotes a part of the late hours of the meeting to learning and perfecting speaking in tongues — the later the hour and the groggier the neophytes the better. Some call it "tarrying" in a lame attempt to find in Luke 24:49 a Biblical precedent for extended efforts to get the gift — a sort of "if at first you don't succeed, try, try again" approach. Learning and practice sessions are calculated to up the percentages. Whatever comes from such sessions, it is not apostolic, it is not Pentecost renewed, it is not "charismatic" — the "*free* gift of God."

Speaking categorically, the baptism of the Holy Spirit is the Divine side of the one baptism into the one body, which is the body of Christ. From the human side it requires "the obedience from the heart to that form of doctrine which was delivered us" (Rom. 6:17), whereby the penitent believer, "transformed by the renewing of the mind" (Rom. 12:2) "presents his/her body unto God as an instrument of righteousness," to "be buried with Christ in baptism unto death (of sin), to be raised to walk in newness of life" (Rom. 6:4,13).

Outwardly (initially) baptism consists of the surrender of the body to the overwhelming waters in an act symbolic of Christ's demonstration of his full surrender to the Father in his death, burial and resurrection. Inwardly, it consists of the surrender of the human spirit to the overwhelming of the Holy Spirit in an act symbolic of the death of our carnal minds and the "renewing of our minds by the Holy Spirit" (I Cor. 12:13; Titus 3:5). Thus it is that Paul could write Romans 6, Colossians 2:12,13, Galatians 3:27 and I Corinthians 12:13, and yet say in Ephesians 4:4,5 "there is one body and one Spirit, one lord, one faith, one baptism."

Baptism is used metaphorically in the Scriptures in other contexts than the baptism of the Holy Spirit. a. It is used of the baptism in fire. Reason precludes a literal meaning in this case. The wicked are not just dipped into the lake of fire. They are "cast therein" and are completely and irrevocably subject to the conditions therein.

b. Jesus spoke of a baptism of suffering. Long after he had been baptized by John in the Jordan he put to his disciples a question that likely supplied the apostle Paul the imagery for I Corinthians 12:13: "Are you able to drink the cup that I drink? or to be baptized with the baptism wherewith I am baptized?" (Mark 10:38). Their answer was, "We are able." At the time they likely had little idea what he was really asking. He answered them, "the cup that I drink, ye shall drink, and with the baptism that I am baptized you shall be baptized" (v. 39).

We speak in the same vein when we speak of raw soldiers receiving their "baptism in fire" when for the first time they are in the heat of battle with shrapnel falling all around them. By the same token we speak of a football team receiving their baptism when the forward wall of the opposing team rolls over them like a tidal wave.

In short, the baptism of the Holy Spirit and the baptism in water of a penitent believer are not two baptisms, but rather two facets of the "one baptism." Outwardly, baptism consists of the surrender of the body to the overwhelming waters in an act symbolic of the death, burial and resurrection of Christ. Inwardly it consists of the surrender of our spirits to the Spirit Divine in an act that calls for the death of the carnal mind and the renewing of the Holy Spirit. A baptism that a) does not engulf both the body and the soul, b) fails to make Jesus both Lord and Christ, c) or is not an obedience that is from the heart to that form of doctrine which was delivered to us, is not the baptism in which "in one Spirit we are all baptized into the one body."

Assisting (Utilitarian) Gifts of the Holy Spirit

Concerning those powers generally classified as the special (or specialized) spiritual gifts, we here suggest their special function would be better designated as the assisting (or utilitarian) gifts of the Holy Spirit. That is to say, these gifts had a definite pragmatic, utilitarian function. However, their function was auxiliary. The gifts were given to assist those otherwise endued with the Holy Spirit to do some specific thing for which special endowment was needed at the time. Unlike the gift(s) of the Holy Spirit that could be spoken of as the "filling" and/or "indwelling" of the Holy Spirit, these supplied a temporary need.

Such gifts were neither a sign of, nor reward for, advanced spiritual attainment. The Corinthian church is witness to that. According to Paul (I Cor. 1:7) the church at Corinth was second to none with respect to spiritual gifts, but they exhibited little (if any) evidence of high spiritual attainment. Moreover, Paul affirms the "moral" manifestations of the Holy Spirit which are "grown," as distinguished from the "miraculous" gifts where were "bestowed," are "greater." One such gift (love) is "the more excellent way" to go if one is wanting to manifest spiritual endowment (I Cor. 12:31). But, paradoxically, the gift of love is not sought that one might have whereof to boast. Apparently tongues, and such like, were, and often are today.

Why were the miraculous gifts given? They were needed

under the circumstances of that time. They were of three classes, and served three functions. In lieu of the NT Scriptures, which were then only in the early stages of their making, the gifts we are speaking of consisted of: 1) gifts of knowledge, providing information, 2) gifts of power (signs), providing confirmation, and 3) gifts of service, which provided administration.

Witness the need for such gifts in the instance of such a church as the church at Philippi. The Philippian church represents the first fruits of Paul's labors in Macedonia. It included a) a traveling saleswoman from Thyatira (and her "household," Acts 16:13), b) possibly "a certain damsel" from whom Paul exorcised "a spirit of divination" (vv. 16-18), and c) a jailor and his household, (vv. 27-34). Apparently, soon after the conversion of the latter, Paul found it expedient to leave the city. In doing so he left behind an infant church of a heterogenous makeup, a solitary Christian colony in the midst of a populous pagan city and a pagan nation.

How were such congregations to be nurtured and sustained? Few, if any of our NT documents had as yet been written, much less copied and circulated. There were no Christian publishing houses from which they could order Christian literature, or Bible colleges from which they could get even fledgling preachers.

The situation at Philippi was oft repeated as new congregations were formed and left pretty much on their own as evangelists moved from place to place. The situation was not always as precipitous and dramatic. Paul, for example, sometimes stayed longer and on occasion converts were made from among patrons of Jewish synagogues and even from their elders (teachers). But in all cases the fledgling congregations had three pressing needs: a) information, b) confirmation of the verity of message that came to them as "the word of the Lord," and c) leadership (administration). Through the laying on of the apostles' hands (Acts 8:18), gifts of the Holy Spirit were given, presumably tailored to the special needs of each congregation. Thus, in lieu of the continuing presence of an apostle, or a gifted understudy (such as Titus and Timothy), and in lieu of our NT documents the young churches were able to survive and grow in the grace and knowledge of the Lord Jesus.

Today, we receive the necessary information from the confirmed and completed canon of the Holy Scriptures (II Tim. 3:16,17; II Pet. 3:19-21; Heb. 2:1-4). Administration is provided for new congregations by leaders developed and drawn from sponsoring congregations or other experienced Christians who have moved to the area. The need for apostles and prophets (present in person), or miracle workers, healers, discerners of spirits, tongue speakers, etc. has long been outgrown. "Now abideth faith, hope, love" (and such like). These, "the greater gifts," (the fruit of the Spirit) are not "zapped" upon us. Fruit has to be grown, and that takes time. In this day of "instant" everything, many would have it otherwise.

The Abiding (Universal) Gift

It was a sad day when the indwelling presence of the Holy Spirit, "given to all them that obey him" (Acts 5:32), came to be called the "ordinary" gift. Technically, that which is not extraordinary, but of general experience, observation or distribution, may be so called. But the term comes across as somewhat depreciatory when applied to a gift of such consequences as the indwelling presence of the Holy Spirit (Rom. 8:11; I Cor. 3:16). A gift of God which, working together with the quickening power latent in the Word of God, and in response to one's desire to be true to the Scriptures in all that one says and does, is far from being "ordinary" no matter how often it is observed in the lives of those about us. It is thus that we "grow in the grace and knowledge of our Lord and Saviour Jesus Christ" (II Pet. 3:18).

The Greek word which suggests the term "indwelling" is *enoikountos* lit., *"in housed"* (Rom. 8:9,11; I Cor. 3:16). Paul speaks of it as "the spirit of adoption whereby we cry, Abba

117

Father, his spirit bearing witness with our spirits that we are children of God" (Rom. 8:15,16; Gal. 4:4-6). That's super-ordinary "in my Book" (the Bible — no less).

Interlude

Before attempting a wrap-up of the subject at hand it seems appropriate to interject at this point a flash-back which may help readers to see where I am coming from. The point of reference goes back some thirty years into the mid 1950's. I was at the time the president of Minnesota Bible College. The FGCBMFI (Full Gospel Christian Business Men's Fellowship International) was just beginning its underground activity aimed at infiltrating the "main-line" churches with what has been dubbed "the Charismatic Revival/Movement," "the Latter Rain," or "Pentecost Renewed."

Minneapolis/St. Paul was a prime place to begin. The Twin Cities area is the home of an unusually large number of church-related collegiate institutions — Bible colleges and institutes, seminaries, and liberal arts colleges. As a gesture of token ecumenicity the schools on occasion shared such features as choral concerts, or guest speakers addressing themselves to sub-jects of general interest. Students of the several colleges occa-sionally formed friendships in the process and dialogues concern-ing doctrinal differences sometimes ensued. Thereon hangs a tale.

Near lock-up time one evening I had occasion to go to my of-fice. A student in charge of locking the building approached me and asked if I had any idea what was going on in a certain classroom on the top floor and far corner of the building. I did not, but gathered that I ought to. So I made my way to the room indicated. From within I heard the voice of a stranger, lecturing on the baptism of the Holy Spirit. No such activity had been scheduled. Upon opening the door I found a score or so students, some from our school and some from a Bible institute serving the Pentecostal churches of the area. Their academic dean was at the podium explaining Joel 2:21-32 from the neo-Pentecostal perspective.

My entrance evoked an awkward silence. To gain some perspective I motioned for the speaker to proceed. He did so with an obvious sense of uneasiness. I was told afterwards that was in marked contrast to his manner of speaking prior to my sudden appearance. Shortly I noted his interpretation followed closely the KJV rendering of verse 33, so I raised my hand (and voice) and asked if he had taken time to research the footnotes accompanying the passage in the ASV. He allowed he was aware of the different light the ASV footnotes cast on the text, and admitted the Hebrew text was likely more accurately rendered thereby.

At that point I took over and began to present the case for the two-episode theory of the baptism of the Holy Spirit. To make a long story short, he "shot me down." Never before had such a thing happened to me. To have it happen in front of an audience, with a number of my students in the audience was doubly embarrassing. My only solace was that I "shot him down" also. Toward midnight we called a truce. The invading dean apologized for his breach of ethics. We agreed to restudy our positions and to meet again. However, we never managed to do so in any kind of confrontational setting.

The following quarter I was scheduled to teach a course on the Holy Spirit. Students who had been somewhat swayed by the interloping dean, and others who cared to do so, were invited to play the role of "the devil's advocate" or "an angel of enlightenment," howsoever they might care to view themselves. A resume of my restudy was presented at the 1966 Show Me Lectureship (Central Christian College of the Bible) under the title: *A Third Look at the Baptism of the Holy Spirit*. The manuscript was published in the *Christian Standard*, May 29 and June 5, 1966, and as an appendix to my book, *What the Bible Says About the Church* (College Press, 1985).

119

SUMMARY

Precisely, what is the baptism of the Holy Spirit? By way of answer the first thing which is needed to be done is to delete the word "precisely." The baptism of the Holy Spirit is not the stereotyped thing usually called to mind when the term is used. Neither the Pentecostalist model nor the two-episode theory conform to the total array of facts. Neither is any episode so designated in the Scriptures exactly parallel to any other.

Generally speaking, at least for most adults, the baptism of the Holy Spirit is a dramatic (and sometimes traumatic) milestone experience — an experience in which one is very much aware of undergoing a change of state as well as a change of life. In some cases the happening can be called a transformation.

The case of Saul of Tarsus is a classic example of the latter. We commonly speak of Saul's conversion, but rarely think of him as having received the baptism of the Holy Spirit. But he most certainly did. Ananias was sent to him that he might a) receive his sight, and b) "be filled with the Holy Spirit," (Acts 9:17). Thus he was able to say: "I reckon that I am not a whit behind the chiefest of the apostles" (II Cor. 11:5). He demonstrated that to be so, again and again.

The case of the twelve apostles who received the baptism of the Holy Spirit on Pentecost, years after they were baptized in water, was as dramatic an experience, but not as traumatic. They had already been baptized "for the remission of sins" (Mark 1:4) and had subsequently undergone a life transformation. Nevertheless, the baptism of the Holy Spirit was for them a milestone experience. It was "crossing the state line" so to speak, chronologically. Peter, in reporting the Caesarean episode, said of the Gentiles, "the Holy Spirit fell on them even as on us at the beginning" (Acts 11:15).

The case of Cornelius and his household was also dramatic, but likely traumatic only to the six Jewish brethren who had come along with Peter. Peter himself had already worked through the trauma of no longer writing the gentiles off as "common and unclean" (Acts 10:14). His three-fold house-top vision had helped to prepare him for the experience he was soon to undergo.

How about the rest of us? According to I Corinthians 12:13, "in one Spirit we are all baptized into one body." Our problem is we likely have been programmed to believe that all who experience the baptism of the Holy Spirit do so in the same manner and for precisely the same purpose. That is tantamount to putting the Holy Spirit in a straight jacket. The truth is that the gifts (pl.) of the Holy Spirit are given "according to his own will"; not according to our theories. The very essence of the baptism of the Holy Spirit is challenged by that notion. It would not be "baptism" in the Holy Spirit if we were in control, dictating the terms, the conditions and even the recipients.

We repeat, the term "baptism of the Holy Spirit" employs the word "baptism" in its metaphorical sense. It speaks of the overwhelming of the human spirit, *by the consent* of the human spirit; but for whatsoever purpose or service God chooses to call us.

In the case of the Corinthians Paul called their attention to the fact that the distribution of Spiritual gifts was not subject to the will of the recipients. Were that so it would appear they would all have chosen to speak in tongues. That is the gift that they too regarded as "Pentecostal." Was that not *the* manifestation of the baptism of the Holy Spirit "at the beginning"? How "apostolic" it must have seemed to "speak in other tongues." So much was that so it may even be conjectured some of them tried to "fake it." Many do so today.

7

NOW CONCERNING SPIRITUAL GIFTS

Good news! Paul wrote three chapters of Scripture (I Corinthians 12-14) that we might not "be ignorant concerning Spiritual Gifts." The passage opens with these words: "Now concerning *pneumatikon* . . ." (spiritual *gifts*). Note that "gifts" is italicized in both the KJV and ASV, and rightly so. *Pneumatikon* is an adjective. It is used twenty-six times in the NT, with reference to a number of different things. (See the special appendix at the close of the next chapter: Spiritual Gifts — Word Study Data). The context determines the noun supplied by the translators — here, and in several other places where the implied word is lacking in the Greek text (Cp. I Cor. 2:13; 9:11; Eph. 6:12).

First Corinthians 12-14 comprises the only discourse on spiritual gifts contained in the Scriptures. Nine specialized gifts are mentioned; some but barely. Three non-specialized gifts are mentioned, one of which (love) is elaborated upon in chapter 13, while two (faith and hope) are mentioned only in passing (v. 13).

Though nine specialized gifts are listed in chapter 12, not all are sufficiently described or named as to be readily identified. It would have aided our study considerably if in the case of each gift listed an example were given of someone so endowed. Especially would that be so if an instance were cited in which each gift was exercised, and how exercised, and why. Were such gifts to be a continuing and necessary endowment it would seem such would surely be called for. Otherwise those possessing such gifts would have no NT precept or precedent to guide them. First Corinthians 12:8-10 simply says:

> (8) To one is given through the Spirit the word of wisdom, and to another the word of knowledge, according to the same Spirit: (9) to another faith, in the same Spirit: and to another gifts (pl.) of healings (pl., cp. vv. 28,29) in the one Spirit: (10) to another workings (pl.) of miracles (pl.) and to another prophecy, and to another discerning of spirits: to another *diverse* kinds of tongues; and to another interpretation of tongues.

Verse 28 and verses 29,30 appear to repeat the listing of gifts bestowed on "some" in the church, but there are some differences to be noted: 1) three offices: apostles, prophets and teachers are named in the place of the word of wisdom, the word of knowlege and (word of) faith; 2) the workings of miracles are placed ahead of the gifts of healings in v. 28 and v. 30; 3) some of the gifts are either omitted or called by another name. Verse 28 and vv. 29,30 read:

> (28) And God has set some in the church, firstly apostles, secondly, prophets, thirdly teachers, then mircles, then gifts of healings, helps, governments, *diverse* kinds of tongues.
> (29) Are all apostles? are all prophets? are all teachers? are all *workers* of miracles? (30) have all gifts of healings? do all speak with tongues? do all interpret?

The differences in the three listings become quite obvious

124

when the lists are set side by side, as follows:

vv. 8-10 "to one is given	v. 28 "God has set"	vv. 29,30 "Are all"
1) the word of wisdom	firstly, apostles	apostles?
2) the word of knowledge	secondly, prophets	prophets?
3) (the word of) faith)	thirdly, teachers	teachers?
4) gifts of healings	then miracles	workers of miracles?
5) workings of miracles	gifts of healings	have gifts/healings?
6) prophecy	helps	————
		(do...? have...?)
7) discerning of spirits	governments	————
8) kinds of tongues	kinds of tongues	speak with tongues?
9) interpret. of tongues	————	interpret?

Note: The word of wisdom (inspiration?) appears to be equated with the apostolic office, the word of knowledge (providential insight and/or direction? cp. Acts 11:28; 13:1-3; 21:10,11) seems to be identified with the prophetic office, and faith with the teaching office. The latter is certainly in keeping with the dictum of Romans 10:17.

SEVERAL GUIDELINES MAY BE DEDUCED

From what Paul has written we may discern, at least tentatively, several guidelines. 1. We learn what some of the gifts were, or at least what they were called, plus the fact the terminology is somewhat variable in the case of some of the gifts.

2. The gifts appear to have been of two kinds, perhaps of two levels. a. Some were apparently "showy," i.e. capable of being exhibited in such a way as to call attention to oneself as one "gifted." This was enough so that those so possessed tended to become vain (see 12:21,22) and those not so endowed tended to feel left out, inferior (see 12:15,16). b. Some were less spectacular, less overtly demonstrable, yet are said to be "greater,"

and to be more "earnestly desired" (12:31, Ch. 13). Except for the terms just noted no other classifying terms such as spectacular, special, showy, etc. are used in the text. Such terms are, however, suggested by what is said of those who were recipients and non-recipients.

3. We have already noted there is considerable variation in the manner the gifts are listed in vv. 8-10 as compared to v. 28 and vv. 29,30. This should prove helpful in the sense that it demonstrates the terminology may not be as precise as we would prefer. For example(s):

a. Again take note of the fact that the first three gifts listed in vv. 8-10 seem to be not primary gifts of the Spirit, but modes of expression or resultants of the primary gift to the church of certain important *offices*. In Ephesians 4:8 we are told that when Christ ascended on high "he gave gifts to men." Following a parenthetical explanation of what is meant by the expression "He ascended" (vv. 9,10), Paul returns to the main theme of the paragraph and specifies the gifts spoken of. They turn out to be gifts of leadership and of service. Note v. 11, "He gave some apostles, some prophets, some evangelists, and some pastors and teachers." (Now, cp. I Cor. 12:8, with vv. 28,29.)

b. Note also that the gift of "prophecy" as mentioned in v. 10 and as distinguished from the prophetic office of v. 8 and vv. 28,29, is called "helps" (Gr. *antilempseis*) in v. 28, and receives no mention in vv. 29,30. The verb means to lay hold upon with a view to giving support or assistance.

c. A third variance is seen in the fact that "the discerning of spirits" (Gr. *diakriseis*) in v. 10 is replaced by "governments" (Gr. *kuberneseis*) in v. 28, and omitted altogether in vv. 29,30. *Diakrino* signifies to learn by discriminating, sifting. It is sometimes rendered to examine, judge. *Kubernao* means to guide or steer, hence metaphorically it is used of governing and of governments. As used here it likely signifies the use of special insight in setting a course of action. Whether it refers to the discernment Peter used in seeing through the pretension of Ananias and

Sapphira, or a more generalized insight, is not made plain. The action taken by Peter seems to be a one-time event serving as a Divine warning. Such drastic action is normally reserved for the judgment day that is yet to come.

4. It appears that the less showy gifts were no more regarded by the Corinthians than they are today as the "greater" gift, else the problem which prompted the penning of the three chapters before us likely would never have arisen. Paul, however, contends the moral gifts, (the fruitage of the Spirit), the gifts that are grown, not bestowed, are the greater, the more to be desired, and the enduring gifts (I Cor. 12:31; 13).

5. From 12:8-10 it appears some viewed their gift as inferior to what others received. Perhaps a contributing factor may have been the manner in which others paraded their gift. For some to consider themselves more favored in God's sight because they had an attention-getting gift would of itself be deplorable. But to make others feel like second-rate Christians at best, and so lacking in spiritual gifts they had nothing to contribute, is unfeeling and absurd. Paul's hypothesis underscores the absurdity. Suppose one member of the body were to say to another, "Because you are not what I am, I have no need of you, you are no part of the body that I adorn." Would the depreciated member be bereft of bodiness? Even if the brunt of such arrogance were so stripped of self-esteem as to accede to that judgment, actuality would not be changed. But functioning would likely wane.

In the light of the foregoing observations, a practical and perhaps personal question arises. Are there "spiritual gifts" today (feigned or for real) which are paraded as a mark of special spiritual endowment? Are there "gifts" so promoted as to again divide the church into the "haves" and "the have nots"? Yea verily.

6. From 12:28-31 it appears only "some" were set in the offices and/or endowed with the special abilities, that gave rise to what one writer has called "the Corinthian catastrophe." The text does not hint that all "the haves" overtly contributed to the

degrading of the "have nots," but enough did so that the non-possessors who likely were the majority of the church were made to feel inept and unwanted.

7. The arrogance of some endowed with special gifts demonstrates the fact one can have a spiritual gift and still not be a *spiritual* person. This could not be said of those whose desire is to produce the "greater gifts," the fruit of the Spirit, love, joy, peace, etc.

8. As for tongues (and its corollary, the interpretation of tongues) some interesting statistics need to be noted. a) Tongues and the interpretation of tongues are mentioned by name no less than twenty-one (21) times in the three chapters. That is as often as the other seven gifts all put together are mentioned. Moreover, b) tongues are cited as the prime source, in fact the *cause* of the disorderly conduct which marred their assembling together. Thus, c) tongues, especially in the form of prophesying in tongues, constitute the only gift(s) Paul saw fit to place under restrictions in order that all things might "be done in decency and in order" (14:40). That has a familiar ring, does it not? That was not true of the tongue speaking on Pentecost. For this reason I choose to speak of the current spate of tongues as neo-Corinthianism, rather than neo-Pentecostalism.

9. In all three lists tongues and the interpretation of tongues are listed last. The gifts by which the church was informed and edified via the offices of apostles, prophets and teachers head the list. But tongues are at "the foot of the class," so to speak. They are cited as a poor substitute for straightforward speaking in the realm of communication (14:19). To those who seek "the gift of tongues" I find myself repeatedly asking, "precisely what have you learned thereby for sure that you did not already know from the Scriptures, if anything?"

10. Obviously not all exhibited the less showy gifts, the gifts which are grown, not bestowed. But they were exhorted to do so. Such are cited as marks of maturity.

11. As noted in numbered paragraph nine (9), tongues seem

to be the gift most often abused and misused.

12. We note (13:8-13) a terminus was predicted for some gifts, e.g. tongues, but not the character trait gifts which are marks of maturity.

WE REMAIN "IGNORANT" OF SOME THINGS DESPITE WHAT PAUL WROTE

1. We do not know whether the bestowed gifts could be received other than through the laying on of the Apostles' hands. See Acts 6:6, cp. v. 8 (Stephen) and 8:6,7 (Philip), cp. 8:13-20 (Note v. 18), 19:1-7, (Baptist disciples at Ephesus), II Tim. 1:6; 4:14 (Timothy). The classic exception, the household of Cornelius (Acts 10:44-48; 11:15-18) is set forth in the Scriptures as a kind of one-time exception, and for the reason cited (see Acts 11:18).

2. We do not know what some of the gifts actually were, nor to whom they were given, nor how they were exercised (e.g. "helps").

3. We do not know if there were non-language (devotional) tongues, or whether such utterances were simply emotional outbursts, or faked. They often are faked today. To equate something that is acquired through imitation, or practice, and particularly to equate something that is learned through classes conducted to teach the "art" is hardly a "charismatic" (gracious, free) gift of God. It smacks of Corinth, not of Pentecost.

Contrast: Abiding (universal) Versus Assisting (utilitarian) Gifts

Abiding	Assisting
a) Moral	a) Miraculous
b) Grown	b) Bestowed
c) Internal	c) External
d) Achieved	d) Bestowed
e) Constant Value	e) Intermittent

Note: The abiding gift is "the fruit" of the Spirit, the goal for which the Spirit is given. The qualities cited represent the perfect blending of the Divine nature and the human spirit at its best. The assisting gifts were (sometimes) imposed upon the human spirit to meet an immediate need, usually external to those endowed. They were service oriented, not merit badges or awards for distinguished service.

HOW WERE THE GIFTS OBTAINED?

The question as to how the specialized (service) gifts were received cannot be answered by a blanket statement. A general principle may be stated, and supported. But there are variables to be noted. Answers to the question fall into two categories.

1. Some teach the spiritual gifts discussed in I Corinthians 12 are a kind of second blessing, "a second work of grace" no less. Many link the gifts with their doctrine of "sanctification." They view tongues in particular as a sign and the seal of the baptism in the Holy Spirit.

2. At the other extreme are those who hold that (with but one exception) such gifts were given only through the laying on of the hands of the apostles. The one exception, the household of Cornelius, was indeed "exceptional." That is generally conceded.

Those holding to the position that the gifts were otherwise given only through the laying on of the apostles' hands espouse a kind of "trickle down" theory. According to this model, the apostles, in the vernacular of our day were "zapped" with the Holy Spirit, and were empowered thereby to bestow through the laying on of their hands the service gifts which were necessary to equip the church in lieu of the New Testament. The Holy Spirit determined what gift was given, whether the word of wisdom or of knowledge, or the teaching office by which faith was produced in the hearts of those who were taught. Gifts of healings, the working of miracles, prophecy, discerning of spirits, tongues, and the interpretation of tongues also may have been distributed in

130

this manner.

The first position is especially fraught with problems. The bizarre behaviour of the Corinthians bears witness to that. Arrogance, unbrotherly attitudes, and disorderly conduct even in Christian worship do not bear witness to a high plateau of spiritual attainment. Yet the Corinthians spoke in tongues and prophesied, apparently in concert.

The case for the second position has somewhat to commend it. The record in Acts generally supports the view that 1) the service gifts were bestowed through the laying on of the hands of the apostles, and 2) the apostles exercised a wider range of powers (gifts) than any one else of record. Note the following facts.

a) In response to Peter's sermon, abetted undoubtedly by the miraculous signs which drew the audience together, three thousand were baptized. According to the promise held forth, they received "the gift of the Holy Spirit" (Acts 2:38,39). But verse 43 reads, "and many wonders and signs were done through *the apostles*." No mention is made of any signs and wonders being done by the multitudes who had received the gift of the Holy Spirit promised to the baptized penitents.

b) In chapter three a miracle was wrought which the intransigent Jewish rulers called "a notable miracle," lamenting "we cannot deny it" (4:18). The miracle was the healing of a man who had been lame from his mother's womb (3:2-9). It was Peter, an apostle, who performed the miracle.

c) In chapter four we read: "the multitude of them that believed were of one heart and soul" (32), but the text goes on to say, "with great power gave the apostles their witness of the resurrection." The manner in which the "great power" was demonstrated is not specified, but it is noteworthy that they, not "the multitude of them that believed," are said to have done so.

d) In chapter five (vv. 1-11) we read of the Ananias and Sapphira episode. It appears the church was taken in by their lying report calculated to make them appear more generous than they were. It was Peter who exercised what would appear to be "the discerning of spirits," and who brought down Divine judgment upon them (vv. 5:3-5,8,9).

e) In chapter six we read of the selection and appointment of seven men to a service role in the church. One of the qualifications stipulated was that they be "full of the Holy Spirit and of wisdom" (v. 3). But not until after the apostles laid their hands on them are any of them reported as doing anything miraculous. Thereafter we read that "Stephen, full of grace and power, wrought great signs and wonders among the people" (v. 8).

f) Chapter seven records Stephen's defense and martyrdom. His vision of "the glory of God, and Jesus standing at the right hand of God," (v. 55) borders on the miraculous.

g) Chapter eight has much to say to us. Philip, another of "the seven" who fled the city in the wake of the mass persecution against the church, went down into Samaria and proclaimed the Christ. There "the multitudes gave heed with one accord when they heard, and saw the signs which he did, for from many of those that had unclean spirits, they came out, crying with a loud voice: and many that were palsied, and that were lame, were healed" (vv. 6,7). Even Simon, the sorcerer was amazed. The result was that "Simon himself believed: and being baptized, continued with Philip; and beholding the signs and great miracles wrought, he was amazed" (v. 13). At this point we are told:

(14) Now when the apostles at Jerusalem heard that Samaria had received the word of God, they sent unto them Peter and John: (15) who, when they were come down, prayed for them that they might receive the Holy Spirit: (16) for as yet it was *fallen* upon none of them; only they had been baptized into the name of the Lord Jesus. (17) Then laid they their hands on them, and they received the Holy Spirit.

The next verse is worthy of special note. "Now when Simon saw that through the Apostles' hands the Holy Spirit was given, he offered them money, saying, Give me also this power, that on whomsoever I lay my hands, he may receive the Holy Spirit" (vv.

132

18,19).

It is interesting that Simon saw that. But today with the inspired account before us in writing many cannot see what Simon saw. We have earlier noted that when the Spirit of God or the Holy Spirit is said to "fall upon" someone, the expression denotes special powers conferred upon someone, not the Spirit working quietly and patiently within. The latter is given as an abiding gift to stimulate the production of the fruit of the Spirit: The other was more or less of a temporary endowment to meet a certain present need.

The rest of the chapter recounts the providential leading of the Holy Spirit that brought Philip and the Ethiopian eunuch together, after which it is said, "the Spirit of the Lord caught away Philip" (lit., "raptured" him, cp. I Thess. 4:17, a provocative phrase, the full import of which we can only guess), "and the eunuch saw him no more" (v. 39).

Chapter nine provides us one of three accounts of the conversion of Saul of Tarsus. Chapters 22 and 26 are Paul's first hand report of the happening. The role of Ananias is stated in 9:17,18 where he is recorded as saying: "Brother Saul, the Lord, (even) Jesus who appeared unto you in the way you came, has sent me that you may receive your sight, and be filled with the Holy Spirit. And immediately there fell from his eyes as it were scales, and he received his sight; and he arose and was baptized." Note the text does not indicate Ananias laid his hands on Saul, and by that means he became spiritually gifted on a par with the chiefest of the apostles, (cp. II Cor. 11:5). Everything Paul said or has written concerning his conversion, apostleship and his credentials strongly suggests otherwise.

Chapter ten, and 11:1-18, have already been duly considered in this discussion, and the reason for the exceptional order of events with regard to that notable occasion. We simply repeat, no broad generalizations can be legitimately drawn from that singular occasion. Acts 11:26 records that during Paul's stay at Antioch the name Christian was called upon that landmark interracial church by Divine direction (Gr. *chrematisai*). (Cp. Matt. 2:12,22; Luke 2:26; Acts 10:22; Rom. 7:3; Heb. 8:5; 11:7; 12:25.) The presence in their midst of the specially appointed apostle to the Gentiles is likely a factor. The chapter draws to a close (vv. 28,29) with mention of a fulfilled prophecy by one named Agabus, to which we will have occasion to refer again below.

Chapter twelve reports an answered prayer event. It is worthy of note that though "prayer was made earnestly of the church unto God" (vv. 5,12) for Peter, imprisoned by Herod and marked for execution, they seemed to have been taken by surprise when the answer to their prayer stood at the door (vv. 13-16).

Chapter thirteen returns the scene to Antioch. Three other men, along with Barnabas and Saul are identified as prophets and teachers. As they were ministering and fasting the Holy Spirit instructed them to set apart Barnabas and Saul for the work to which he had called them (vv. 1-3).

Acts 13:4-22:21 records Paul's missionary journeys, ended by his arrest in Jerusalem. A dozen extra-ordinary events are recorded:

1) 13:9-12, Paul, "filled with the Holy Spirit" temporarily blinds Elymas.

2) 14:8-10, Paul heals a congenital cripple at Lystra.

3) 14:19,20, Paul, though stoned, rises apparently from death.

4) 16:6-10, Paul, against his inclinations, is led to Macedonia.

5) 16:16-18, Paul cast a spirit of divination out of a slave girl.

6) 16:25,26, Paul, via an "unearthly" quake is freed from prison.

7) 18:9,10, Paul is comforted and assured via a night vision.

8) 19:6,7, Paul laid hands on 12 men. They "tongued," prophesied.

9) 19:11,12, Cloths from Paul's body cured ills, exorcised demons.

134

10) 19:13-16, Paul's imitators (7 sons of Sceva) failed miserably.

11) 20:8-10, Paul raised Eutychus, apparently from the dead.

12) 21:10,11, Agabus, a prophet, predicted Paul's coming arrest. As noted above, cp. 11:28,29. Every other extra-ordinary event recorded involved actions of Paul. None are attributed to travel companions.

Chapters twenty-two to the end record Paul's defense addresses, his Caesarean imprisonment, the ill-fated sea voyage to Rome and Paul's Roman imprisonment. Three extra-ordinary events are recorded. 1) At the height of the storm which resulted in a shipwreck and loss of the cargo, an angel informed Paul there would be no loss of life, nor even harm befall any of the 276 men on board (27:23, cp. vv. 34-37). 2) Paul suffered no ill effects from the viper which sprang from a fire and fastened its fangs into Paul's hand, (28:5,6), and 3) upon learning that the father of Publius, the chief officer of the island on which they came ashore, was ill with fever and dysentery, Paul healed him, and all on the island who were sick he also cured (vv. 7-9).

Granted that Peter is the central figure in the book of Acts up to the middle of Chapter 11, and Paul is the central figure in the narrative from that point on. But in the earlier chapters, when Peter was front and center, Luke did not hesitate to mention that "many signs and wonders were done by the apostles" (Acts 2:43, cp. 4:32). And he did not hesitate to point out that persons upon whom the apostles had laid their hands wrought signs and wonders also (6:8; 8:6,7,13,18). If we are to believe that others as well did so, to go along with popular theory, it is up to those who so believe to explain why the inspired historian failed not only to mention it, but failed as well to even hint at it.

THE DURATION OF THE SPECIAL SERVICE GIFTS

This brings us to the question as to the duration of the gifts of which we have been speaking. On the basis of what we have observed it would seem reasonable to suggest that 1) when the last apostle died, and 2) the last person on whom they "laid their hands" died, the signs and wonders imparted thereby ceased, or at least waned.

The truth appears to be they may not have lasted even that long. For the further we advance in New Testament history and literature the less emphasis and mention is made of confirming signs and extraordinary powers. Paul, for example, near the end of his life, wrote: "Trophimus, I left at Miletus, sick" (II Tim. 4:20). And to his dear son in the gospel, Timothy, he wrote: "Take a little wine for your stomach's sake, and your oft infirmities" (I Tim. 5:23). At the time Timothy was serving in Ephesus, whereof it was earlier written: "God wrought special miracles by the hands of Paul: insomuch that unto the sick were carried away from his body handkerchiefs or aprons, and the diseases departed from them, and evil spirits went out" (Acts 19:11,12).

Heb. 2:1-4 has somewhat to say concerning this. Following an exhortation to give the more earnest heed to the things we have learned, lest haply we drift away from them, we read:

If the word which was spoken through angels (messengers) proved steadfast, and every transgression and disobedience received a just recompense of reward, how shall we escape if we neglect so great a salvation, which (note the verb tenses and the order of events) having *at first* been spoken through the Lord, *was* confirmed unto us by them that heard, God also bearing witness *with them* (not us) both by signs and wonders, and by manifold powers, and by gifts of the Holy Spirit, according to his own will.

8

MARK 16:17,18 REVISITED

Many find it disturbing to learn that the Gospel according to Mark has come down to us with three different endings. 1) The renowned Codex Sinaiticus and Codex Vaticanus, among others, end abruptly with verse eight, hence with the dismal announcement: "and they (the three women who had come to the tomb) said nothing to any one; for they were afraid."

2) In the margin of the Syriac versions there is a somewhat contradictory addition which states:

> And they declared briefly all that was commanded, to them that were with Peter. Afterwards Jesus himself published by them the holy and incorruptible preaching of eternal salvation. Amen.

3) Other ancient authorities end with the verses familiar to us in our common English versions. However, the text of the NIV and the New KJV include a footnote calling attention to the fact

that "the two most reliable early manuscripts do not have Mark 16:9-20." Hence verses 17,18 are lacking in our oldest and, (generally regarded) most reliable early manuscripts.

In the midst of verses 9-20, following Mark's statement of Jesus' "great commission," are found two of the most controversial verses of the New Testament: The verses read:

(17) And these signs shall accompany (KJV, follow) them that believe: in my name they shall cast out demons; they shall speak with new tongues; (18) they shall take up serpents, and if they drink any deadly thing it shall in no wise hurt them; they shall lay their hands on the sick, and they shall recover (ASV).

The introductory announcement, "these signs shall accompany them that believe," plus four of the five specific actions which follow, employ the third person plural, future indicative form of the verbs which appear. The actions (accomplishments) predicted are thereby said to be things which shall surely come to pass. The one variance relates to the drinking of some deadly thing. In this instance the verb form is the third person plural, aorist subjunctive. The subjunctive accounts for the word "if" which appears in connection with that particular prediction. The other actions cited, except possibly the taking up of serpents, are such things believers (if empowered to do so) might conceivably do intentionally.

Incidentally, in the lone New Testament report of anyone taking up a serpent, so to speak, Paul did not actually "take it up." Instead, the serpent sprang out of a fire being kindled and fastened itself onto Paul's hand. He forthwith shook it off into the fire. To the surprise of the witnesses, Paul suffered no harm (Acts 28:1-4).

What are we to make of what is said in Mark 16:17,18? What are our options, if any? There are three possibilities. All three deserve to be carefully explored.

OPTION ONE: WE CAN REJECT
THE PASSAGE AS SPURIOUS

Many have taken this option. I am not one of them; for three reasons. 1) Although the passage, along with its immediate context, is lacking in some significant manuscript sources, it is inconceivable to me that Mark would close his account of the life and work of Jesus, and the impact made upon those who were his witnesses, with an expression so negative as: "for they were afraid."

The twelve verses (9-20) which make up the ending of Mark's gospel as we know it would make up approximately one page of a manuscript. It would be much easier to believe the final page of a copy of Mark's gospel serving as the source of some later copy (or copies) was accidentally lost than to believe Mark would close his account so direly as with verse eight. The fact that the shorter ending of the Syriac version first appears as a marginal note, suggests that the scribe thereof was aware that a closing statement was missing, and needed. Hence the one supplied is an innocuous statement, perhaps indicating a reticence to take liberty with the received text.

2) My second reason for not rejecting the passage as spurious is that I consider that a "cop out." I would no more take the easy way out in order to avoid a doctrinal difficulty, than I would build a doctrine on such a basis were I on the other side of the issue. The oft repeated Biblical dictum to which I make frequent reference, Deut. 17:6, etc., deserves to be recalled at this point. If what is said were intended by Christ to be the norm for all who believe, throughout the whole of Christian history no less, it seems strange there is not a second witness to the same in one of the other three gospels. It seems strange also that the record of Acts does not chronicle the fact that such proved to be the case at least at the onset of the Christian era. Of that we will have more to say later as we review the Divinely recorded history of the church of the apostolic era.

3) Suppose the passage is genuine. Suppose Jesus actually said that. Can one prove he did not? Since that cannot be done, we do well to consider what options are ours, if any, on the assumption the passage is genuine. It is a dangerous procedure to look for excuse or reason to doubt, or in some way disallow the veracity of a saying, because it does not fit into one's own experience, or mold of thinking.

Questioning the authenticity of the text does not solve the difficulty. Aside from the drinking of some deadly thing, the one "sign" prefaced with the word "if," every other sign is prefaced by an expression of certitude. The future active indicative verb form is used in each case. Moreover the record in Acts chronicles the fact that miracles of the sort predicted actually happened in the formative history of the church. Option One is out insofar as I am concerned. I consider the passage genuine.

OPTION TWO: THE PREDICTION
WAS RESTRICTIVE, NOT GENERAL

Those who take this option assume the prediction applied only to the apostles, and such persons as may have been provisionally empowered through the laying on of the apostles' hands. Witness for example the case of Philip and the Samaritans (see Acts 6:3-6; 8:5-7,13-18). Philip was one of seven men "full of the Holy Spirit and of wisdom" chosen to minister to the needs of the widows of the Jerusalem church. Aside from inferred moral qualities (e.g. "of good report") no hint of miraculous powers is attributed to him or to others of the seven prior to the laying on of the apostles' hands (6:6, cp. 8:18).

Following the report of that action attention is focused upon two of the seven, Stephen and Philip. Forthwith we are told: "Stephen, full of grace and *power*, wrought great wonders and signs among the people" (Acts 6:8). The rest of Chapter 6 and the whole of Chapter 7 is given over to Stephen's run-in with the synagogue of the Libertines, climaxed by his stoning and his vision of Christ in glory.

Chapter 8 opens with a brief account of the ensuing persecution against the church which scattered the disciples abroad. Now the focus falls upon Philip's Samaritan sojourn. Verse 6 reports that "the multitudes gave heed with one accord unto the things that were spoken by Philip when they saw the signs which he did."

Two of the five certain signs predicted in Mark 16:17,18, are given special mention: a) "From many that had unclean spirits, they came out, crying with a loud voice," b) "and many that were palsied, and that were lame were healed" (v. 7). Even the local occult leader, Simon the Sorcerer, believed and was baptized. "Beholding signs and great miracles wrought, he was amazed" (v. 13).

The report of this reached the church at Jerusalem who dispatched Peter and John to look into the matter. Note: Despite the fact that the Samaritans were now numbered among "them that believe" and many among them were beneficiaries of miraculous gifts, it is said: the Holy Spirit was not was yet "fallen upon them" (v. 16). That phrase uniformly denotes the endowment to perform miracles. Note when the apostles laid their hands on them they "received the Holy Spirit" in a form that caught the attention of the astute Simon. The account says: "When Simon saw that through the laying on of the apostles' hands the Holy Spirit was (thusly) given" he tried to buy the power he saw resident in the apostles. Isn't it strange he could see that? But even with the inspired record before us many today cannot.

May I suggest there may be a reason. Perhaps the view that sees the facts otherwise is excusable. The view we have been outlining has one count against it. It is not the conclusion to which one would be readily drawn in reading Mark 16:17,18 in context. Taken for what it seems to plainly say, the passage says nothing to the effect that the signs would be visited upon believers selectively; for many, in a sense, second handedly. The inference seems to be that the signs (pl.) are promised to be accompaniments of the state of believing. This brings us to the third option.

OPTION THREE: THE PROMISE IS TO ALL WHO BELIEVE

This option is really beset with problems, not the least of which is both stated and elaborated upon in I Corinthians, chapters 12-14. The one point Paul drives home is that such gifts as tongues and healings were *not* possessed by all that believed. Such gifts were selectively, possibly even sparingly given. Moreover, it was the Holy Spirit who did the selecting and the distributing. (See I Cor. 12:8-11, particularly v. 11, and cp. Heb. 2:4.)

Lest anyone should miss the point he was making, beginning with v. 12 and continuing to the end of the chapter 12, Paul introduced an analogy which he painstakingly explained and applied. The inference that is to be drawn, and which is re-enforced by chapter 13, is that some of the believers who made up the church in Corinth did not have any of the specialized gifts with which some were endowed. Nonetheless, they were in no wise less spiritual than those who did. And they certainly were not reckoned as unbelievers. In fact, if they were loving they are said to manifest a greater gift of the Holy Spirit than those who gloried in the signs they could display (or simulate). The latter possibility cannot be disallowed.

Witness the Case of the Samaritans

The record in Acts plainly attests the fact that the signs listed in Mark 16:17,18 did not automatically accompany all who believed. Note again the case of the Samaritans. They are definitely identifed as "believers" (Acts 8:12,13). But though Philip had wrought such signs among them that even Simon the sorcerer "believed, and being baptized, continued with Philip" (v. 13); the fact remains that neither the signs listed in Mark 16:17,18, nor any other manifestation of special spiritual endowment (visible or audible) "followed" as an inevitable accompaniment of faith.

Despite the fact that Philip exhibited *amazing* signs and wrought great miracles (v. 13), having received the laying on of the apostles' hands (Acts 6:6), the Holy Spirit did not "*fall upon them*" until the apostles, Peter and John, came down to Samaria and laid their hands upon them (8:18). Yet, from the time of their acceptance of the gospel they are reckoned as believers.

The Case of the Twelve "Believers" at Ephesus

Ponder the case of the twelve believers at Ephesus who had received the baptism of John out of dispensation. They did not even know the Holy Spirit was given (Acts 19:2). Note Paul did not question their faith. He questioned instead their baptism. Upon their submission to Christ's (Christian) baptism, Paul laid his hands upon them. At that the Holy Spirit "came upon" them, evidenced by the fact that "they spoke with tongues and prophesied" (v. 6).

No explanation is given as to the reason Paul exercised his apostolic power in behalf of the twelve men. The fact that they had been "short changed," so to speak, in that they had received only the baptism of John, may have had something to do with it. Unlike Christian baptism, John's baptism carried no promise of the gift of the Holy Spirit. With the laying on of the apostles' hands an immediate and dramatic endowment was experienced. The "fruit of the Spirit" which grows out of the gift of the Holy Spirit which accompanies Christian baptism is not so readily manifested.

As previously noted, the phrase "came upon them" is akin to

OT descriptions of special spiritual endowment. It speaks of the Spirit making use of persons so endowed. The gift of the Holy Spirit which accompanies the baptism of penitent believers works with, and from within, one's own spirit.

On the surface it may seem that the language used in Acts 8 and 19 with reference to the Samaritans and the twelve of Ephesus is at variance with the promise of Acts 2:38,39. The key to the seeming contradiction is in the langauge we have just noted. The "spirit of adoption" which "bears witness with our spirits that we are children of God (Rom. 8:15,16) is the gift promised in Acts 2:38 to baptized believers (cf. Acts 5:32). Miraculous endowment of the Holy Spirit is described in the kind of language we have noted in the examples cited above, and in their OT counterpart.

The Case of Cornelius Compared

The conversion of Cornelius and his household, at first glance, seems to provide a proof text for those committed to the third option. They received the Holy Spirit, evidenced by the gift of tongues, apart from the laying on of the apostles' hands, and prior to water baptism. But there was a good reason for that. For one thing, it is generally conceded that theirs was a special case. They were the first strictly Gentile converts. They were providentially chosen to be so, and providentially put in contact with Peter, and he with them. But all that not withstanding, Peter likely would not have laid his hands on them even to baptize them in water, much less impart to them some spiritual gift, if God had not baptized them in the Holy Spirit before Peter's very eyes; and manifested the same by "giving them the like gift" which had been poured out upon the apostles "at the beginning" (Acts 10:45-47; 11:15-18).

At Pentecost the preachers (the apostles) were thusly accredited for the sake of their audience. At Caesarea the audience was similarly credentialized for the sake of the preacher, and the six Jewish brethren whom Peter providentially took along as witnesses. That is precisely what Peter made of it, on two occasions: see Acts 11:15-18; 15:7-11.

What Happened at the Beginning?

This seems the appropriate time to inquire as to what actually happened "at the beginning," and in the early history of the church thereafter. It is recorded that about 3,000 "received the word, and were baptized" (Acts 2:41). But nothing is said to the effect that the phenomena that caught their attention and brought them together or that the sign which credentialized the apostles were visited upon any one of them when they believed. Much less did the signs listed in Mark 16:17,18 accompany their faith. To the contrary, verse 43 reports that it was through *the apostles* that "many wonders and signs were done."

In chapter seven, "Now Concerning Spiritual Gifts," we took time to sketch, chapter by chapter, the record of miraculous activity, as it is chronicled in the book of Acts. It should not be too repetitious to at least highlight the facts once again in this context.

Chapter 3 reports the first healing in the church age (vv. 1-10). It was through an apostle (Peter) that the healing was done. Chapter 4 reports that the multitude of them that believed were of one heart and soul (v. 32), but adds: "With great power they (the apostles) gave their witness of the resurrection" (v. 33). Chapter 5 notes: "By the hands of the apostles were *many signs and wonders* wrought among the people" (v. 12). But there is no mention of *any* signs and wonders being done *by* the people.

Chapter 6 introduces us to Stephen and Philip, men "full of the Holy Spirit" even before the apostles laid their hands upon them. But it is worthy of our note that not until after the apostles laid their hands on them that anything miraculous is attributed to any one of them. Thereafter Stephen (see Acts 6:8) and Philip

145

(see Acts 8:6-8,13) did so. Note especially Acts 8:13. And so it goes throughout the book of Acts.

OPTION TWO: RECONSIDERED

This brings us back to option two as our only viable option. This is not to limit God's power or his promises. It is simply to observe the limitation which God, according to his own recorded word, saw fit to place upon the predictions under consideration. In the epistle to the Hebrews there is a verse to which we have previously alluded, (Heb. 2:4). We do well at this point to again note the verse, and to take note of its context.

(2) If the word spoken through angels (messengers) proved sted-fast, and every transgression and disobedience received a just recompense of reward, (3) how shall we escape if we neglect so great a salvation? which having at the first been spoken through the Lord, *was confirmed* unto us by them that heard; (4) God also bearing witness with them, both by signs and wonders, and by manifold powers, and by gifts of the Holy Spirit, *according to his own will* (Heb. 2:2-4).

Read it again, carefully, noting the time clauses and their implications. The ancient manuscripts carried the title, *Pros Hebraious*, "to Hebrews." Recall that Paul said, "Jews ask for signs," (I Cor. 1:22). And they received signs aplenty, more so than the Gentiles. But that was fast drawing to a close. It could be the time was already past. The passage before us speaks of the confirmation which miracles provided, as an end already accomplished. The word which a) at the first was spoken by the Lord, b) was confirmed unto us by them that heard, c) God also bearing witness with them (not us) both by signs and wonders and manifold powers, and gifts of the Holy Spirit, according to his own will." That would seem to indicate that already in Christian history the role of signs and wonders had served its purpose, and

146

at least was no longer a common phenomenon.

Following through with the inference of the foregoing passage, it deserves to be noted that the further we advance in both NT history and literature, the less emphasis is placed upon confirming signs.

In view of what we have just noted, let us return to Mark 16:17,18 and consider the text from the perspective of New Testament history. Again, several sub-options are to be considered and evaluated:

1) The things predicted either did or did not happen. One accepting the Scriptures as trustworthy should have no serious difficulty in choosing between those two possibilities. Except for the drinking of "some deadly thing," the one sign spoken of as "iffy," and one of two which, if done intentionally, would border close on "making trial of the Lord, our God" (Matt. 4:7), the book of Acts records the fact the others signs did indeed "follow." For example:

a) Casting out demons is reported four times: Acts 5:16 (by Peter), 8:7 (by Philip), 16:16-18 and 19:13-16 (by Paul). b) Speaking in tongues is recorded three times: Acts 2:3-11; 10:44-46; 19:6. c) Healings are recorded seven times. Four are attributed to Peter: Acts 3:1-12, the lame man at the gate of the temple; 5:15,16, "multitudes from cities round about Jerusalem," including bed-ridden and demon possessed; 9:32,33, palsied Aeneas of Lydda; and 9:36-40, Dorcas, raised from the dead. That was more than was promised in Mark 16:17,18 — a "healing plus." Three healing occasions are ascribed to Paul: Acts 14:8-10, a cripple was healed at Lystra; 19:11,12, cloths carried from Paul's body effected healing of diseases, and even exorcising of demons. (This passage somewhat parallels "the shadow of Peter" phenomenon reported in Acts 5:15,16). Acts 20:9,10 records the account of Eutychus, raised (possibly) from the dead.

d) "The taking up of serpents" and e) "the drinking of some deadly thing" apparently were not a part of the apostolic agenda.

They were not "show offs." The inadvertent snake bite episode recorded in Acts 28:1-4 suggests what might have been were poison taken inadvertently or forced upon one of them.

Sub-option 2). The things predicted accompanied the state of believing, at least generally so, or they did not. If one takes the affirmative position, one then has the apostle Paul to combat. In I Corinthians 12, Paul expounds the point that such was not the case. And were it so, the church as "the body of Christ" would be ludicrous, even freakish.

Sub-option 3). The things predicted still happen, or they do not. The negative position is supported by a) the developing trend reflected in the NT literature, and b) the history of the church through the ages, and c) observable human experience.

As for the first mentioned, Hebrews 2:1-4, as has been noted, contains a strong inference that confirming signs and wonders, even at that point in NT history, were no longer extant. He speaks of the confirmation for which they were given as an already accomplished fact, rather than an ongoing phenomenon. In saying the word which was first spoken by the Lord "*was* confirmed (past tense) *unto* us" (rather than "*by* us") we are given further cause to conclude that the primary purpose served by the signs already had been fulfilled.

Picking up again on the observation that the further we proceed in NT history and literature the less emphasis is placed upon confirming signs, two texts in Paul's letters to Timothy, should be noted. Near the close of his own life, and the nearing end of the apostolic age, Paul writes: a) "Trophimus (a traveling companion) I *left sick* at Miletus" (II Tim. 4:20). And b) to his beloved son in the gospel, Timothy, he wrote: "Take a little wine for your stomach's sake, and for your oft infirmities" (I Tim. 5:23). At the time Timothy was in Ephesus where earlier, cloths carried from Paul's body to the sick caused diseases and evil spirits to depart (Acts 19:11,12). Why was Timothy not told to rub Paul's manuscript on his stomach?

While reflecting on the gimmickry of the current spate of big-time (and not-so-big) pushers of the "health and wealth" gospel(?) the snide thought crossed my mind: "What a healing ministry Paul might have had were kleenex available in his day!" Were healing miracles, and other wonders divinely designed to be the ongoing certification of faith, there are many things hard to explain. Why Paul left Trophimus sick, and why he proffered Timothy such mundane advice are among the least of them, as will be noted from what follows.

Four Conundrums to Be Considered

If Mark 16:17,18 is to be interpreted as applying to all who truly believe, for all the time, we have four conundrums to be considered:

1) Take the case of the beacon lights of the reformation: John Hus, Luther, Calvin, the Wesleys, the Campbells (to name a few). Were all these unbelievers? Did God by-pass sign-credentialized believers to use unbelievers to usher in and extend the reformation? Oh how those men could have used such signs as are listed in Mark 16:17,18, but they were no part of the reper-toire of any of them.

2) Take the case of the evangelists who ushered in "the Great Awakening" of the 19th century: George Whitefield, John Knox, Jonathan Edwards, D.L. Moody, Billy Sunday. While I would not endorse for a moment Billy Graham's "faith only" stance, I would hardly count him an unbeliever. The man who has likely preached to more millions than any other man, has never spoken in tongues, exorcised a demon, or resorted to snake handling or healing shows to credentialize his ministry.

3) And what shall we say of the renowned missionaries? William Carey, often called "the father of modern missions," Judson, Livingston. Taylor, Shelton, and a host of men and women from among ourselves who in the past two generations have accomplished as much or more than those we have come to

honor through history. Untold numbers of men and women who have carried the gospel to the four corners of the earth have done so without exercising a one of the powers listed in Mark 16:17,18. Were they, and scores of others like them, all unbelievers? If Mark 16:17,18 as interpreted by the neo-Corinthian "charismatics," is the "litmus test," the answer would have to be "yes!"

4) But that is not all. What shall we say of the translators of the Scriptures, men who braved death to give us the Bible in our own language? Were Wycliffe, Tyndale, Coverdale, and the like, unbelievers? Consider the missionaries, and the translators of present day Bible societies who go into malaria-infested jungles, facing head hunters, jealous witch doctors and tribal chieftains, military and doctrinaire revolutionists, and obliged to live in squalid huts and eat nauseous foods, in order to learn the native languages, reduce the same to writing and teach them to read so they can know Christ as Lord. Are these also unbelievers?

Why does not the gift of tongues follow those who could really use it to God's glory (not their own ego), and to bring the light of salvation to multitudes in darkness? Is it not strange that those who often show the greatest evidence of being believers do not exhibit a one of the signs of Mark 16:17,18? But men (and feminine counterparts) who grow rich hustling the *select* signs which turn out to be crowd pleasers and money makers — simulated tongues, psychosomatic healings, these, if Mark 16:17,18 is the test, are the only true believers.

Some Final Questions

To those who choose to differ, some parting questions are in order. To the "rope holders," the bank account bulgers of those who, like Simon Magus see in certain "signs" a way to make gain, to those whose "love offerings" have graduated the big-time operators from the proverbial "gravy trains" to private jets we beg to ask some questions:

1. When did you as a sincere and fervent "believer" exorcise a demon — really? That is to say, when have you done anything of the sort that was visible, audible, and convincing even to unbelievers?

2. What new tongue has the Holy Spirit given you lately? Or are you still mouthing the same mumbo-jumbo you started with? Have you edified anybody thereby, besides yourself? (if indeed you can demonstrate that you are really edified, informed, or enlightened). Or do you just "do your thing" to get attention, or to assure yourself (and perchance others) that you are part of the "in" group?

3. Have you taken up any deadly serpents lately? Or do you leave that demonstration to the back-country mountaineers? Oral Roberts, in his paperback *The Baptism of the Holy Spirit*, confesses backhandedly that he elects to by-pass the snake handling attention getter, saying: "This is an idiom of the East that referred to enemies. It means what Jesus referred to in Luke 10:19 . . . . This was power enabling them to overcome their enemies who would attempt to impede their spiritual progress, or would seek to prevent their being witnesses of the Lord Jesus Christ" (p. 16). Obviously the famed Tulsa evangelist and "healer" does not (to adapt a phrase) "cotton to that snake bit."

4. Have you drunk some deadly thing, with no ill effects? Roberts also disallows that this promise is to be taken literally. It only means that missionaries and itinerant preachers will not get sick from eating tainted food. Ah, but they do. Are they then unbelievers?

5. And what is your box score on miracle healings? Does your power work best on simple things, such as headaches, stomachaches and the like? Have you lengthened or strengthened any withered limbs? Or has the best that you have done so far been to convince someone they can hear a little better out of their left ear? Pardon me if I am not impressed.

151

CONCLUSION

The wheel has come full circle. We have reviewed three options. The only one that passes: 1) the test of time, 2) the test of sound exegesis, and 3) the test of experience in the lives of millions of believers, past and present, is the one that squares with Acts 8:18 and Hebrews 2:3,4. The word which was first spoken by our Lord himself, was indeed confirmed unto us by those who heard him speak (his chosen apostles, no less); God also bearing witness *through them*, both by signs and wonders, and by gifts of the Holy Spirit, according to his own will.

That said, let us revisit Mark 16:17,18 one more time, and note the setting in which it is found. The two verses immediately preceding are Mark's characteristically terse statement of Jesus' commission to his disciples. And the two verses which follow are the summary verses with which Mark brings his gospel to a close. Having recalled Christ's promise that certain "signs" would "follow alongside" of them, (Gr. *para-kolouthesei*) he closes in a somewhat matter of fact fashion, typical of his writing throughout:

> After the Lord Jesus had spoken to them, he was taken up into heaven and sat down at the right hand of God. Then the disciples went out and preached everywhere, and the Lord worked with them and confirmed his word by the signs that accompanied it (vv. 19,20, NIV).

That is the way it was predicted. That is the way it happened. The text really presents no problems: unless it is taken out of context. It has been well said: "a text taken out of context is a pretext."

9

THE ABIDING GIFT OF THE HOLY SPIRIT

We have company! We may have more than we have been led to expect, or less. It is a common thing to hear someone speak of "the indwelling (or indwelling presence) of the Holy Spirit." Although that precise phraseology is not used in the Scriptures, there are several texts which suggest it.

THE INDWELLING PRESENCE OF THE HOLY SPIRIT

Jesus, in what is commonly called his farewell address, said to the apostles:

> I will pray the Father, and he shall give you another Comforter, that he may be with you for ever, (even) the Spirit of truth: whom the world cannot receive; for it beholdeth him not, neither knoweth him. You know him, for he *abideth with* you, and shall be *in* you (John 14:16,17).

Paul charged Timothy, "That good thing (the pattern of sound words), which was committed unto you, guard through the Holy Spirit which *dwells in* us" (II Tim. 2:14). To the Corinthians he wrote: "Know you not that your body is a temple of the Holy Spirit, which is *in* you, which you have from God?" (I Cor. 6:19). Thus we have the "two or three witnesses" the dictum the Scriptures prescribe "for a thing to be established" (Num. 35:30; Deut. 17:6; Matt. 18:16; II Cor. 13:1).

GOD DWELLS IN US

Now hear this. God dwells in us also. In fact this is more often said of God (yea, and of Christ also!) than of the Holy Spirit. Even in the New Testament, apart from the more extensive scope of the Old Testament, this is true of God. Note the OT witness to this teaching:

Most of the Old Testament references which speak of Jehovah's presence among his people are not as intimate as the passages just noted but there are exceptions. For background let us note the general references. Exodus 25:8 and 29:33-36 speak of God's desire to dwell "with" and "among" his people, by his presence in the tabernacle. A recurring phrase speaks of Jehovah as he who "sits above the cherubim," (II Sam. 6:2; II Kgs. 19:15; Psa. 80:1; Isa. 37:16). The verb (Heb. *yashab*) is used 728 times in the OT, and 616 times it is translated by such words as dwell, abide, remain. Its general import therefore communicates the idea of residency. It is so used to denote Jehovah's regal presence in the throne room of both the tabernacle and the temple.

It needs to be noted that this is not to suggest that God actually dwelt where the tabernacle was pitched, or later, in the temple. Such texts as I Kings 8:27 and II Chronicles 6:18 make that plain. (See also Isa. 66:1; Jer. 23:23,24; Psa. 139:7-16; Acts 7:40, 17:24.) The passages communicate that God is not a god who is far off and unapproachable.

At least four New Testament texts intimate that God dwells in us. In Ephesians 4:4-6 Paul's cites seven facets of the unity of the church:

There is one body, and one Spirit, even as also you were called in one hope of your calling; one Lord, one faith, one baptism, one God and Father of all, who is over all, and through all, and *in* all.

Note also the words of Paul in Romans 8:9a, "You are not in the flesh but in the Spirit, if so be that the Spirit of God *dwelleth in you*." Second Corinthians 6:16 closely parallels I Corinthians 6:19, except here it is said that God dwells in us: "We are a temple of the living God; even as God said, I will *dwell in* them, and *walk in* them: and I will be their God, and they shall be my people."

The apostle John also bears witness to the fact that God dwells in us. In I John 4:12,13,16 it is written:

(12) No man has beheld God at any time: If we love one another, God *abides in* us, and his love is perfected in us. (13) Hereby we know that we *abide in* him, and *he in* us, because he has given us of his Spirit . . . . (16) And we know and have believed the love which God has in us. God is love, and he that abides in love *abides in* God, and *God abides in* him.

CHRIST DWELLS IN US

There's an old saying, "There is always room for one more." That needs to be so just now. At least four texts state that Christ, the Son of God, dwells in us also. In fact, we are told in Romans 8:9b "if any man has not the Spirit of Christ, he is none of his." Verses 10,11 should be noted as well.

(10) If Christ is in you the body is dead because of sin, but the spirit is life (alive) because of (his) righteousness. (11) But if the

Spirit of him that raised up Jesus from the dead dwelleth in you,
he (God) that raised up Christ Jesus from the dead shall give life
also to your mortal bodies through his Spirit that *dwelleth in you*.

Galatians 4:6 informs us that because we that are in Christ are
sons, "God has sent forth the Spirit of his son in our hearts, crying, Abba, Father." In Ephesians 3:16ff. Paul pens a prayer in
which he entreats that a double portion of the Divine nature may
be ours, asking that we might be "strengthened with power
through his (God's) Spirit in the inward man: that *Christ may
dwell* in (our) hearts, through faith . . . that (we) may be filled
unto all the fulness of God" (vv. 17-19).

The apostle John also writes concerning this in his first epistle.
He sees no contradiction in noting that the Father (I John
4:12,15), the Son (v. 14, cp. 3:24), and the Holy Spirit (v. 13)
are all said to be in us. (See also I John 2:20,24,27; 3:23,24.)
The indwelling of Christ in our hearts may be only inferred from I
John 4:14, but the fact of it has already been set forth in the closing verses of chapter three, wherein John stated:

This is his (God's) commandment that we should believe in the
name of his Son, Jesus Christ, and love one another even as he
(Jesus) gave us commandment. And he that keeps his (Christ's)
commandments abideth in him, and he (Christ) in him. And
hereby we know that he (Christ) abideth in us, by the Spirit which
he gave us (I John 3:23,24).

A FLURRY OF QUESTIONS

Some ponderous questions arise in our minds as we reflect on
these things. 1) What are we to make of them? 2) Would it be best
to ignore them? 3) Are there three personalities, three Spirit beings besides our own human spirits, dwelling in our bodies? 4)
Have we been belittling our favored and gifted state by speaking
only of the indwelling of the Holy Spirit? 5) Are the Father and

156

the Son unwittingly slighted, (perhaps offended) thereby? 6) Or are we dealing with figurative language in a crassly literal fashion? Thus the questions we are pondering rise to trouble us, but needlessly. 7) Could it be that a higher regard for the unity of the Godhead versus the creedal dogma of the Trinity would ameliorate such questions? It is worthy of reflection that such questions did not trouble the minds of believers until the philosophic speculations of the Graeco-Roman world crystalized in the doctrine of the trinity as set forth in the Nicene Creed (325 A.D.).

PERTINENT PASSAGES

Several passages are particularly pertinent to a study of the indwelling (abiding) presence of the Holy Spirit. The doctrine may not be demanded by such texts but they certainly give rise to the belief that the Holy Spirit is given to obedient believers and intended to be a lifetime endowment, and perhaps even an internalized resident.

1. In Luke 11:13 Jesus concluded a familial illustration by saying: "If you (fathers) know how to give good gifts to your children, how much more shall (your) heavenly Father give the Holy Spirit to them that ask him?" Matthew's phrasing of the saying is, "How much more shall your Father who is in heaven give good things (gifts) to them that ask him" (Matt. 7:11). We take the liberty to insert the word gift parenthetically, since it is implied in the context. The Holy Spirit is not a "thing," but it is a "good thing" to receive such a gift from God.

2. In Acts 2:38,39 the multitude stricken with guilt by Peter's sermon was promised that upon the condition of repentance and baptism they would receive not only the remission of their sins but "the gift of the Holy Spirit" also. Moreoever, Peter affirmed the promise was not limited to that assembly and that occasion, but "unto as many as the Lord our God shall call unto him." No

specifics are included concerning the precise nature, function or duration of the promised gift. However, the prophecy of Joel, cited by Peter at the beginning of his sermon, would likely be called to mind. That raises an engaging question. Would they (the audience on Pentecost) assume that upon receiving the Holy Spirit whenever they spoke thereafter all hearing them would hear as though the speaking were in the listeners' home town dialect? Should we so reason? One might so assume, but there is no indication *they* did, and there is certainly no intimation that any of them so spoke that day, or any time thereafter.

3. In Acts 5:32 Peter repeats, in effect, the promise of Acts 2:38, saying: "We are witnesses of these things; and so is the Holy Spirit whom God gives to all them that obey him." Were this not self-evident the obverse certainly would be. Disobedience is a repudiation of authority. How could one expect to receive the Holy Spirit when one's own spirit is in a state of rebellion? And how could the Holy Spirit dwell within, or even abide with one in whom what Paul calls "the spirit that works in the sons of disobedience" (Eph. 2:2) is at work? The answer is found in the context of Acts 5:32. Peter is justifying the apostle's refusal to obey the Jewish council. He declares that he and his fellow apostles witnessed the facts they were proclaiming concerning Jesus. He further declares the Holy Spirit also to be a witness to the same. He then concludes that God gives the Holy Spirit (God's faithful witness) to those who *obey* him — that is, those who submit to (God's) authority.

4. Romans 8:15 informs us we have received "the spirit of adoption, whereby we cry, Abba, Father." Verse 16 goes on to say: The Spirit himself bears witness with our spirit, that we are children of God." Galatians 4:6 is somewhat more precise. Therein, Paul says: "And because (we) are sons, God sent forth the *Spirit* of his Son *into our hearts*, crying, Abba, Father." From this text the concept of the Holy Spirit dwelling within is inferred.

5. John 14:16,17, is at least compatible with that inference. However it needs to be kept in mind that not everything promised

158

the apostles is necessarily capable of generalization. To the apostles he said: "He (the Father) shall give you another comforter, that he may be with you for ever; even the Spirit of truth . . . . You know him, for he abides in you, (i.e. he will do so, when given) and shall be *in* you."

6. On the assumption John is not using the "editorial we" (or "*us*," as the case is in the texts we are next to consider), John, in his first epistle, is commonly regarded as extending the promise of the Holy Spirit (as recorded in his gospel) to believers generally. In I John 3:24 he said: "Hereby we know he (Christ) abides in us, by the Spirit which he gave us." Actually this verse would serve as a better proof text for the doctrine that the person of Christ somehow dwells within us. First John 4:13 says much the same things. "Hereby we know that we abide in him (Jesus) and he (Christ) abides in us, because he has given us of his Spirit" (lit., "the Spirit of himself," i.e., Christ's own Spirit).

BACK TO SQUARE ONE

This brings us back to square one, so to speak. The doctrine of the Trinity is an engaging paradigm. As a philosophical concept it makes sense of a number of Scriptures. But when it is pressed to the point of an overriding creedal dogma whereupon all Scripture must be interpreted in the light of the Nicene formula, many a text has to be shaded and adapted to fit the format. We have just noted two of them (I John 3:24; 4:13).

As I "girded up the loins of my mind" (I Pet. 1:13) to set forth a convincing case for the doctrine of the personal indwelling of the Holy Spirit I found myself torn between what I was wanting to say and what the Scriptures I was researching seemed to be actually saying. Since the purpose of the series of studies of which this work is a part is to set forth *What the Bible Says About the Holy Spirit*, conscience and Scripture must be given priority over prior personal opinion and popular opinion, and indeed over opinion *per se*.

IN WHAT SENSE DOES THE HOLY SPIRIT INDWELL US?

How then does the Holy Spirit indwell us? Or is this just a figure of speech? The answer to the second question is, No. While there is an element of analogy involved in the expression, it is not "just a figure of speech." Hence the first question. Since I do believe in the indwelling of the Holy Spirit (despite what may seem to have been said) the question is, in what sense does the Spirit dwell within us? To answer this question we need to note the *modus operandi* of God's self-revelation as it has prevailed from the beginning.

THE MODUS OPERANDI OF GOD'S SELF-REVELATION

The Biblical revelation records that following the creation of man, God saw fit to reveal himself. He did so by means of communication. He spoke of Adam (Gen. 1:27-31). There is no suggestion that Adam had any other knowledge of God. It is never said that he saw God or touched him. John has declared, "No man has seen God at any time" (John 1:18). God told Moses, "No man shall see me and live" (Exod. 33:20). Only in dreams and visions is anyone said to have "seen God." But Adam heard God speak. They conversed about several things (See Gen. 2:16,17,19,20,23). And "the fellowship and communion of *his holy Spirit*" (Isa. 63:10), was sweet and blessed until another spirit gained the ear of Eve (and, through her, Adam), whereby they believed Satan's seductive lies. In the wake of that folly they again "heard the voice of God," but fearfully so (Gen. 3:8). The gist of the conversation is recorded in verses 9-19.

The balance of the Old Testament, generally speaking, is the record of God's further revelation through chosen mediators, "in diverse portions and in diverse manners" (Heb. 1:1); chiefly the prophets. As Peter phrased it: "Holy men spake from God, being moved by the Holy Spirit" (II Pet. 1:21).

It is an illuminating experience to trace the course of God's self-revelation through the ages by noting the interplay of the terms "Spirit of God," "Spirit of Jehovah" (KJV, of the Lord) and the phrase: "and God (or Jehovah) said." Add to those references the voluminous number of times in which the prophets declared, "the word of Jehovah (God) came unto me," and proceeded thereupon to speak, or to write, and/or carry out a God-given directive. From such a study one will gain an insight into the *modus operandi* of God's revelatory process, and his purpose in making *himself* (and in the process, *his will*) known.

The activities of those individuals to whom God spoke resulted in the "word of the Lord (Jehovah)," and His will, being made known. How else? The prophets did not know His will instinctively. Neither do we. No voice within us, "the Holy Spirit dwelling within us" not excepted, tells us what to do. David stated it succinctly: "The entrance of thy word giveth light" (Psa. 119:130).

What God communicated to the prophets they in turn communicated to the people. In so doing they used the vernacular and idiom of their time and place. And God so approved of what they said, it has come down to us as the Word of God, "written for our admonition upon whom the end of the ages is come" (I Cor. 10:11).

The Old Testament revelation was but preparatory to a fuller revelation yet to come. The coming of Christ "in the fulness of time" (Gal. 4:4) climaxed God's revelation of himself, and of his will, "for in him (Christ) dwells all the fullness of the Godhead bodily, and in him (who is the head of all principality and power) are you made full" (Col. 2:9,10). The New Testament discloses God's will for the Christian dispensation as the Old Testament did for the Mosaic.

WHAT EVER GOD HAS DONE
HAS BEEN DONE THROUGH HIS WORD

From the inception of the primordial creation God has accomplished his purpose through his word. Is it not written, "We understand that the worlds have been framed by the word of God, so that what is seen has not been made of things which appear" (Heb. 11:2). In the beginning God brought entity out of non-entity and order out of waste and void by his word. "God said, Let there be light, and there was light" (Gen. 1:3). Seven times the phrase is repeated, and each time a major facet of the present created order came into being, climaxed by the creation of man.

In the prologue of his gospel John sums up the creation of the world and they that dwell therein by saying:

> In the beginning was the Word, and the Word was with God, and the Word was God. The same was in the beginning with God. All things were made through Him, and without Him was not anything made that has been made . . . . And the Word became flesh and dwelt among us, and we beheld His glory, glory as of the only begotten of the Father, full of grace and truth (John 1:1-13,14).

WHERE DOES THE HOLY SPIRIT FIT INTO THIS?

What we have just noted does not emaciate the Holy Spirit, or diminish his role in either creation or redemption of the primordial. Creation it is said that "the Spirit of God moved upon (brooded over) the face of the deep" (Gen. 1:2). And he was in the beginning, he is now and ever shall be. As the Biblical revelation draws to a close the Holy Spirit is still found moving upon the face of the earth, brooding as it were over the lost. Is it not written: "And the Spirit and the bride say, Come. And he that is athirst, let him come; he that will, let him take the water of life freely" (Rev. 22:17).

The term, the Holy Spirit, appears to be a synonym for the presence or power of God (and/or of Christ) at work in the world through his word. This is not to say that the Holy Spirit has no ex-

162

istence except as God or Christ speak, or apart from the written word. But it does point up the fact that whatever level of self-consciousness or personhood the Holy Spirit possesses, his primary role is in the field of communication. In that role he does not occupy a free-lance status. Jesus' words in John 16:13,14 underscore that fact:

> When he, the Spirit of truth, is come, he shall guide you into all the truth: for he shall not speak from himself; but what things soever he shall hear, *these* shall he speak: and he shall declare unto you the things that are to come. He shall glorify me: for he shall take of mine and shall declare *it* unto you.

It has been said "the pen is mightier than the sword." And oft times the spoken word is mightier still. We are all well aware of the ability of some persons to subject the mental and physical powers of others to their own will. Hypnosis is a short-term, dramatic example. On a long-term basis thousands, sometimes millions, surrender their minds and wills with fanatical unthinking devotion to such persons as Adolf Hitler, Jim Jones, the Ayotollah Khomeni. They thoughtlessly mouth the utterances of men whose vile spirits they allow to possess them, and become slaves of megalomaniacs whom many have never seen.

If it is possible for persons to submerge their minds and wills to fellow mortals, it is certainly possible to be immersed in the Holy Spirit, and in so doing reflect the mind of Christ. The difference is that we are ennobled when we have the mind of Christ in us. The Spirit of Christ, the Spirit of God, the Holy Spirit never enslaves, dehumanizes nor depreciates those so "possessed."

THE GIFT OF THE HOLY SPIRIT VERSUS SPIRITUAL GIFTS

How are we to differentiate between the gift of the Holy Spirit and spiritual gifts? We suggest the following: 1) The gift of the Holy Spirit is more personal. The relationship involved is interpersonal. The benefits which evolve relate to the realm of personal development. More than a half century ago a father, whose daughter I was courting, gave her to me in marriage. That was a tangible, visible, physical gift. The gift abounded with potentialities which were metaphysical. But these he could not give. For example, he could not give to me her love, her fidelity, her trust, her confidence. These, and such like, are gifts which could only be mine as she took up residence with me, and our lives intertwined and knit together in the bonds of matrimony.

God has given us the Holy Spirit. From the relationship formed thereby proceed gifts which cannot be bestowed. Love, for example, can be lavished upon us. But love, as a virtue welling up within us, cannot be bestowed. The same is true of the other spiritual qualities which Paul calls "the fruit of the Spirit" (Gal. 5:22,23).

2) The gift(s) of the Spirit enumerated and discussed in I Corinthians 12 represent a domination of the human spirit from without. The tongue speaking of the apostles on Pentecost was surely acceptable to them. One could imagine they were as amazed by it as were the multitudes who heard them, and no doubt as favorably impressed. They spoke "as the Spirit gave them utterance." But the gift which Paul called "the Holy Spirit of promise" (Eph. 1:13) represents a melding of the human spirit and the Divine, resulting in "the strengthening of our inner man" (Eph. 3:16). 3) The bestowed gifts were of temporary and sporadic utility whereas the moral gifts are apropos to all occasions, and for all time. Were the choice yours, (and it is!) which would you prefer?

SPIRITUAL GIFTS — WORD STUDY DATA

I. SPIRITUAL — *pneumatikos* (adj.) Used 26 times in Greek NT, with reference to a number of different things. Sometimes the "things" referred to must be conjectured from the context. *Words in parenthesis have been added by translators.

Rom.	1:11	that I may IMPART UNTO YOU SOME *SPIRITUAL* GIFT (charisma)
	7:14	the law is *spiritual*
	15:27	partakers of their *spiritual* (things)*
I Cor.	2:13	combining *spiritual* things with spiritual (words)*
	15	but he that is *spiritual* judgeth all things
	3:1	speak unto you as *spiritual*
	9:11	if we sowed unto you spiritual (things)*
	10:3,4	they did all eat the same *spiritual* food, and all drank of the same spiritual drink, for they drank of a *spiritual* rock
	12:1	NOW CONCERNING *SPIRITUAL* (things?, *gifts?*)*
	14:1	DESIRE *SPIRITUAL* (gifts)*
	37	if any man be a prophet, or *spiritual*
	15:44	it is raised a *spiritual* body . . . there is also a spiritual body
	46	that is not first which is *spiritual* . . . afterwards the *spiritual*
Gal.	6:1	ye which are *spiritual*, restore
Eph.	1:4	blessed us with every *spiritual* blessing
	5:19	speaking one to another in psalms, hymns and *spiritual* songs
	6:12	against *spiritual* (hosts)* of wickedness
Col.	1:9	in all wisdom and *spiritual* understanding
	3:16	in psalms and hymans and *spiritual* songs
I Peter	2:5	ye are built up a *spiritual* house . . . to offer spiritual sacrifices

II. GIFT, GIFTS — the term appears 56 times in the NT (58 times in KJV). *Seven* different Greek words are so translated (9 in KJV) the KJV translates 1) *anathema* (used 10 times in the Greek text, and 2) *charis*, "grace" (used 154 times) "*gift*" in Luke 21:5; II Cor. 8:4.

1. *Charisma* (s.), charismata (pl.) — a "gift (or gifts) of grace"

Romans 1:11   that I may impart unto you some spiritual *gift*
          5:15   so also is the (free)* *gift*
          5:16   but the (free)* *gift* is of many offences
          6:23   BUT THE (free)* *GIFT* OF GOD IS ETERNAL LIFE IN CHRIST JESUS
        11:29   FOR THE *GIFTS* AND THE CALLING ARE OF GOD
         12:6   HAVING *GIFTS* DIFFERING ACCORDING TO THE PROPORTION OF YOUR FAITH [prophecy, v. 6, ministry and teaching, v. 7, exhortation, giving, (sharing), ruling (leadership) and showing mercy, v. 8 — charistmatic]

I Cor.   1:7   I come behind you in no *gift*
          7:7   every man hath his proper *gift*
        12:4   there are diversities of *gifts*
        12:9   to another *gifts of healing(s)*
          29   then *gifts of healing(s)*
      12:30   have all *gifts of healing(s)*?
          31   desire earnestly the greater *gifts* (love, e.g., see Ch. 13)
II Cor. 1:11   for the gift bestowed upon us by means of many
I Tim.   4:14   neglect not the *gift* that is in thee, which was given thee by prophecy, through the laying on of the hands of the elders
II Tim. 1:6   Stir up the *gift* of God, which is in thee through . . . my hands
I Peter 4:10   AS EACH HATH RECEIVED A *GIFT* [speaking oracles of God, ministering]

2. *Doron* 19 times — *Gifts* given as an expression of honor

Matt.   2:11   they presented unto him *gifts*, gold . . . .
        5:23   if thou bringeth thy *gift* to the altar, and there remember
        5:24   leave there thy *gift* before the altar, go . . .
                . . . then come and offer thy *gift*
        8:4   offer the *gift* that Moses commanded
       15:5   it is a *gift* by whatsoever thou sayest (Corban)
    23:18   whosoever sweareth by the *gift*

	19	which is greater the *gift* or the altar that sanctifieth the *gift*?
Mark	7:11	corban, that is to say, it is a *gift*
Luke	21:1	casting their *gifts* into the treasury
	4	cast in unto the *offerings* of God
Eph.	2:8	not of yourselves (salvation) is the *gift* of God
Heb.	5:1	May offer both *gifts* and sacrifices
	8:3	to offer *gifts* and sacrifices
	4	there are priests that offer *gifts* according to the law
	9:9	were offered both *gifts* and sacrifices
	11:4	God testifieth with respect to his (Abel's) *gift*
Rev.	11:10	shall send *gifts* one to another

3. *Dorea* 11 times — *Gift*, used with reference to *gifts* Divinely given

	4:10	if thou knewest the *gift* if God
John		
Acts	2:38	and ye shall receive the *gift* of the Holy Spirit
	8:20	thou has thought to obtain the *gift* of God with money
	10:45	because that on the Gentiles was poured out the *gift* of the Holy Spirit
	11:17	if God gave unto them the like gift which he did unto us
Rom.	5:16	not as is the trespass . . . much more the grace and the *gift*
	17	the gift of righteousness
II Cor.	9:15	thanks be unto God for his unspeakable *gift*
Eph.	3:7	according to the *gift* of that grace of God given me
	4:7	the measure of the *gift* of Christ
Heb.	11:4	tasted of the heavenly *gift*

4. *Dorema* 2 times

Rom.	5:16	so is the *gift*
James	1:17	every perfect *gift* is from above

5. *Doma* 4 times — Gift, emphasizes the *gift* per se — the thing given

Matt.   7:11   knoweth how to give good *gifts* to your children
Luke   11:13   knoweth how to give good *gifts* to your children
Eph.   4:8   gave *gifts* to men
Phil.   4:17   not that I desire a gift

6. *Dosis* 2 times — Gift, emphasizes the acts of giving

Phil.   4:15   in the matter of *giving* and receiving
James   4:17   every good *gift* (giving) and every perfect gift

7. *Merismos* 2 times — Gift, emphasizes the distribution of the gift

Heb.   2:4   and *gifts* of the Holy Spirit according to his own will
cf.   4:12   (unto the dividing of both soul and spirit)

10

DO ALL (SHOULD WE) SPEAK IN TONGUES?

PART ONE

It should not take long to set forth what the Scriptures say about speaking in tongues. They actually say very little. The Old Testament says next to nothing, if anything. As for the New Testament, the phenomenon is mentioned in only five places. 1) in the Gospels it is mentioned only in Mark 16:17 — a lone verse in the midst of a passage that is lacking in the two oldest and most reliable manuscripts, 2) it is mentioned but three times in the whole of the book of Acts, the history of the early church, (2:4,11; 10:46; 19:6), 3) in the 21 NT epistles tongues are mentioned only in one, I Corinthians, Chs. 12-14 and 4) not at all in the Apocalypse.

Thus 3 of the 4 gospels, 12 of Paul's 13 epistles, all seven of the epistles of miscellaneous authorship — Hebrews, James, I & II Peter, I, II & III John, and Jude — along with the Apocalypse are all silent about tongues. John, the second most prolific writer of the NT, and the writer who has so much to say about the Holy Spirit otherwise, neither in his gospel, his epistles nor the Apocalypse has anything to say about the gift of tongues. Moreover, I Corinthians 12-14, the lone epistle which discusses tongue speaking, is openly critical of the practice, and suggests its days are numbered.

Datewise, a) Mark's gospel is generally regarded as the earliest of the four to be written, b) I Corinthians is generally accepted as one of the earlier of Paul's thirteen epistles, and c) the last mention of tongues in Acts (19:6), relates to an event which occurred prior to the writing of I Corinthians. This has some implications.

TEXTUAL DATA ANALYZED

A careful analysis of each text in which the tongue speaking phenomenon is mentioned is incumbent upon us. Fortunately there is not the plethora of Biblical references that many have been led to expect. The few there are 1) belong to the earlier NT documents, and 2) except for the unique Caesarea/Cornelius episode they relate to situations in which sign-oriented Jews were front and center. Even at Corinth, a Gentile city, this proves to be the case. (See Acts 18:2-17.) Jews dominate the historical data recorded.

Old Testament

Isaiah 28:11 is quoted by Paul in I Corinthians 14:21, leading some to believe that speaking in tongues was predicted in the Old Testament. That is neither the use Paul made of it, nor the obvious meaning of the text taken in context. In answer to the questions: Whom will he (God) teach knowledge? and whom will he make to understand the message? Innocent babes newly weaned from their mother's milk? "Nay," Isaiah writes, "but by men of strange lips and with another tongue will he (God) speak."

170

There is no hint in the passage that spokesmen would speak in a tongue unknown to themselves. It simply means that since Israel refused to listen to their own prophets he would humiliate them by using barbarians to instruct them the hard way. The passage is a prophecy of Israel's forthcoming exile in which God would use barbarians to teach them the lessons they refused to learn aforehand from their own prophets. In I Corinthians 14:21 Paul uses the passage to point out that not even then did Israel really learn. Thus prophesying (instruction) is for them that believe. Tongues were a sign to the unbelieving, as were the lessons Israel learned in exile from the barbaric Chaldeans.

Joel 2:28-32 actually says nothing about speaking in tongues. The fact is it is not even hinted at. In retrospect it might be inferred from the fact that the universality of mankind is sometimes expressed by such language as "all nations and tongues" (Isa. 66:18) and "every nation and all tribes and peoples and tongues" (Rev. 7:9; 10:11; 11:9; 13:17; 17:15). But the language of Joel is quite dissimilar. Joel's expression, "all flesh" is not primarily multi-national in its application. He first defines "all flesh" as "sons and daughters, old men and young, servants and handmaids" (2:28,29). Only in closing the passage cited by Peter did Joel give the prediction an international application, adding: "and it shall be delivered (saved)" (2:32).

In short, the Old Testament says nothing about the phenomenon of tongue speaking. The tower of Babel episode is sometimes lifted out of context and used by the "babblers" in support of their premise that their utterances are a gift of God, but that is "a sword which they grasp by the blade." Confusion, not communication, and Divine judgment, not blessing, are the essence of the tower of Babel episode (Gen. 11:1-9).

New Testament References

Mark 16:17,18
This passage was discussed in depth in the preceding chapter.

The text is the lone reference to tongue speaking in the gospels and hence the only recorded saying of Christ which relates to the topic at hand. Beginning with the beatitudes, (Matt. 5:1-16) he had much to say about showing evidence we are his disciples. Love is the grace most often cited (John 13:34,35; 15:12). Fruit bearing, of which love heads the list, is enjoined upon us in John 15:1-8. But of tongues Jesus said next to nothing. Were tongue speaking the sure sign we are his Spirit-filled disciples, he would surely have discoursed on that somewhere.

Acts 2:1-11

The phenomena described in this passage signalized the inauguration of the New Covenant. Both the Mosaic covenant and the covenant of Christ were certified by demonstrations of the Divine presence. At the giving of the Law on Mt. Sinai the presence of God was signalized by a mount that "burned with fire," and from which smoke ascended "as from a furnace," and which "greatly quaked," and from whence the voice of an "exceeding loud" trumpet "waxed louder and louder" insomuch that all the people (Moses included) did "exceedingly fear and quake" (Exod. 19:16-19, cp. Heb. 12:18-21).

At the inauguration of the New Covenant "there came from heaven a sound as of a rushing mighty wind," but without the terrifying physical effects — else those who heard would not have made their way to the source of the sound. Upon their arrival a visual phenomenon was added to the audible wonderment which had claimed their attention. "Tongues parting asunder, like as of fire" are said to have "sat upon each one of them (the twelve apostles, cp. Acts 1:26-2:1) and they were all filled with the Holy Spirit and began to speak with other tongues (Gr. *glossais*, languages) as the Spirit gave them utterance" (Acts 2:1-4).

The dual phenomena of Pentecost (audible and visual) are reminiscent of the two-fold facet of the phenomena that claimed Israel's attention at Mt. Sinai. In each case God used attention-getting phenomena to set the stage. But there the parallel ceases.

The signs and wonders he employed were suited to the Divine purpose being served.

The tongue speaking on Pentecost served precisely the function Paul attributes to the phenomenon in I Corinthians 14:22. They were "for a sign, not to them that believe, but to them that believe not." That which caught the auditors' attention was the fact that "each of them heard in his own tongue (Gr. *dialecto*) the mighty works of God" (Acts 2:8).

Acts 10:44-48

Tongue speaking is often inferred to have ensued at Samaria upon the visitation of Peter and John, (Acts 8:14-25). From verses 15,16 we learn that Peter and John: "prayed for them that they might receive the Holy Spirit (v. 15): for as yet it was *fallen upon* none of them; only they had been baptized into the name of the Lord Jesus" (v. 16). Verse 16 needs to be read in the light of Acts 2:38; 5:32. There is no contradiction here. When the Scriptures speak of the Spirit of Jehovah or the Holy Spirit as "fallen upon" or "come upon" someone, it uniformly designates special endowment whereby extraordinary powers are imparted, (cp. Acts 19:6; Num. 24:2; Jdgs. 11:29; 13:25; 14:6,19; 15:14; I Sam. 10:6,10; 11:6; 16:14-16,23; 19:20,23). The powers imparted upon the Samaritans are not specified. They may have included tongues, but not necessarily. (See I Cor. 12:4-11, noting particularly v. 11, cp. Heb. 2:4).

The gift of tongues was definitely visited upon the Gentile household at Caesarea — in their case *without* the laying on of the apostle's (Peter's) hands. This was a case calling for Divine demonstration in an area wherein at least the six Jewish brethren Peter brought with him were "unbelievers." The fact the Gentiles spoke in tongues made "believers" also of the brethren to whom Peter had to give account upon his return to Jerusalem. (See Acts 11:2-18.) And it made "believers" also of the Jerusalem conference delegates. (See Acts 15:8 and context.)

The fact that the Jews looked askance at the Samaritans

could be used to infer that tongues were included among the gifts Peter and John bestowed on them. But Luke did not see fit to say so. And in their case Peter and John apparently were not "unbelievers" needing such evidence. They laid their hands upon the Samaritans, imparting special powers apart from the sign which tongues would have provided.

Acts 19:1-12

Verses 8-12 are added to this citation because they may provide some additional context. The incident recorded in verses 1-7 is the final reference to tongue speaking in the book of Acts. The text is somewhat enigmatic. The purpose of the gift of tongues in this instance, and of the gift of prophecy which was also given, is not clear. In fact the only facet of the episode which conforms to the pattern is that the gifts mentioned were received through the laying on of the hands of an apostle (v. 16).

In every reference to tongue speaking up to this point (Mark 16:17; Acts 2:6,7,12,13; 10:44-47; cp. 11:15-18), the gift served as a "sign to the unbelieving." If such was the purpose in this instance the unbelievers for whose sake the gift was given are not specified. However the verses which follow (8-12) indicate the ministry of Paul in Ephesus began amid a hostile setting. Early on some of Paul's hearers were so "hardened and disobedient, speaking evil of the Way before the multitude" (v. 9), that Paul was obliged to depart from them, taking his disciples with him, into the school of Tyrannus where he apparently found relief from the disruption of the rabble crowd.

It is significant Paul's greatest display of miraculous powers (of record) were performed in that hostile setting. Verses 11,12 note that "God wrought *special* miracles by the hands of Paul insomuch that unto the sick were carried away from his body handkerchiefs or aprons and the diseases departed from them, and evil spirits went out."

Apart from the initial description of the manner in which the gift of tongues functioned "at the beginning" (Acts 2:6-8), no insight is provided as to whether that pattern prevailed in each instance. Nothing is said to the effect that it did not. Only as we come to the final reference (I Cor. 12-14) could anything else be reasonably inferred.

I Corinthians 12-14

These three chapters provide the final reference to tongue speaking (*glossolalia*) in the Scriptures. Up to this point mention of the phenomenon is found in a positive setting. The gift had a telling and desired effect upon the hearers.

Nothing is said of the emotional or mental state of those exercising the gift. From the fact some of those who heard the apostles speaking in tongues on Pentecost sought to dismiss the phenomena with the snide remark, "they are full of new wine," it is sometimes inferred the apostles were giddy with euphoria. The fact that the subject of their conversation appears to have been a recital of "the mighty works of God" (Acts 2:11) would suggest their mood may have been one of elation. In that it is generally inferred they were all speaking at once, that, if true, would lend some credence to the snide remark to which we have already alluded. But were they all speaking at the same time, none of them listening to any of the others, but each "doing his own thing"? The text of Acts two does not say that.

The emphasis of Luke's account of the happening is placed on the fact that those who heard them, at least those who took time to listen, heard them speaking as it were in their own "back home" dialect — whether Parthian, Mede, Elamite, Mesopotamian, Judean, Cappadocian, Pontusian, Asian, Phrygian, Pamphylian, Egyptian, Cyrenean-Libyan, Roman (both Jews and proselytes), Cretan, and Arabians — fifteen locales listed, and all heard them speaking as though each of them were listening to their next door neighbor. Where hear we, where does *anyone* hear such "tongue speaking" today? Whatever it is that is heard it is not "*Pentecost* renewed." However, it has definite affinity with the aberration of the "tongue speaking" phenomenon that was

175

creating division and disorder at Corinth.

First Corinthians, Chapters 12-14 introduce a new perspective in the "tongue-speaking" phenomenon. For the first time the exercise is spoken of critically, even accusatorially. If what the Corinthian "tonguers" were doing really was a gift of the Holy Spirit, the gift no longer appears to be serving its original purpose. Instead of serving as "a sign of the unbelievers" (14:22), those professing to speak in tongues were coming across to those who heard them as "barbarians" (14:11) or even as ones who were "mad" (v. 23). The term "barbarian" denotes in Greek an ignorant, crude stranger. The word translated "mad" is derived from the verb *mainomai* from whence our English words mania and maniac are derived.

An overview of Paul's observations of the Corinthian mania for tongue speaking and the guidelines he laid down provides a critique and corollary instruction which read as though he anticipated our day as he addressed himself to what has been called "the Corinthian catastrophe." At least twenty relevant observations are set forth in chapters twelve through fourteen.

1. Tongues are *not* "for everybody." They never were, much less are they now, *the* sign of the baptism of the Holy Spirit and of the true and credentialized believer (12:10,11,28-30). When Paul says "to one is given . . . kinds of tongues, and to another the interpretation of tongues," etc. (v. 10), he is not saying that each of the various gifts listed would be restricted to one person, but he was most certainly saying that not one of the specialized service gifts would be given to any and every one. And in verse 11 he plainly states that the distribution of such gifts is the province of the Holy Spirit. They are given "according to *his* own will" (Cp. Heb. 2:4). The rhetorical questions in verse 28-30 are to be answered with a resounding, "No!" All are *not* apostles, prophets . . . tongues speakers, etc., etc.

2. Tongues belong to the lower rank of spiritual gifts. The offices of apostle, prophet and teacher are numbered — firstly, secondly, thirdly, (v. 28). The order is plainly on a descending

scale. The six unnumbered services which are then cited are also listed in a descending order of importance to the functioning of the church. Tongues and its counterpart, interpretation of tongues, are at the bottom of the list in all three catalogues (vv. 8-10, v. 28 and vv. 29,30). Moreover such gifts are specifically designated as lesser gifts when compared to "the greater gifts" which constitute " a most excellent way" of service (v. 31) that is open to all — the way of love (Chapter 13).

3. Tonguers are only a noisome clamor apart from love (13:1). The sound of a voice ultimately dissipates in the air. Even those words which are pleasing to the ear (when heard) become empty and vain unless re-enforced by tangible demonstrations of love.

4. Tongues belong to an order of gifts that shall cease (13:8). Even the gift of prophecy, one of the three numbered service gifts, and the "knowledge" mediated thereby, belong to the non-permanent order of special ministrations of the Holy Spirit. Tongues, being of a lesser order still, could the more be reckoned as transitory at best. This was especially so of the non-communicating babbling of the Corinthian tonguers to say nothing of their modern counterparts, however sincere though misled.

5. Tongues of the Corinthians and neo-Corinthian sort are profitless insofar as our fellowmen are concerned (14:2). Such tonguers may "speak unto God" (Paul gave them the benefit of the doubt, and so may we). It is possible that some have contrived a kind of "prayer language" which may not be altogether void of personal edification. But he that "speaks mysteries," even *in the Spirit*, provides no "understanding" for others (v. 2, cp. 3).

6. Tongues may edify (build-up) the speaker (in his own eyes) but not those who hear (14:4). Note what is said here: "He that speaks in tongues edifies himself, but he that prophesies edifies the church." This could not be said of the tongues speaking on Pentecost (see Acts 2:5-12). The modern counterparts of the Corinthian tonguers aver they have been given "a prayer

177

language" as a very personal gift, and that is why what they "speak in tongues" understood only by themselves. If so, the only Biblical precedent is the Corinthian debacle. Paul was not at all supportive of what the Corinthians were doing on their premise they were being "led by the Spirit" (cp. I Cor. 12:2). Again the "self-interest" of the Corinthians was showing, and gave cause to call in question their claim of special spiritual endowment.

This seems a good time to pause and consider a possible explanation for the manner in which Paul handled the Corinthians situation. He obviously had the spiritual gift he calls "the discerning of spirits" (12:10). He exercised that gift in his encounter with a) Elymas, the sorcerer of Cyprus (Acts 13:6-11), b) the soothsaying maid at Philippi (16:16-18), and c) Sceva's seven exorcist sons whom he encountered at Ephesus (19:13-16).

Since Paul had the gift of the discerning of spirits why did he not openly expose the Corinthian claimants of special spiritual endowment? Two reasons may be cited. One, he was not there in person to observe, discern and confront pretenders head on as his custom was. Two, he may have been using an age old debate technique: namely, "Concede a point in order to make one." Again and again it appears that Paul did this. In effect he was saying: "Suppose we give you the benefit of the doubt. Assuming your gift is genuine, who except for yourself is profited by it? or convinced of it?"

The principle to which we have alluded is illustrated in the opening words of chapter 13. Paul picks up on the exhortation with which he closed the preceding chapter. Recall that he closed chapter 12 by addressing both the "haves" (those glorying in the showy gift(s) they could display; and apparently did at every opportunity), and the "have nots" (those who were intimidated thereby). He challenged them, one and all, to "desire earnestly the *greater* gifts." Moreover, he said, "a most excellent way (to do so) show I unto you" (12:31).

Note what he says next, and consider its implications. His opening words are, "If I speak with the tongues of men and of angels, but have not love . . . ." Pause, and note what is implied. He is saying in effect: "If I speak in the tongues of men — ah, I will go you one better, even if I speak in the tongues of *angels*, but have not love, I am become sounding brass, or a clanging cymbal." Thus Paul conceded a point which, considering his insight, he might have openly challenged. But he conceded a point in order to make one. The lowly "have nots," those who had no miraculous powers they could display, nor could even pretend they did, if they had the gift of (*agape*) love — that "other regarding" love which is exercised always with regard for the one being loved — *that* person has a greater gift than the gift of tongues, *even of* angels. The church could survive without the gift of tongues, but not without the outpouring and sharing of (*agape*) love.

7. Tongues are inferior to prophecy (14:2). They must be interpreted to do what prophecy does unaided (14:4). This could not be said of the gift of tongues as elsewhere mentioned in the NT. It was not so on Pentecost. It would not appear to be so of Cornelius and his household, else it could not be described as "the like gift" which was poured out upon the Apostles "at the beginning" (Acts 11:18).

There appears to have been no need of an interpreter for the twelve men who received such a gift at Ephesus. The fact is, it could well be that when it is said of them that "they spoke with tongues and prophesied" (Acts 19:6) that the latter phrase is simply explanatory of the first. The tongues predicted in Mark 16:17 would not have been a very convincing "sign" if it consisted only of the mouthing of jargon which the unbelievers who heard them speak could in no way understand.

This raises a question. Why then was the gift of "the interpretation of tongues" given at Corinth? If the gift of tongues at Corinth was also the "*like* gift which was poured out (upon the apostles) at the beginning" why were interpreters now needed? And if the gift was not the same, but rather a gift that required the presence of interpreters before it could be exercised legitimately,

179

why the difference?

The question just raised is rarely addressed. Either it does not occur to commentators that there is a problem, or, if it does, like the priest and the levite they choose to "pass by on the other side." The few who see the problem generally conclude that tongue speaking is, and always has been, *ecstatic* utterances. They labor the point that at least some who heard the apostles speaking in tongues thought they were drunk (Acts 2:13). But the truth is those who heard them "got the message," and in "their own dialect," no less, and without an interpreter. The record reports their hearers as saying: "We hear them speaking in our own tongues the mighty works of God" (v. 12).

How could ecstatic jargon be a sign of the Holy Spirit? Drunkenness, drugs, hypnotism, excitement produce the same. Paganism abounds with similar phenomena. The Holy Spirit is capable of better demonstration. Why interpreters of tongues were needed at Corinth is beyond my discernment at this point. The case of the Corinthian church presents many riddles. Corinth hardly provides a pattern to be emulated.

8. Tongues of the Corinthian and neo-Corinthian order are inferior even to senseless harps and pipes (14:7-9). Even things without life, hence without mind or self-determination, are capable of sending forth a clear message, readily understood by those who hear. If the trumpet is caused to give an uncertain sound confusion arises, and the inherent worth of the trumpet is voided. The trumpet of course is not to be blamed when that occurs. The trumpeter is at fault. Consider the implications of that. We are not lifeless, senseless things. And the Holy Spirit is not an inept or conniving bugler nor a traitor to God's people and his plan. "God (whether the Father, the Son or the Holy Spirit) is not a god of confusion" (I Cor. 14:33).

9. Tongues of the Corinthian sort are inferior to all kinds of voices (14:10). There are indeed "many kinds of voices in the world, and no kind is without signification." This is true of birds, beasts, even of insects. It is true of the sounds of the wind and of

the sea, of landslides and falling trees. Hence to profess to speak as the Spirit gives utterance, yet say nothing that has any signification, is to devalue the most versatile and highly perfected speech mechanism in all of God's creation. Blame not that on the Holy Spirit.

10. Tongues of the Corinthian variety (the forte of the current tongues movement also) are as uninformative as the voice of utter strangers (14:11). The Greek word (*barbaros*, translated barbarian) was generally used derogatorily. It was used of anyone who could not speak or understand Greek. Paul uses it here to disparage an activity in the guise of Christian worship which would make the participants appear as barbarians. This poses a conundrum. Would such an activity be "led of the Spirit?" Was Paul then second guessing the Holy Spirit?

11. Tongue speakers, so zealous of spiritual gifts, ought to set their sights higher. Paul phrases it on this wise, "Since you are zealous of spiritual gifts, seek that you may abound unto the edifying of the church" (14:12). Aren't they one and the same thing? By no means. The overriding thrust of Paul's extended discourse on spiritual gifts is that tongue speaking is ego-centric, self-interest oriented. It is not the means by which the church is edified. It is not the most excellent way. It is not the way of love.

12. Tongue speakers ought to be more concerned with communicating than with toying with their tongues (14:13). Specifically Paul exhorts: "Wherefore let him that speaks in a tongue, pray that he may interpret." Tongue speaking is often called by its claimants a "special prayer language." If it be so, then according to Paul, the main thing they ought to be praying for is the gift of interpretation so that they can say something others can understand and be edified thereby.

13. Tongue speakers ought to get their understanding in gear with a view to answering the prayer Paul has just enjoined upon them. First Corinthians 14:14 reads: "If I pray in a tongue, my spirit prays (theoretically at least that is so) but my understanding is unfruitful." How long can a mature person be satisfied with a

181

practice devoid of mental acumen?

14. Tongue speakers would do well to follow the example of Paul. In verse 15 he writes: "I will pray with the spirit (the thing tongue speakers were professing to be doing) and I will pray with the understanding also. I will sing with the spirit, (perhaps David, the sweet singer of Israel, came to his mind as he wrote this) and I will sing with the understanding also." Knowing and understanding what one is doing in the exercise of worship is certainly not to be disparaged. It could also edify those who are worshipping with you. (See v. 16.)

15. Tongue speakers of the Corinthian order provoked a note of sarcasm even from Paul. In 14:17 he went on to say: For you verily give thanks well, but the other is not edified. In the colloquial language of our day, Paul is saying: "So you are doing a great job of giving thanks to God. Big deal! Who is edified? Who else has any idea of what you are saying, and hence is reminded of blessings for which they should give thanks?"

16. Tongue speaking is a poor bargain in the communication field. The odds against it being of practical value are 2000 to 1. In verse 18 Paul intimates he may have resorted to the practice in his private prayers, a fact difficult to understand against the backdrop of his extensive discourse on the subject. But he goes on to say, (v. 19) "Howbeit, in the church I had rather speak five words with my understanding than ten thousand words in a tongue."

Jesus Christ is my Lord! The average sermon is comprised of about three thousand words. Theoretically, one would have to preach the equivalent of at least three sermons while speaking in tongues to communicate the equivalent in propositional truth contained in the five italicized words heading this paragraph. No wonder he reserved tongue speaking for private prayer situations. If his lone supportive statement has any message for us, it is: "Keep it to yourself. Don't flaunt it."

17. Tongue speaking of the Corinthian order can be malicious in effect, if not by intent. In verse 20 Paul suggest his

readers were being immature in their thinking and use of tongues. They were babbling like babes, but they ought rather to be "in *malice* as babes," that is, at least there should be no *malice* aforethought. Their offense should cease as soon as they mature enough to realize what they were doing. For the Corinthian tonguers it was high time they grew up.

18. Tongues, properly used, were "for a sign, not to them that believe, but to the unbelieving" (14:22). That certainly has been turned around. Are Paul and modern claimants of the gift talking about the same thing? Tongue speaking of the order described in Acts 2:4-11 had a positive effect upon the unbelieving Jews. But the tongue speaking Paul is dealing with in the text before us was having a negative effect. Verse 23 reads: "If therefore the whole church be assembled together and all speak with tongues, and there come in men unlearned or unbelieving, will they not say, you are mad?" He then goes on to say that prophesying (preaching) will have the opposite effect.

19. Tongues, at best, should be subject to rules of decorum. In verses 26-28, under the heading of an overriding rule: "Let all things be done unto edifying" (26b), Paul cites four guidelines: a) tongue speaking should be limited to two, or at the most three, b) and that in turn, c) let one interpret (v. 27) and d) if there be no interpreter let him (the tongue speaker) keep silence in the church" (v. 28). He may talk to God, and to himself, but not so as to be heard by others.

20. Ignorance about spiritual things, as with most things, is relative. What Paul has written in I Corinthians has lessened but not alleviated mine. One thing has been underscored. Tongues, the easiest of the display gifts to simulate, was then, as it is now, the center of the most controversy, the occasion of the most vexing problems when introduced into the assembly of the church. While it is true that the abuse of a thing is not a valid argument against its proper use, the question remains. Considering the potential of tongues for simulation and disorder why was the gift given? From the fact Corinth was apparently problem and

disorder prone, perhaps the tongues problem was not general. There is no hint of the same in any other epistle, or place.

PART TWO

In Part One of this study we took note of what the Bible says about speaking in tongues. Upon first thought it appeared this sector of our inquiry into the Biblical teaching concerning the Holy Spirit would be relatively brief. The Scriptures seem at first to say but little about tongue speaking. The phenomenon is only predicted once, and there but barely mentioned (Mark 16:17). It is chronicled as having occurred only three times in the whole of the book of Acts (Chs. 2, 10 and 19). The latter two references are of the "in passing" kind. Only one significant detail is cited. In the instance of the Caesarean episode it evidenced the fact that "to the gentiles also God had granted repentance unto life" (11:18). No explanation is given of the happening at Ephesus, only the fact that it occurred.

The text of chapters 12-14 of I Corinthians is another story. The tongue phenomenon dominates the passage. And whereas the other references to the activity are set in the context of divine approval, quite the contrary is true of "the Corinthian Catastrophe" (to borrow a descriptive phrase from the title of a perceptive study by George E. Gardiner, Kregel Pub.). The debacle at Corinth seems to have little in common with the historical references in Acts. That leads me to say that if one seeks to understand the usage and meaning of the gift of tongues, one should view the practice from an *historical* perspective rather than the *hysterical* scenario of Corinth.

It goes almost without saying that the tongues movement in our day has much more in common with the scenario at Corinth than with the phenomenon which attended the descent of the Holy Spirit and birth of the church on Pentecost. Hence, the term neo-Christianism is often more descriptive of the distinctive exercises of the groups whose most common self-designation is pentecostal. Non-aligned pentecostals of recent vintage prefer the title charismatic. However, the Greek word from which it is taken (*charismata*) is nowhere used in the Scriptures in a context in which tongues are included under that general heading.

Many other gifts of grace are so identified, singly as in Romans 6:23; 11:29; I Corinthians 12:9,29, and collectively as in Romans 12:6-8; I Peter 4:10,11. But tongue speaking is nowhere so catalogued, or otherwise identified in the Scriptures as a "charismatic gift."

Charismatic is a word which has only recently been coined and introduced to the masses. It stems from the Greek root "*charis,*" commonly translated "grace" and defined as "unmerited favor." Thus a familiar derivative "charity" signifies "the state of being gracious." Hence any gift or good deed extended on behalf of some one generally regarded as undeserving of such favor is called "charity." The Greek word for a *gift* of grace is "*charisma*" (pl. "*charismata*").

Romans 6:23 tells us "the *wages* (Gr. *opsonion, pay*) of sin is death but the *free* gift (Gr. *charisma*) of God is eternal life in Christ Jesus." That makes every saved person a charismatic and a charismatic church of every congregation of redeemed persons. And in addition to the general gift of grace, our great salvation, purchased for us by the blood of Christ and bestowed upon us freely through his grace, many other charismatic gifts are available, and operable in the church today.

Romans 12:6-8 lists seven *charismata* (gifts) differing "according to the grace that is given to us" — a) *prophecy*, a general word for preaching. Generically it simply means "one who speaks for" another. b) *ministry*, Gr. *diakonian* — lit., deaconing, serving. c) *teaching* (no qualifying or limiting terms or situations are included in the text). d) *exhorting*, Gr. *parakalon*, cp. *paraclete*, elsewhere translated comforter, lit., "to call along side," to rally, encourage, admonish. e) *giving* (sharing) *with liberality*, or "simplicity," making no show of it. f) *ruling*, lit. "taking the lead."

The Greek, *proistemi*, means to go before, as one who leads (shows) the way. g) *showing mercy, with cheerfulness*; not a martyr to forgiving, but one glad to do so.

This may seem far afield from a discourse on tongues. But we do well to inform one another of the options which are beckoning to us through the grace of God. No wonder Paul said to the Corinthians who were caught up in tongue speaking, "Desire the *greater* gifts" (I Cor. 12:31), and launched into a rhapsody on the grace of love (I Cor. 13).

ETYMOLOGY

In the NT the word commonly translated tongue(s) is *glossa(ai)*. It appears fifty times in the Greek NT. Twelve times it refers to the member of the body we call the tongue. Once (Acts 2:3) it is used metaphorically. The visual phenomenon which attended the descent of the Holy Spirit on Pentecost is said to have appeared unto them "as tongues parting asunder, like as of fire." Otherwise, and generally, the term is used with reference to languages.

Today, *glossa* is often coupled with *lalia*, the Greek word for speaking, to form the word glossolalia. Glossolalia is the code name for what is currently being promoted as "speaking in tongues."

Glossolalia, "speaking in tongues," real or imaginary, has lately caused a greater stir in Christendom than any other spiritual gift — if indeed what is being promoted under that catchword is either spiritual or a gift. This is the issue we need to evaluate.

HISTORY OF THE TONGUE SPEAKING: POST APOSTOLIC

Tongue speaking in post apostolic times has had a checkered career. The various groups that have made a specialty of the performance have had one thing in common. Invariably they have reckoned themselves to be living "in the last days," in the eschatological sense of the term. A verse in the prophecy of Joel, preceding the verses Peter quoted on Pentecost, has been commonly given "end time" prophetic application. Specifically, Joel 2:23 is cited as predicting a renewal of spiritual gifts at the apostolic level, as the sign of the end time. It reads:

> Be glad then ye children of Zion, and rejoice in Jehovah your God; for he giveth you the former rain in just measure, and he causeth to come down for you the rain, the rain, the former rain and the latter rain, in the first *month* (lit., "at the first").

The passage is interpreted as predicting two seasons of the outpouring of the Holy Spirit, the first at the inception of the Gospel age (on Pentecost) and the latter "in the end time," the consummation of the church age. Those who so interpret are unimpressed by the fact that Peter quoted the verses quickly following, verses 28-31, announcing: "It shall come to pass *in the last days* saith God. I will pour forth of my Spirit upon all flesh . . ." and prefaced the quotation by saying: "*This is that* which has been spoken through the prophet Joel" (Acts 2:16, cp. v. 33). According to Peter, "the latter days" began when "the former days," the Mosaic dispensation, came to an end. (Cp. Heb. 1:1,2; I John 2:18; Jude 1:17,18.)

Montanists

In the middle of the second century A.D., Montanus, a Phrygrian cult leader hailed as the incarnation of the Paraclete, determined the end of the church age was near and that credentializing miraculous powers, including tongue speaking, were available to true believers. He and his prophetesses, along with a smattering of prophets, were given to ecstatic unintelligible utterances. Despite the fact that the celebrated Tertullian became an enthusiastic convert to Montanism, their failing "prophecies" along with the weariness that protracted emotionalism ultimately engenders brought an end to Montanist pentecostalism.

Pre-Reformation Drought

Montanism represents the only authenticated account of tongue speaking between the apostolic age and the Protestant Reformation. Tongue speaking had no significant role in the onset of the Reformation. Spiritual gift cultism and the eminent expectation of a pre-millennial second coming of Christ commonly go hand in hand. Historically the mind-set that triggers the one tends to engender the other.

French Cevennes

The A.D. 1685 revocation of the Edict of Nantes brought to the Huguenots some relief from the bitter persecution they had suffered at the hands of the Catholic church. In the aftermath a "spiritual renewal" broke out among a peasant group in southern France. Extravagant claims of spiritual gifts, including the gift of tongues and of prophecy spread among them. Their exercises were particularly noted for the participation of little children, of whom it was claimed that when they were "in the Spirit" the children (though peasants) spoke eloquently in classical French. But retaliatory night raids against their long time enemies and their record of unfulfilled prophecies combined to discredit them utterly.

Jansenites

The Jansenites were a group of Roman Catholic reformers who were out of the main stream of the protestant reformation, but who were bitter antagonists of the Jesuit priests. Circa 1730 they held nocturnal meetings about the tomb of a revered leader. Ecstatic experiences, including "tongue speaking," were reported among them. Kendrick, a Pentecostal apologist, credits the Jansenites as being the first group in modern times to exhibit the characteristic marks of pentecostal renewal (The Promise Fulfilled, p. 20).

188

The Shakers

In the latter half of the 18th century arose one who presented herself as "Mother" Ann Lee, the female counterpart of Christ. In short she professed Christ's second coming was fulfilled in her. In 1776, an important date in American history (but for other reasons), she founded a Shaker community near Troy, New York. Her "revelations" included the prohibition of sexual relations, even in marriage. But at the same time she is said to have initiated the incongruous practice of having male and female devotees of her cult "mortify their flesh" by dancing naked together, while "speaking in tongues," no less.

Irvingites

This early 19th century sect, followers of Edward Irving, erstwhile Scotch Presbyterian clergyman, taught that all the apostolic gifts were available and should be evidenced in the church. "Tongue speaking" and "prophecies," the prevailing pattern in all such cults, proliferated among them. But their prophecies not only failed, they were self-contradictory, and flagrantly so of the Scriptures. In time Mary Campbell, the leading priestess of the movement, confessed her utterances to be fraudulent. Robert Baxter, Irving's most noted convert, renounced the cult, and hastened its demise.

The Mormons

While the Mormons are somewhat "low key" in their advocacy of tongue speaking, beginning with their founder, Joseph Smith the cult has avowed that the apostolic gifts, tongues included, are available for "the latter days" as of old. Brigham Young professed to pray in the "pure Adamic language," a feat which is hardly capable of verification. Their citadel temple in Salt Lake is reported to have been dedicated amid the prayers of hundreds of elders praying in the Spirit, "in heavenly languages," no less. (Would such be a cut above "pure Adamic language" per chance, or just a tad lower?)

189

Miscellany

A miscellany of short-lived cults and sects have risen and faded away. For the most part they have been devotees of a clever manipulator, or at times of a sincere but misguided personality with a "messiah complex." It is a hallmark of the tongues movement that when the authority figures fail — recant, become discredited, or otherwise fade or fall, their devotees scatter. Some abandon the movement *en toto* in disillusionment. Others seek a new authority figure, perchance of an altogether different persuasion, but almost always a leader and/or teacher in a movement that is aberrant in some way.

THE PROLIFERATION OF MODERN PENTECOSTALISM

The proliferation of modern pentecostalism could scarcely be traced or evaluated in this brief overview. Among others, Charles R. Smith (*Tongues in Biblical Perspective*, BMH Books, Winona Lake) cites four factors which have figured prominently.

1. *The Holiness Movement.* In eastern Tennessee and western North Carolina a "holiness revival" was initiated by two Baptist preachers, R.G. Spurling, Sr. and Jr. In 1902 a "Holiness Church" was formed. The year following A.J. Tomlinson became the preacher and founder of the Church of God which headquarters in Tennessee.

2. *Bethel Bible College.* In 1900 Charles Parham, often called "the father of the modern Pentecostal movement," founded Bethel Bible College at Topeka, Kansas. In December, as he was preparing to leave the campus for a preaching engagement, he assigned the students the task of answering the question, "What is the evidence of the baptism of the Holy Ghost?" They concluded speaking in tongues was the evidence and began to fervently pray for that experience. New Year's day, 1901 a female student, Agnes Ozman, reputedly received the baptism of the Holy Ghost, and the gift of tongues. That date is commonly

cited as the birthday of the pentecostal renewal of the church. Selective signs of the order predicted in Mark 16:17,18 have characterized all facets of the movement from the beginning unto now.

3. *Azusa Street Mission*. In 1906 a black student from a new school Parham had founded in Houston, Texas was invited to speak in a mission church in Los Angeles. Tongue speaking broke out in a prayer meeting. A bi-racial congregation of blacks and whites outgrew their quarters and moved to a building on Azusa Street, and became known as the Azusa Street Mission, and the spawning bed of another Pentecostal movement that numbers approximately two million.

4. *Ecumenicity through infiltration*. In the post World War II era pentecostalism has successfully penetrated "the mainline churches." Through the Full Gospel Christian Business Men's Fellowship International an astute program of infiltration has been worked with significant success. Key persons, at times preachers, are targeted and drawn into business men's prayer breakfasts, luncheons, etc. Home Bible study and prayer groups target key women. Proselyting is low key but artfully executed. Neo-Pentecostalim has become respectable.

FACTORS CONTRIBUTING TO SUSCEPTIBILITY TO TONGUE SPEAKING

Several factors have been observed to contribute to susceptibility to tongue speaking. Clinical research solidly supports personal observations. In fact, objective evaluation by persons with no vested interests, no doctrinal position to disprove or maintain, no cause to defend, or against which to defend oneself — in short, persons pressure-free to examine objectively the reference data uniformly conclude that modern tongue speaking is a psychic phenomenon. It can be induced, and/or reproduced by several means completely apart from "spiritual" endowment.

Six factors, rarely singly, but in various combinations other-wise, result in the psychic phenomenon promoted as the restoration of the apostolic-era gift of tongue speaking. The first three, and if all else fails, the last, are essential to the success of the now popular quest.

1. *Susceptibility to hypnotism.* John P. Kildahl (*The Psychology of Tongues,* Harper & Row), among others, documents this observation. Kildahl, a clinical psychologist, is singled out for special mention in that his documentary represents a ten-year empirical and clinical research. His research, financed by the *National Institute of Mental Health,* set out with "no doctrinal axe to grind." *Glossolalia* had become a sufficiently widespread sociological phenomenon that it claimed the attention of sociologists and psychologists, if for no other reason than the fact they found themselves called upon to deal with some of the aftermath in the form of the "fall out" from the emotion-charged practice. Kildahl notes "hypnosis and glossolalia are induced in a similar manner" (p. 37).

Kildahl cites the standard reference work by Ernest Hilgard (*Hypnotic Susceptibility,* Harcourt, Brace & World), wherein it is noted:

> The hypnotist has essentially a two-pronged strategy: that of sensory deprivation and that of developing a "special kind of relationship," i.e., a regressive transference based on a relationship to the hypnotist, as in the sense of a parent substitute (p. 25 in Hilgard, p. 38 in Kildahl).

Extended clinical research demonstrated when initiates into the practice of glossolalia spoke in tongues "they always manifested positive feelings for their group leader." In fact it was found that "a profound trust in a leader is necessary to initiate speaking in tongues (just as it is for induction into hypnotism)." Moreover, "a persisting relationship of trust appears to be equally vital if the practice is to continue" (Kildahl, pp. 44,45). This observation leads to the second essential to the practice of glossolalia.

2. *The Need for an Authority Figure.* This is a fact well documented and readily observable. A corollary is that matriarchal family units are much more susceptible to the practice than families wherein the husband and/or father is seen as the head of the family. A wife who does not see in her husband a man to whom she can look for guidance is prone to look elsewhere for an authority figure. If she is religiously oriented she may find such in her "pastor." Or she may find such in a forward woman who appears to be spiritually gifted and a leader. She may see in that woman one who has found an answer to her need. If that woman professes to have an "in" with the Lord, a relationship of trust and dependency often develops. If the authority figure (man or woman) is a "charismatic," likely the admirer soon will be also.

As intimated above, husbands and children in matriarchial homes are readily susceptible to glossolalia. Attainment of the "gift" normally calls for the surrender of one's autonomy to an authority figure. But in compensation the "gift of tongues," when promoted as a gift of Divine favor, is an ego-expanding experience. Glossolalists are induced to count themselves to have become recipients of a gift which places them a cut above the uninitiated.

Early on, Pentecostalism proved especially attractive to women. The reason is not difficult to discern. Pentecostal assemblies, particularly on Sunday evenings and revival services, are generally quite informal in their structure, hence allowing more freedom of expression — especially for women. With the introduction of a combination of "tongue speaking" and "prophetic utterances," intelligible or otherwise (mostly otherwise), presumably induced by the Holy Spirit, women could now "do their thing" quite uninhibited. Traditional masculine protestations citing Biblical admonitions designed to keep "the weaker vessels" submissive, and "silent in the assemblies" (except for singing, which does not do too well without feminine participation) were ostensibly overruled by the Holy Spirit!

Soon it was noted that Philip, the evangelist, "had four daughters that prophesied" (Acts 21:9). Since prophesying appears to be more directly prompted by the Holy Spirit than mere preaching, it was readily reasoned that if women can prophesy they can surely preach. With the meteoric rise and success of Aimee Semple McPherson of the famed Angeles Temple (Los Angeles, California, circa the 1920's), "gifted" women gained a measure of "liberation" through Pentecostalism long before the current Women's Rights movement came to prominence in the political arena.

3. An anxiety syndrome is the third factor Kildahl's research determined to conditon one for susceptibility to tongue speaking. Kildahl cites the research of Dr. Paul Qualben in which it was noted that more than 85 percent of the tongue speakers had experienced a clearly defined anxiety crisis preceding their speaking in tongues. My own observation is that if one does not have an anxiety syndrome the pressures that devotees impose upon the uninitiated are calculated to produce one. Christians who have found their faith and Christian experience rewarding and fulfilling are not prime candidates. But this is often set upon by the initiates as a form of self-righteousness which does not allow the Holy Spirit to work. This is "the last" of the factors to which we have previously alluded. When all else fails, the promoters of the phenomenon frequently resort to this tactic. If a guilt complex can be induced an anxiety syndrome will likely follow.

The spate of literature evaluating the tongues movement has peaked and is now perceptibly waning. Perhaps the tongues movement itself is waning also. At least the novelty has sufficiently worn off that initiates are no longer as gung ho as when the outbreak first became the "in thing" a few years ago.

Of the scores of books familiar to me two stand out as being especially helpful in evaluating the phenomenon objectively. Mention has already been made of the work of Dr. John P. Kildahl, a psychotherapist who conducted in depth interviews with tongues speakers over a period of ten years. He traveled from coast to coast listening to devotees describe their practice, and observing their group sessions in progress.

A companion volume by W.J. Samarin, *Tongues of Men and of Angles* (Macmillan Company) reports the work of linguists who taped hundreds of hours of purported "tongue speaking," representing a comprehensive cross section of the phenomenon in many lands and among many cultures. The vocalizings were then subjected to language analysis by linguists. Among them were persons so devoted to the dissemination of the Word of God that they have devoted many years to sojourning among tribes which have heretofore had no written language and little, if any, knowledge of the grammatical construction of their communication. From such study the linguists note patterns which enable them to identify the parts of speech they may employ (nouns, verbs, adjectives, etc.) and the syntax. From this their vocalizations are reduced to writing, using symbols to which the natives can relate. The grammatical patterns they have used, often unwillingly, are explained to them and they are ultimately taught thereby to read and write.

According to the extensive study of Samarin and his associates the utterings of the tongue speakers have no syntax, no pattern that can be identified with ideas, concepts, parts of speech, etc. Many pages in Samarin's report are filled with print-outs of the sounds recorded in tongue speaking sessions. The conclusion is the only thing the syllables have in common with language is that sounds are emitted via the vocal apparatus.

Claims have sometimes been made to the effect that as someone was "speaking in an unknown tongue" a stranger from a foreign land passed by and "heard in his own language" what was said. Such claims were investigated by those engaged in the research reported by Samarin. They report no such claims have been verified.

The final refuge of the claimants of tongue speakers, that they are speaking in the language of angels, is at variance with the

Biblical record. Throughout the Scriptures when angels spoke in the presence of men they spoke in the language of those who heard. No interpreter was required. Nonsense syllables are sometimes used in nursery rhymes, "fun songs," and other occasions when a mood rather than a message is being communicated. But to equate such an exercise in frivolity with Christian worship and communication is nonsense!

Sometime ago I sat with my colleagues in the company of a visitor who spoke very complimentarily of our chapel services. He had observed some things he said he would like to see incorporated in the chapel services of the school over which he presided — the leading school of a major segment of the Pentecostal movement. Out of curiosity I asked him to what extent tongue speaking was involved in their chapel services. To my surprise he answered, quite readily: "Practically none, rarely ever in fact." Apparently noting my look of surprise he added thereto by stating: "I haven't spoken in tongues in years." He then went on to explain that as one "grows older and matures in Pentecostalism" tongue speaking is engaged in less and less. And without further prompting he concluded by saying that in conducting revivals, particularly when planting a new church in a community, tongue speaking may be used "as an attention getter" (pause) "like it was on Pentecost." He then hastened to repeat what he had said earlier: "As one matures in Pentecostalism one rarely resorts to tongue speaking, even in prayer."

At that I ventured to think out loud, saying somewhat reflectively: "Might that have any bearing upon what Paul said in I Corinthians to the effect that when he was a child he spoke, felt and thought as a child, but when he matured he put away childish things" (I Cor. 13:11). "And if so (I further reflected) was he speaking only for himself, or was he thinking of the maturing of the church also?" His response was: "That's a thought worth pondering." That it is indeed. That ended that particular topic of discussion. And it may well serve as a fitting end to this present discussion of the topic. So be it!

11

GIFTS OF HEALINGS

In I Corinthians 12 "gifts of healings" (pl.) are mentioned three times: verses 9, 28 and 30. In each instance the same is prefaced with the Greek word *charismata*, from which the popular code words of our time, "charisma" and "charismatic," have been derived. Transliterated, the phrasing in the Greek text reads: *charismata iamaton*, (which is, by interpretation) "gracious gifts of healings." The other "gifts," "powers" (or whatever) which are listed in the three catalogues of *pneumatikon* — "spiritual _____(?), gifts(?), matters(?), things(?)," are not prefaced with any one of the Greek words commonly translated "gift(s)." Neither *charisma(ta)* nor *doron* and its derivatives, nor *merismos* is used in direct reference to anyone of them.

The reader may have noted that even in the KJV the translators have put the word "gifts" in italics to indicate it is added as a translator's gloss. The NIV translators have elected to gloss over the matter more fully by entering the word "gifts" non-italicized.

197

The context of the passage allows for it, since the word "gifts" is obviously implied. But be that as it may, only "the gracious gifts of healings" are prefaced by the term "charismata." *Iamaton* (healings) is so prefaced in all three listings in which the several special powers, functions, gifts, are named. See verses 7-9, 28 and 29,30.

An overview of the healing miracles of the Bible is overdue. Aside from the record of Jesus' ministry, they prove to be not nearly as numerous, nor the power so widely distributed, as is commonly supposed.

COMPREHENSIVE LISTING
OF BIBLICAL HEALINGS

Old Testament

Only nine of the thirty-nine Old Testament documents record any semblance of miracle healings: six healings, of a sort, are recorded in the Pentateuch: Genesis (4) and Numbers (2). In only two of these was a "healer" (in the sense of a fellow human being) used as an agent through whom the power of God was mediated. Otherwise God appears to have operated directly.

One, perhaps two, exceptions might be cited: a) Miriam, whom God struck with leprosy, was presumably healed in response to Moses' prayer, in which he cried unto Jehovah, saying: "Heal her, O God, I beseech you" (Num. 12:13; see verses 9-15). b) Those bitten by the fiery serpents were spared from death when they looked upon the brazen serpent God commanded Moses to raise aloft on a pole (Num. 21:9-15).

The first "healing," of a sort, is predicted in Genesis 17:15-21. God promised Abraham that Sarah's lifelong barrenness would be interrupted in her old age that she might bear for Abraham the son of God's promise. But though this was the most remarkable birth chronicled in the Old Testament the phrase "God opened her womb" is not used of Sarah. Instead it is written of her: "And Jehovah *visited* Sarah as he had said, and Jehovah did unto Sarah as he had spoken. And Sarah conceived and bare Abraham a son in his old age." In view of the language of Genesis 20:17 this is indeed the first "healing" miracle recorded.

To some degree this miracle was repeated three times in the Genesis record. a) God reversed his punitive closing of the wombs of Abimilech's wives and maidens. In fact it is said God "healed" Abimilech also. Ponder that. Incidentally, Genesis 20:17 marks the first time the word "healed" appears in the Scriptures. b) In Genesis 29:31 God is said to have "opened Leah's womb," and c) in Genesis 30:22 he is said to have opened Rachel's womb. Curiously, that phrase was not used of Sarah of whom it was even more true, considering the advanced age at which she was caused to conceive and to bare a son who was healthy in every respect.

In view of the Hebrew penchant for the use of a figure of speech called "Hebrew verticalism" some of the references to God's opening and closing of wombs may be regarded as akin to our usage of the phrase "an act of God" — except for the fact the Hebrew people were generally more inclined to view God as directly and personally involved rather than operating through "laws" (forces) he has set in motion in nature. Their reasoning was that since God is omniscient, he knows all things. Therefore whatever occurs happens within the sphere of his knowledge and observation. Since he is omnipresent and omnipotent also, he is not so far removed nor bereft of power but that he could, if he would (if he so willed), prevent anything from occurring that does occur. Hence whatever takes place is "an act of God," whether for good or for ill. Hence, such expressions as "The Spirit of Jehovah departed from Saul, and an evil spirit from Jehovah troubled him" (see I Sam. 16:14, cp. v. 23; 18:10; 19:9; I Kgs.

22:19-23; etc.)

First Classic Healing Miracle

The first classic healing miracle recorded in the Bible is the account of the healing of Miriam's leprosy, a dire punishment that was divinely inflicted upon her, and from which (presumably) she was divinely relieved (Num. 21:9-15). From this passage some have wrongly speculated that all maladies are a form of Divine punishment.

Healings in the OT Books of History

Healing miracles in the books commonly called books of OT History are few. Joshua, Judges and Ruth contain none, though they abound in reports of miraculous happenings. First Samuel 1:6-10 reports a healing of the sort noted four times in Genesis. In answer to Hannah's fervent prayer and the intercession of Eli, the high priest (v. 17), God who is first said to have "shut up her womb" (v. 6) "remembered her" (v. 19), and "she conceived and bare a son . . . and called his name Samuel" (v. 20). Eli is not to be reckoned as having the "gift of healing" from this incident. It is nowhere stated that Eli was miraculously gifted.

The most remarkable healing miracles of the Old Testament are the three resurrection miracles recorded in I & II Kings. a) I Kings 17:17-24 records Elijah's dramatic resurrection of the son of a widow who had provided him hospitality in the course of an extended drouth, and for whom in recompense he had miraculously extended her meagre food supply. b) II Kings 4:17-37 records a similar miracle performed by Elisha in behalf of a Shunammite woman. c) II Kings 5:1-9 records the healing of Naaman, the Syrian leper. d) II Kings 13:20,21 records the most amazing and inexplicable "healing" miracle of the Bible. Verse 20 makes mere mention of the death and burial of Elisha by way of noting a miracle which occurred apparently some time afterwards. Another corpse had been brought to the burial grounds but the interment was interrupted by the appearing of a band of Moabites.

To make a hasty departure without leaving the corpse for the Moabites or wild beasts to desecrate, they opened the tomb of Elisha and cast the corpse onto his bones. Verse 21 records: "As soon as the man touched the bones of Elisha, he revived, and stood on his feet."

An observation is in order at this point. Almost every time a series of reference data seems to point towards a pattern one can thereafter cite as a rule, an exception to "the rule" appears. God cannot be bound. He is not capricious and wholly unpredictable, but neither is he grooved into a set pattern from which he cannot deviate. In our study of the tongues phenomenon we noted that subsequent to the initial outpouring of the Holy Spirit on Pentecost the Holy Spirit ordinarily did not "fall (or come) upon" those who believed except through the laying on of the apostles' hands. But God saw fit for it to happen otherwise at Caesarea when "to the Gentiles also was granted repentance unto life." Here in a review of healing miracles in the monarchian era of Israel, as it was beginning to appear that miracles of whatever kind were performed only by God's select prophets, we have an episode in which no living soul acted as God's intermediary. Be it noted we can only observe principles. God alone can establish laws. But in doing so he is in no wise bound by them, though we are until such time as he sees fit to inform us otherwise.

There remains one other healing miracle recorded in the OT books of history — a healing chronicled also in the book of the prophet Isaiah. Second Kings 20:1-11 (cp. II Chron. 32:24) records the prayer of Hezekiah that his life might be extended. From Isaiah 38:1-9 we learn Isaiah had been sent to Hezekiah to admonish him, saying: "Set your house in order, for you shall die, and not live" (v. 1). At the announcement the king besought the mercy of Jehovah, and "wept sore" (v. 3). Through Isaiah he was then informed his life would be extended fifteen years (v. 5), and was provided a visual miracle via the sun dial of Ahaz to assure him it would be so (v. 11). In this episode the prophet was but an informant, not a medium through which the miracle was wrought.

Healing Miracles in the Books of the Prophets

Surprise! Though miracles were sometimes performed by the prophets, however not nearly as often as is commonly supposed, there is no mention in any of the seventeen books which we call the Major (longer) and Minor (shorter) Prophets, of any one of them healing anybody. And as has already been noted, the non-writing prophets such as Elijah and Elisha did not spend their time in "healing crusades" in behalf of the maimed and physically ill. They were preachers concerned about truth and righteousness.

Healing Miracles in the Poetical Books

The same observation just noted also holds true of the five books commonly designated books of poetry. Job, who held the leading role in the book which bears his name, is believed by the Jews to have lived in the early patriarchial period. With God's foreknowledge and provisional consent, Job was afflicted by Satan with boils, and bereaved of sons, daughters, servants, and possessions. When his trust in God was fully tested and proven unshakable, God restored his health (as implied in Job 42:10-17) and his estate. Among the lessons learned from the book of Job this comes across loud and clear: righteousness, trust, spiritual steadfastness are greater values than physical health and/or wealth. Yet it is the "gospel(?) of health and wealth" that is being proclaimed and highly received today.

Post Monarchian Era

Neither the books which chronicle the history nor the preaching of the post-monarchian era record healing ministries or episodes. The deliverance of the three Hebrews cast into the fiery furnace (Daniel 3) was a miracle of great magnitude, but God did not use some miraculously endowed human intermediary to accomplish the feat.

Summary of the OT Miracle Healings

Of the thirty-nine documents which constitute the OT, only seven record any semblance of miracle healings. 1) Healings in Genesis, using the term loosely, are limited to female infertility abatement. Four such are recorded. 2) A similar healing(?) is recorded in I Samuel (the case of Hannah). 3) Two miracle healings are reported in Numbers. Both were in the form of relief from punitive afflictions Divinely inflicted for disobedience.

4,5) I & II Kings report the first resurrections, on record. a) The resurrection (via Elijah) of the Zarephath widow's son (I Kgs. 17:17-24), b) the resurrection (via Elisha) of the Shunammite's son (II Kgs. 4:18-27) and c) of an inexplicable, seemingly unplanned resurrection (II Kgs. 13:21). Elisha also was the agent through whom Naaman, the Syrian leper was cleansed (II Kgs. 5:1-14).

6) Job's boils were apparently healed apart from any known human agency. 7) Isaiah reports a fifteen-year extension of life to King Hezekiah but he is not said to have been the agency thereof (Isa. 38:5, cp. II Kgs. 20:6). No healings are attributed to Jeremiah or Ezekiel. Daniel reports a healing(?) only in the sense that three Hebrew youth suffered no harm when cast into a fiery furnace. The Twelve (minor prophets) report no healings.

Only a handful of healing miracles (even when the term is used loosely) appear in the OT — five cases of feminine fertility abatement, three resurrections, two cases of Divinely imposed affliction rescinded, one case of life extension granted, and Job's bout with boils presumably ended miraculously, but nowhere so stated.

In a day of wonder drugs, skilled doctors and surgeons and ever advancing techniques, except for the resurrections, particularly the one cited in II Kings 13:21, the list is not impressive. But miracles other than healings make up for that. Such, however, are not attributed to the Holy Spirit. In fact the designation "the Holy Spirit" does not appear in the whole of the Old Testament.

New Testament Healing Miracles

Miracles in the realm of nature much more abound in the Old Testament than in the New Testament. That is partly due of course to the difference in the time span covered. But not altogether so. From the call of Moses to the fall of the monarch, nature miracles dominate God's manifestation of Himself and his power.

Proportionately speaking, the life of Jesus of Nazareth, particularly the three and one-half year span of his public ministry more than makes up for any seeming lack of evidence of God's presence and power. There is good reason for that. John stated it expressly when he wrote:

> Many other signs did Jesus in the presence of his disciples which are not written in this book. But these are written that you may believe that Jesus is the Christ, the Son of God, and that believing, you may have life in his name (John 20:30,31).

Healings Recorded in the Gospels

Two persons are predominant in the four Gospels. For a limited time John the baptizer was front and center. But despite the fact it was foretold of him that he would be "full of the Holy Spirit, even from his mother's womb" (Luke 1:15); and his mother, Elizabeth, was "filled with the Holy Spirit" (v. 41) as she carried him in her womb; and Jesus said of him, "Of them that are born of a woman there is none greater than John" (Matt. 11:11; Luke 7:28): it is nonetheless true that it is not recorded of John that he performed a single miracle. He healed no one. He promised none.

But with the ministry of Jesus it was quite a different story. He claimed to be the Son of God, and the long awaited Messiah. Isaiah had foretold concerning him that he would be credentialized by miracles of healing and mercy (Isa. 61:1-3, cp. Luke 4:16-21).

Healing Miracles Performed by Jesus

Person(s) Healed: Episode	Matthew	Mark	Luke	John
"All manner of diseases"	*4:23,24			
Nobleman's son				4:46-54
Synagogue demoniac		1:23-28	4:33-37	
Peter's mother-in-law	8:14,15	1:29-31	4:38,39	
Mass: sick, blind, demoniac	8:16,17	1:32-34	4:40,41	
Demons cast out (Galilee)		1:39		
Leper outside of Capernaum	8:1-4	1:40-45	5:12-16	
Palsied man, borne of four	9:1-8	2:1-12	5:17-26	
Impotent man, Bethesda pool				5:1-9
Plagues, demoniacs at Tyre		3:11		
Centurion's palsied servant	8:5-13		7:1-10	
Resurrection: widow's son			7:11-17	
Gaderene demoniac	8:28-34	5:1-20	8:26-39	
"A few sick"		6:5		
Jarius' daughter	9:18-26	5:21-34	8:40-56	
Hemorrhaging woman	9:20-22	5:25-34	8:43-48	
Two blind men	9:27-31			
Dumb demoniac	9:32-34			
"All manner of sickness"	9:35			
Apostles authorized . . .	10:1,2	6:7-12	9:1,2	
"They that had need"			9:11	
Man with speech impediment		7:32-37		
Man with withered hand	12:9-14	3:1-6	6:6-11	
Blind and dumb demoniac	12:22,23	3:22	11:14-23	
Syro-phoenician daughter	15:24-30	7:24-30		
Multiple, varied healing:	***15:29-31			
Blind man at Bethsaida		8:22		
Demoniac boy	17:14-26	9:14-29	9:37-43	
Man born blind				9:1-7
Crippled woman straightened			10:13-17	
Man with dropsy			14:1-6	
Raising of Lazarus				11:17-44
Ten lepers cleansed			17:11-19	
Blind Bartimaeus:	****20:29-33	10:46-52	18:35-43	
High priest's servant's ear			22:50,51	
CHRIST'S RESURRECTION:	28:1-10	16:1-11	24:1-11	20:1-18

Notes:

   * The text states he healed "all manner of diseases and sicknesses among

205

the people," and when the report of it went out, "they brought him all that were sick, holden with divers diseases and torments, possessed with demons, and epileptic, and palsied; and he healed them."

** Jesus gave the twelve (vv. 2-4) "authority over unclean spirits, to cast them out, and to heal all manner of diseases, and all manner of sicknesses." However, it is not recorded that they used that authority ere they were endued with power from on high on Pentecost.

***The only two-stage miracle recorded. Others were instantaneous.

****Matthew notes two blind men were healed, not just one.

Summary of Jesus' Healing Ministry

Christ's healing ministry touched human maladies in almost every form — whether mental, physical, social, or spiritual. The blind, the cripples, congenitally malformed or maimed, the deaf and dumb, demon possessed, epileptics, hemorrhaging, insane, lepers, palsied, paralyzed, plagued. "All manner of diseases and all manner of sicknesses" responded to his command. Even the dead were raised up.

Jesus did not specialize in the routine aches and pains engendered by the daily stress of life, the stock and trade of the modern "healers" and "charismatics" — headaches, stomach aches, and psychosomatic complaints. He likely ministered to them on occasion, as in the instance of his alleviating the fever of Peter's mother-in-law, but normally he devoted his attention to ills beyond the power of physicians.

Jesus certainly did not have his disciples screen out the basket cases, the hopelessly and helplessly maimed. They did not hold back the familiar indigents of the villages, such as were well known to those standing by, and who would be in the public eye after he had departed to enjoy the luxury his healing campaigns provided him.

The healing of the paralytic brought to Jesus by four enterprising friends is instructive. Upon finding the house packed where Jesus was they removed a part of the roofing and "let their friend down" (in a non "proverbial" way). He was lowered on a pallet before Jesus. Jesus promptly attended his most pressing need. To the man sick of the palsy Jesus said: "Son, be of good cheer, your sins are forgiven" (Matt. 9:2). But that did not go over well with certain of the crowd. And it likely was disappointing to the four men who had gone to such trouble to get their crippled friend into Jesus' presence.

The scribes said within *themselves* (note that!): "This man blasphemes" (v. 3). Jesus, "knowing their *thoughts*" (v. 4) said: "Wherefore think ye evil in your hearts? Which is easier, to say: Your sins are forgiven: or to say, Arise, and walk? But that you may *know* the Son of man has authority on earth to forgive sins (then said he to the sick of the palsy), Arise and take up your bed, and go unto your house" (vv. 4-7). And that is precisely what he did.

Note that the man's greatest need, the forgiveness of his sins, was a blessing Jesus bestowed as an act of unsolicited mercy. That is grace, "amazing grace," grace indeed. That is the "charismatic" gift supreme. Physical healing, the lesser gift, also a ("charismatic gift" (cp. Greek text of I Cor. 12.9,28,30), demonstrated Christ's power at the level of popular appeal (then, as now). The "greater gift" (I Cor. 12:31, cp. Rom. 6:23) is an expression of his love and power at the point of our greatest need. Hallelujah! What a Saviour!

A Moot Question: Did the Apostles Heal Prior to Pentecost?

A question deserves our attention. Did the apostles heal during Jesus' earthly sojourn? On one occasion they are reported as having attempted to do so, but failed (Luke 9:38-40). Yet Jesus readily healed the boy, an epileptic, at the foot of Mt. Hermon (vv. 41-43). Luke, however, places this prior to the commission to "the Seventy," (Luke 10:1-16). It would seem from Luke 10:9 that not only "the Twelve" but "the Seventy" could, and even should, "heal the sick." They returned from their first assignment with joy, exclaiming "even the demons are subject to us" (v. 17). To that Jesus replied, "I beheld Satan fallen as lightning from heaven" (v. 18); an apocalyptic and eschatological saying much too involved to treat adequately at this time. See my work *What the Bible Says About the End Time*, pp. 71-85, (College Press).

Matthew places the commission to the twelve apostles before the transfiguration episode. In that commission it is said he "gave them authority over unclean spirits to cast them out, and to heal all manner of diseases, and all manner of sicknesses (Matt. 10:1). In view of the happening in the aftermath of the transfiguration, and of the lack of any citation of a miracle having been performed by Jesus' disciples prior to "the pouring out" of the Holy Spirit upon Pentecost, the promise of Matthew 10:31 might have been proleptic (anticipatory). Some so insist.

Prolepsis is a term which relates to a manner of speaking defined as: 1) the describing of an event as taking place before it could have done so; 2) the treating of a future event as though it had already happened. A classic example of a prolepsis is the statement in Genesis 3:20 wherein it is said: "And the man (Adam) called his wife's name Eve, because she was the mother of all living," whereas in fact she was not yet the mother of anyone.

Miracle Healings in Acts

Eleven miracle healings are recorded in the book of Acts. They have one thing in common. They were performed either by an apostle, or one upon whom the apostles had laid their hands. 1) Four healing episodes are credited to Peter: a) The healing of the lame man at the temple gate (3:1-12). b) Sick and demon-possessed were placed along Peter's pathway in the hope at least his shadow might fall on them (5:15,16). However, it is not said that any were actually healed in that manner (cp. 19:11,12). c) Aeneas of Lydia, palsied, bedfast and lame eight years was healed (9:32,33). d) Dorcas was raised from the dead (9:36-40).

2) Five healing episodes are credited to Paul. a) At Lystra, Paul healed a man crippled from birth. "He leaped and walked" (14:8:10). b) Paul exorcised a "spirit of divination from a damsel

at Philippi (14:8-10). This calls to mind that Paul pronounced judgment upon Elymas, a sorcerer he encountered on the isle of Cyprus (13:8-11). Since the curse of blindness brought upon him was datelined in its duration ("for a season"), the passing of the curse in due season was not so much a miracle of healing as the curse was a miracle of judgment.

c) The most notable of Paul's healing miracles is recorded in Acts 19:11,12 where it is reported that cloths carried from his body caused diseases to depart and even exorcised demons. Many a modern pretender has since distributed "prayer cloths" to devotees who have been exhorted to send an offering to "sustain their ministry." But the results promised to be "forthcoming" have not "come forth."

d) When Eutychus fell asleep while Paul was preaching and fell from a third-story window "and was taken up dead," Paul went down and embraced him, and apparently restored his life (20:9,10). Paul could rightly say that he was not one whit behind even the chiefest of the apostles in anything (II Cor. 11:5).

e) A healing miracle of a sort took place when Paul was unharmed by the viper which sprang from a fire he was kindling, fastening itself upon his hand (28:3-5).

f) As word of the miracle spread throughout the island, Publius, the chief officer on the island, invited Paul into his home. Publius' father, in bed with fever and dysentery (v. 8), was healed by Paul with the result that "when this was done, the rest also that had diseases came, and were cured" (v. 9).

3) Two other healing miracles are recorded in Acts: a) Philip, the evangelist, having received the laying on of the apostles' hands (6:6) went into Samaria. There he exorcised demons and "many that were palsied and lame were healed" (8:5-7). b) Ananias was commissioned (details are not cited) to go to Damascus that Saul (Paul) might "receive (back) his sight, and be filled with the Holy Spirit" (9:17,18). No doubt Paul was given pause to remember this when he later was on the other side of the miracle in the case of Elymas (Acts 13:8-11).

Overview of Healing Miracles in Acts

Once again we have occasion to ponder a matter we do well to bear in mind. There are few absolutes in the Scriptures, if any. Consider the implications of Hebrews 9:22, "According to the law, I may *almost* say, all things are cleansed with blood, and apart from the shedding of blood there is no remission of sins." Why "almost"? Why not "absolutely"? Because God, not man, has specified the exceptions, and stated the conditions thereof (see Lev. 7:5,11).

A cursory reading of Acts would suggest only the apostles performed miracles. But Acts 8:7,8 cancels that dictum. It remains as a general principle, but not as an absolute. If we broaden the principle to affirm that according to the record in Acts only the apostles and ones upon whom the apostles laid their hands performed miracles we are confronted with the case of Ananias (Acts 9:17,18). We may reason that Ananias had received the laying on of the apostles' hands, but that is eisegesis, not exegesis. The Scriptures do not say so. The best we can offer as an explanation which fits the general principle is that the conversion of Saul was a very special case, in a sense one on a par with the conversion of Cornelius. Hence God chose to bypass the apostolic channel lest Saul (Paul) might be ever afterwards beholden to "the twelve." In Galatians 1:11,12 he affirms his apostleship and his message came "by revelation." Acts, chapter 9, supports what Paul claimed.

Does not this then open the door to others? Only if they can produce the credentials. God is not bound, but we are. Paul came to the apostleship outside of the circle from which Matthias was chosen, but he came not with "another gospel." Even "an angel from heaven" would be "anathema" should one of them attempt to do that (Gal. 1:8,9).

Healing Miracles and/or Instruction in the Epistles

1. Of the thirteen epistles which bear Paul's autograph, only one, I Corinthians, makes mention of the "*gracious gifts* (Gr.

charismata) of healings." (See I Cor. 12:9,28,30.) No healing episodes or examples are cited. In fact the opposite is more nearly the case. No less than four non-healing episodes are cited.

a. Paul prayed earnestly that a vexation which he called "a thorn in the flesh" (Gr. *skolops*, lit. "a sharp stake") be removed (II Cor. 12:7). It wasn't. b. While Paul was imprisoned in Rome, Epaphroditus, an emissary from Philippi, took ill and nearly died. The illness lasted long enough for the news to travel all the way to Philippi, and a report of the deep concern of the Philippians to travel back to Rome ere Epaphroditus was well enough to return to them (Phil. 2:25-30). There is no hint that a miracle healing had taken place. The account suggests that it was not. c) From II Timothy 2:20 we learn that Paul left one of his travelling companions, Trophimus, "sick, at Miletus," and d) Paul's mundane advice to his dearest friend, Timothy, was that he should "take a little wine for (his) stomach's sake, and oft infirmities" (I Tim. 5:23).

2. In the eight epistles of miscellaneous authorship, only James has anything to say about healing. James 5:13-15 reads:

Is any among you suffering? Let him pray. Is any cheerful? Let him sing praise. Is any among you sick? Let him call for the elders of the church: and let them pray over him, anointing him with oil, in the name of the Lord: and the prayer of faith will save him that is sick, and the Lord will raise him up; and if he has committed sins, it shall be forgiven him.

The procedure enjoined does not conform to the prevailing practice of those who profess to be called of God to healing ministries. James is not speaking of staged public healing shows conducted for public viewing. He speaks of a relatively private intimate setting.

Anointing with Oil

James instructs the sick to "call for the elders." The elders are instructed to "pray over him, anointing him with oil, in the name

211

of the Lord." The Greek participle translated "anointing" is not derived from *chrio*, the word that commonly designates sacramental and/or ceremonial anointing. The word used is *aleipsantes* derived from *aleipho*, a general term for rubbing oil or balm upon the body, whether for moisturizing, lubricating the skin after bathing (Matt. 6:17), or as a balm to protect the bed-ridden from bed sores, or even anointing a dead body in preparation for burial.

Recall that because of the onset of the Sabbath, Jesus was entombed too quickly to permit the customary anointing of the body with aromatic spices and oil. Thus Mark informs us the women who came to the tomb at daybreak the day following did so for the express purpose of "anointing him" (Mark 16:1). The verb used is *aleipho*, not *chrio*. Recall also the episode in which Mary Magdalene washed Jesus' feet and "anointed" them with a precious ointment. The verb used is *aleipho*, (Mark 14:8; Luke 7:38,39; John 11:2,3).

Chrio, the word for sacramental anointing, is the root from which the term *Christos* (Christ, "the anointed one") is formed. Thus Jesus, in announcing his messiahship in the synagogue of his home town in Nazareth, read from the book of Isaiah this prophecy: "The Spirit of the Lord is upon me, because he has anointed (Gr. *echrisen*, 3rd. pers. sing. of *chrio*) me to preach good tidings to the poor" (Luke 4:18).

In James' instruction to the elders called to the sick room, the "prayer of faith" is enjoined, having anointed (*aleipsantes*) with oil. Instantaneous, "arise from your bed and walk" healing is not guaranteed by James 5:14. And rarely, rarely does it occur.

Note that James speaks only of the sick (Gr. *asthenei*, 3rd pers. sing, pres. indic. of *astheneo*, lit. weak, without strength). *Astheneo*, *asthenei* and *astheneia*, the three most common forms of the term appearing in the NT, are rendered "weak, weakness" 31 times; "weak thing, without strength, feeble, impotent, impotent folks" (pl.), 1 each; "infirmity," primarily a general term for feebleness, 17 times; "sick," 17 times. Twice it is rendered "diseased." That the term can, on occasion, rightly be translated "sick" may be inferred from Philippians 2:26,27 where it was said of Epaphroditus, "he indeed was sick, nigh unto death." The precise application of the term in James 5:14 is not that clear. The one thing that is clear is that the "sick" mentioned are not so much so that they cannot think or act for themselves. It is they who are to call for the elders. Desperate friends or relatives are not the prescribed initiators. Death bed repentance and/or last ditch prayer and anointing rituals are not to be inferred from the text.

Again let it be noted that James speaks only of the weak or sick, not of "all manner of diseases" (Gr. *malakai*, cp. Matt. 4:23; 9:35; 10:1). He says nothing of the victims of dread diseases, plagues or calamities, nor of the congenitally deformed, the maimed and halt, the blind, epileptics, demoniacs, lepers, paralytics. Jesus healed "all manner of sicknesses and diseases." He gave sight to the blind, hearing to the deaf. He caused the dumb to speak and even congenital cripples to walk and leap and praise God. He raised the dead. He did not avoid obviously difficult cases nor did he cast blame for failure upon others. He had no failures.

The apostles, primarily Peter (of record) and Paul, at least in the beginning days of the church, exhibited kindred healing powers, though to a lesser degree. The fact that the epistle of James is one of the earliest NT documents, reflecting a time when the church was Jewish dominated and synagogue oriented (cp. James 2:2) may cast some light on this enigmatic passage of Scripture.

Summary of NT Miracle Healings

By way of summary three things need to be taken into account. 1. We have noted that the further forward we move in New Testament history and literature, the less mention is made of miraculous happenings, particularly miracle healings. For example, we noted that of the twenty-one epistles only two, I Corinthians and James, make any mention of healing, and no healing episodes are recorded in either of them. To the contrary, four epistles (II Cor. 12:7; Phil. 2:25-30; I Tim. 5:23; and II Tim. 4:20) report non-healing episodes.

2) The book of James belongs to the earliest of the New Testament literature. It reflects a time when congregations were composed principally (if not altogether) of Jews, represented a mingling of the synagogue (Gr. *sunagogon*, James 2:2), and the "church" (Gr. *ekklesia*, James 5:14). If the instruction in James 5:14,15 is intended to be the procedure for the church everywhere and always, it seems strange that none of the score of epistles which followed make any mention of the practice. Neither is it alluded to in the book of Acts. All the healings reported in Acts are attributed to the apostles — none to the elders of the church(es).

3) The oft-repeated dictum of the Scriptures that "by the word of two or three witnesses a thing shall be established (Deut. 17:6) is still valid. God does not have to say a thing two or three times to make it so, but even that dictum is repeated by two or three witnesses in both testaments, and Jesus is one of the "witnesses" (Matt. 18:16). Compare (OT) Num. 35:30; Deut. 17:6; 19:15; (NT) Matt. 18:16; II Cor. 13:1.

For a revealing clinical report of miracle healings, see the Appendix: "In Search of a Miracle," William A. Nolen, M.D., reprinted by permission, *McCalls*, September, 1974. Dr. Nolen, a devout Roman Catholic physician, reports his clinical follow-up research of purported "healings" by the late Kathryn Kuhlman.

Section Three
SPECIAL INTEREST TOPICS

12

BLASPHEMY AGAINST THE HOLY SPIRIT

PART ONE

What does the Bible say about blasphemy against the Holy Spirit? It says surprisingly little in view of the dire consequences which await those who commit the sin. Jesus warned that whosoever blasphemes against the Holy Spirit "is guilty of an *eternal* sin" for which there is "*never* forgiveness" (Mark 3:29) — "neither in this world, nor the world to come" (Matt. 12:32).

It would seem that a sin of such awesome consequences would be 1) described and explained in detail, so as to be readily identified, and 2) that repeated warnings, readily recognized, would be found in the Scriptures again and again. Such is not the case. The term is found only in a conversation of Jesus, hence is reported only in the Gospels. If other dire warnings such as Hebrews 6:4-8, 10:26-31, II Pet. 2:20-22, and I John 5:16,17, have reference to the blasphemy of the Holy Spirit, none of the writers expressly said so. Readers and students of the Scriptures can only infer that one or another, or perhaps all of the references cited are an elaboration or explanation of what Jesus spoke of in one lone conversation.

Fortunately, the dire warning voiced by Jesus (along with its setting, i.e. the circumstances which gave rise to it) is reported in all three of synoptic Gospels. We have seen fit to place the three texts in parallel columns to facilitate comparison of the three accounts.

MARK 3:7-11,22-30	MATTHEW 12:22-32	LUKE 12:1-10
7 And Jesus with his disciples withdrew to the sea: and a great multitude from Galilee followed . . . . 9 And he spoke to his disciples that a little boat should wait on him because of the crowd, lest they should throng him: 10 for he had healed many; in somuch that as many as had plagues pressed upon him that they might touch him. 11 And the unclean spirits, whensoever they beheld him, fell down before him, and cried, saying, You are the Son of God.	22 Then was brought unto him one possessed of a demon, blind and dumb, and he healed him, insomuch that the dumb man spoke and saw. 23 And all the multitude were amazed, and said, Can this be the Son of David? 24 But when the Pharisees heard it they said, This man does not cast out demons, but by Beelzebub, the prince of the demons. 25 And knowing their thoughts he said unto them, Every kingdom divided against itself shall not stand: 26 and if Satan casts out Satan, he is divided against himself: how then shall his kingdom stand? 27 And if I by Beelzebub cast out demons, by whom do your sons cast them out? Therefore shall they be your judges. 28 But if I, by the Spirit of God, cast out demons, then is the kingdom of God come upon you. 29 Or how can one enter into the house of a strong man,	1 In the mean time, when many thousands of the multitude were gathered together, insomuch that they trod one upon another, he began to say to his disciples, first of all, Beware of the leaven of the Pharisees, which is hypocrisy. 2 But there is nothing covered up that shall not be revealed, and hid that shall not be made known. 3 Wherefore whatsoever you have said in the darkness shall be heard in the light; and what you have spoken in the ear, in the inner chambers shall be proclaimed from the housetops. 4 And I say unto you, my friends, Be not afraid of them that kill the body, and after that have no more that they can do. 5 But I will warn you whom you shall fear: Fear him, who after he has killed has power (authority) to cast into hell: Yea, I say unto you, Fear him. 6 Are not five sparrows sold for two pence?
22 And the scribes that came down from Jerusalem said, He has Beelzebub, and by the prince of the demons casteth he out demons. 23 And he called them unto him, and said unto them in parables, How can Satan cast out Satan? 24 And if a kingdom be divided against itself, that kingdom cannot stand.		

218

25 And if a house be divided against itself, that house will not be able to stand. 26 And if Satan has risen up against himself, and is divided, he cannot stand, but has an end. 27 But no one can enter into the house of the strong man, and spoil his goods, except he first bind the strong men; and then he will spoil his house. 28 Verily, I say unto you, all their sins shall be forgiven unto the sons of men, and their blasphemies wherewith they shall blaspheme; 29 But whosoever shall blaspheme against the Holy Spirit has never forgiveness, but is guilty of an eternal sin: 30 because they said, he has an unclean spirit.

and spoil his goods, except he first bind the strong man? And then he will spoil his house. 30 He that is not with me is against me; and he that gathers not with me scatters. 31 Therefore I say unto you, Every sin and blasphemy shall be forgiven unto men; but the blasphemy against the Spirit shall not be forgiven. 32 And whosoever shall speak a word against the Son of man, it shall be forgiven him; but whosoever shall speak against the Holy Spirit, it shall not be forgiven, neither in this world, nor in the world that is to come.

and not one of them is forgotten in the sight of God. 7 But the very hairs of your head are numbered. Fear not: ye are of more value than many sparrows.

8 And I say unto you, Everyone who shall confess me before men, him shall the Son of man confess before the angels of God: 9 But he that denies me in the presence of men shall be denied in the presence of the angels of God.

10 And every one who shall speak a word against the Son of man, it shall be forgiven him; but unto him that blasphemes against the Holy Spirit, it shall not be forgiven.

IMPORTANCE OF THE SUBJECT

The importance of the subject is underscored by the gravity of the warning with which it has been delivered to us. It is not just an unforgiven sin, or unforgiven sin in general, that is, sin that could be forgiven were forgiveness sought. It is rather a sin that is unforgivable — ever, even were forgiveness sought. Jesus describes it as an "eternal sin," for which the sinner "has never forgiveness, neither in this world nor the world to come" (Mark 12:32).

TWO COMMON ERRORS

This observation leads to the next aspect of this subject which deserves attention. There are two common errors which hinder a serious study of the blasphemy against the Holy Spirit. 1) One is oversimplification. Again and again one hears it said that the sin is simply "the final rejection of Christ." That write-off has this going for it. The final rejection of Christ indeed places a sinner in a state of unforgiveness for which there is no provision for pardon "in the world to come." But to equate the ultimate state of unrepentant, hence unregenerate, sinners with the warning of Jesus concern- ing the blasphemy of the Holy Spirit is to completely ignore the context in which the warning of Jesus was given (Luke 22:65).

All sin for which pardon is refused right down to the moment of death is by that very fact unpardoned in this life, and therefore unpardonable in the world to come — unless God has some "second chance" redemptive system reserved for those who want "this world and heaven too." Don't count on that. Has not Jesus warned: "It is written. You shall not make trial of the Lord our God" (Matt. 4:7, cp. Deut. 6:16).

2) The other common error is to go to the opposite extreme, and succumb to the error of overcomplication, thus to say: "It's too confusing. I'll just ignore it, and let the theologians thrash it out, if they can." I suspect the two errors are somewhat related. To beg off on the basis of the latter conjecture sets one up to settle hopefully along the lines of the first conjecture.

ANALYSIS OF THE TERM

Our words "blaspheme" (verb) and "blasphemy" (noun) are derived from the Greek root *blapto* "to hurt," and the verb *phemi* "to speak," hence the basic meaning is: "to speak to hurt." That definition precisely fits the context in which the warning against the blasphemy against the Holy Spirit is found. Rancor, intransigence, jealousy, spite, a deep desire to discredit, to hurt, to cripple the effectiveness of Jesus' ministry is particularly manifest on the part of the Pharisees, Jesus' inveterate and implacable enemies.

While the terms "the blasphemy of" and "blasphemy against" the Holy Spirit are found only in the synoptic Gospels, the noun "blasphemy" and verb "blaspheme" are used several times in both testaments.

OLD TESTAMENT REFERENCES

Four Hebrew words are translated "blaspheme," "blasphemy," (5 in the KJV). Each of the four terms legitimately rendered "blaspheme" shares the common core of the above definition.

1) *Gadeph* signifies "to revile, to cut." It is used seven times in the OT Scriptures. Six times it is translated "blasphemed" (II Kgs. 19:6,22; Psa. 44:16; Isa. 37:6,23; and Ezek. 20:27). In Isaiah 43:28 a derivative of the verb is translated "reviling."

2) *Naqab*, "to pierce," "to strike through with holes" is used eighteen times. Three times it is translated "blaspheme" (Lev. 24:11,16, twice in the latter verse). Six times it is translated "curse" (Num. 23:8,28; Job 3:8; 5:3; Prov. 11:26; 24:24). It is also rendered "pierce" (II Kgs. 18:23; Isa. 36:6), "pierced through" (Job 40:24) and "pierce through" (the head, with staves, Hab. 3:14).

3) *Na-ats* also signifies "to pierce," or "to sting." It is sometimes translated "blaspheme" (II Sam. 12:24; Psa. 74:10,18; and Isa. 52:5). A derivative of the verb is also so translated in II Kings 19:3 and Isaiah 37:3.

4) *Charaph*, signifying "to cut into," is rendered "blaspheme" in Isaiah 65:7.

The aggregate of these many references, particularly in the light of the root meaning of the several Hebrew words so translated points up the heinous mind set which motivates the sin of blasphemy.

221

NEW TESTAMENT REFERENCES

Besides the three texts in the synoptic Gospels which record Jesus' warning against blasphemy against the Holy Spirit (Matt. 12:31,32; Mark 3:28-30; Luke 12:10), thirty-four other NT texts use the terminology.

1) *Jesus* was accused of blasphemy by those who conducted the farce of a trial against him (Matt. 26:57-65; Mark 14:60-64; Luke 22:65). His statement that they would "see the Son of man (himself) sitting at the right hand of God" was the primary basis of their outrage. Almost from the outset of his ministry the charge of blasphemy was laid against him. "Why (his critics asked) does this man speak blasphemies?" (Mark 2:7).

2) *Paul* speaks of himself as having been once (in ignorance) "a blasphemer" (I Tim. 1:13). At the time he sought to incite Christians into saying something whereby he could so charge them (Acts 26:11).

3) Jews who could not withstand the logic of Christian witnesses accused them of blasphemy, or became so inflamed that they themselves resorted to blasphemy. Stephen was so accused (Acts 6:11,13). The success of Paul's preaching provoked those at Antioch of Pisidia to blaspheme (Acts 13:45). Those at Corinth became so enraged they "contradicted themselves and blasphemed" (Acts 18:6).

4) The "name of God" (Rom. 2:24; I Tim. 6:1) and "the worthy name by which we are called" (James 2:7) can be blasphemed. What might that worthy name be? It is doubtful that the party names of sectarian preference are what James had in mind.

5) The Word of God can be blasphemed (Titus 2:6). Thus men need to be taught and warned, "that they might learn not to blaspheme" (I Tim. 1:20).

6) Jesus warned that "out of the heart proceeds blasphemies," along with other carnal behavior, (Matt. 15:19, KJV) and Colossians 3:8 includes blasphemy in listing similar

manifestations of carnality.

7) Blasphemy is included in the indictment of gross behavior eight times in the Apocalypse, (2:9; 13:1,5,6; 16:9,11,21; 17:3).

The force of these many passages underscores the fact that blasphemy is a heinous sin, a mark of the carnal mind, and subject to the wrath of God. But sinful though it is, up to a point it is a sin of which one can repent and be forgiven, as witnessed by the case of Saul of Tarsus (I Tim. 1:13). The towering question is, how and at what point does one become a blasphemer against the Holy Spirit, and thus become guilty of an eternal sin, for which there is never forgiveness, neither in this world nor the world to come?

POSSIBLE PARALLEL PASSAGES

At the outset of this chapter we called attention to the fact the Scriptures say surprisingly little about the blasphemy of the Holy Spirit, in view of the dire consequences said to await those who commit such a sin. In view of the awesome consequences one might expect repeated warnings to appear, in which the sin would be described and explained in detail. But at first glance, at least, that does not seem to be the case. The precise terminology is used only in reporting a warning Jesus on one occasion levelled against the Pharisees when they accused him of casting out demons by Beelzebub, the prince of demons. He did not indict them of having committed the unpardonable sin, but he warned them that they were dangerously near to doing so. If they persisted in the way they were then going they would surely do so, and likely some of them did.

There are several passages of Scripture which closely parallel the warning of Jesus, but in sufficiently different language that a positive identification must be recognized as only tentative. The following texts may be cited as viable reference data. Those asterisked are particularly germaine to the discussion, as bearing reference to sin or a state of sinfulness in which the persons spoken of would appear to be beyond the hope of redemption or pardon.

Acts 5:3	*Rom. 1:18-32	*Heb. 3:14-16
Acts 7:51	*Eph. 4:17-19,30	*Heb. 6:4-8
I Thess. 5:19	*I Tim. 4:1,2	*Heb. 10:26-31
Gal. 5:17-21	*II Pet. 2:20-22	*Heb. 12:15-17
Heb. 2:1-4	*I John 5:16,17	*Rev. 16:8-11

INTERLUDE: SIN DEFINED

This would seem to be a good time to call to mind the Biblical view of sin in general. The principal Hebrew words thus translated are *chata*, and *chattath*. Both, along with other derivatives, stem from the same root. The primary meaning is "a missing" — whether of a goal, or a turn in the road, the road itself, or whatever. To note this is not to suggest the word is ambiguous, only that it is broad in its application and comprehensiveness.

The principal Greek word is quite similar, though more precise in its primary application. *Hamartia* signifies to "miss the mark." It is primarily an archery or lancing term. The target was not a series of concentric rings with a "bullseye" at the center. It was a slender, peeled willow-like rod normally no thicker than the shaft of the marksman's arrow. Hence the marksman did one of two things with each shot taken. He missed the mark or he hit it. There were no "near misses" recorded, no points for landing an arrow in one or another of the encircling rings. There were none. The marksman either split the sapling, or he sinned (*hamartano*) — that is, he missed the mark of being a perfect marksman.

There are, of course, several modes of "missing the mark." a) One's shots may "fall short" (Gr. *husterountai*) of the mark.

224

Spiritually, we all so "sin" (Rom. 3:23). b) One may overshoot the target, hence trespass, (*paraptoma*). Spiritually we may sin by going beyond prescribed limits. Or one may c) "err" (*astocheo*) by swerving either to the right or the left. One is as erroneous as the other. Be not led astray by either the "rightists" or the "leftists." Jesus warned, "Beware of the *leaven* of the Pharisees, *and* of the Saducees" (Matt. 16:6).

WHERE DOES THE BLASPHEMY AGAINST THE HOLY SPIRIT FIT IN?

Where does the blasphemy of the Holy Spirit fit into the foregoing analysis? It may be best described as an unconscionable sin of trespass. It is transgression, trespass (*paraptoma*) of the *nth* degree. The Greek term signifies initially to step aside, but then to forge on by, to go beyond limits.

Contextually, the blasphemy against the Holy Spirit takes the outward form of a sin of speaking. Inwardly it has to do with the motivation which moves one to blaspheme. Grammatically, to blaspheme is to speak with the intent to hurt, to sting, to injure, to revile, to cut, to pierce. It is the epitome of public, malicious slander.

Whatever else may be involved in the blasphemy of the Holy Spirit, contextually and grammatically, it is a public display of contempt and/or deceit. It is borne out of a malignant and malicious spirit. In the setting in which Jesus warned, the blasphemy in which the Pharisees were indulging rooted in the sin of jealousy. The intent of their malicious slander was to equate the spiritual (supernatural) power Christ was manifesting (which power they could not, and did not, deny) with the kingdom of Satan rather than of God.

Note that Jesus did not charge that they had already committed the ultimate sin, but they were well on their way to doing so. Whether one can commit the sin unknowingly is a moot question.

225

It would seem one would have to be so depraved in one's heart that one could sidestep (Gr. *paraptoma*) knowledge and reason, and thence "speak to hurt" in order to blaspheme. Of that we may be sure. At what point blasphemy becomes blasphemy against the Holy Spirit is yet to be determined.

PART TWO

SUNDRY THEORIES

Many and varied are the theories concerning the nature and identification of the sin of blasphemy against the Holy Spirit. Some are easily disposed of when compared with the Biblical data. Others deserve consideration. None may be set forth as the only viable interpretation, beyond question, and thus beyond need of further study.

1. It Is Simply the Final Rejection of Christ

Many simply write off the warning as but a graphic statement of the eternal loss of those who die out of Christ. Thus it is simply the final rejection of Christ. To die unrepentant, heeding not the call of the Spirit, through the Scriptures or otherwise, is to be "guilty of an eternal sin" in the sense it has eternal consequences. Hence Jesus is simply warning that there is no such thing as "a second chance" in the hereafter.

We readily agree that there is no such thing as a second chance in the hereafter, either through the route of some purgatorial system, or otherwise. But that is not the focus of what Jesus was communicating to the Pharisees in his warning concerning blasphemy against the Holy Spirit. Jesus was in no sense

226

intimating the Pharisees were at that time receiving their final opportunity to accept Him as their Messiah. Neither was he saying, "If you keep on as you now are, one day you will reject me for the last time." He was warning them of a state of heart and mind that could well seal their eternal and irrevocable doom in the here and now. Eternal damnation can be brought upon oneself irrevocably in this present life, even though one's life may continue for some time in this present world. The blasphemy against the Holy Spirit is in some way involved in that awesome state.

2. It Is Using the Name of the Holy Spirit Profanely

Some have opined that the sin of blasphemy against the Holy Spirit consists of speaking of him without due reverence, perhaps using the term profanely. This too is an over simplification. A certain plus benefit may have accrued from the notion. It is of interest that few by-words, euphemisms and minced oaths have been coined to use as substitutes for the term Holy Spirit, though God and his Son are politely profaned and blasphemed by saints, keeping stride thereby with sinners.

Bywords are to speech what bypasses are to cities. One can closely circumvent a city, take advantage of its proximity, and reach a destination just beyond without actually entering the city, simply by using a bypass. Bywords for Divine beings permit one to come ever so close to swearing and gain whatever advantage swearing is supposed to provide (without actually doing so), by taking the "byword route."

For a starter consider these: golly, gosh, gosh-allhemlock, by Jove, Jehoshaphat, doggone, dadgum, goldarn, for goodness sakes. These are ever handy euphemisms by which church folk can keep in verbal proximity with our profane neighbors as we move along life's journey. So too with the name and title of Jesus, the Christ: Jeepers creepers, geez, gee whiz, cripes, cripes on a broomstick (Christ on a cross), jiminy cricket. (Oh so near

227

and yet so far.)

For the Holy Spirit few by-words have been coined. Holy Smoke, and Harry Carey's "Holy Cow" are all that come to mind. Perhaps Christ's warning has had some effect. It is more likely the less prominent role of the Holy Spirit accounts for it. Be that as it may, it is not the key to the warning of Jesus which we are in the process of reviewing.

3. It Is a Sin that Cannot Be Committed Today

Many are persuaded that due to the change in circumstances, the sin of blasphemy against the Holy Spirit cannot be committed today. This is because there are virtually no comparable miracles today. Few, if any in our contemporary religious community could be accused of being as prejudiced against the array of "Divine healers" abroad in our times as the Jewish hierarchy was against Jesus. Yet, whereas the hostile Jews did not deny the reality and actuality of the miracles Jesus and his apostles performed, few even of the supporters of the "health and wealth" performers attest to having witnessed anything comparable today. Indisputable miracles, miracles which even gainsayers cannot deny, are not performed openly, along city streets, on the spur of the moment, without theatrical mind-bending build-up, sans careful screening of the healees, and en masse: "healing all manner of sicknesses, diseases, torments, epileptics, palsied, demoniacs . . . maimed, lame, blind, dumb, and many others" (Matt. 4:24,25; 15:29-31) and even the dead raised up (John 7:11-17; 11:1-5; etc.)

Note that the Pharisees, whose charges against Jesus evoked the teaching now under review, did not deny that he had cast out demons. They could not. Their only resort was to charge he had done so by the power and spirit of Beelzebub, rather than by the power and Spirit of God.

So, too, of the healing miracles performed by the apostles. Of the lame man Peter healed at the gate of the temple (Acts 3:1-10), the high priest and the elders had this to say (among themselves), "What shall we do with these men? For that indeed a notable miracle has been wrought through them is manifest to all that dwell in Jerusalem. But that it spread no further, let us threaten them that they speak no further in this name" (4:16,17).

The miracles of Christ, and of the apostles and prophets, effectively "confirmed the Word." Their modern counterparts(?) often produce the opposite effect. When do we see anything that compares to the signs and wonders which authenticated the Divine sonship of Jesus and the inaguration of the New Covenant era?

The lame man whom Peter healed "walked and leaped" in the sight of all. He did not thereafter, when the excitement subsided, again become a cripple. The blind did not just see a little, enough to no longer need to feel their way along with the help of a cane. In the case of mass healings, "they were healed everyone," not highly selectively. Congenital cripples, those crippled by diseases, those maimed by accidents, all manner of sicknesses, epilepsy, lepers, blind, deaf, dumb — their wretched state was not just helped a bit. They were healed.

We repeat the healings were not denied even by the most inveterate enemies of Christ and his disciples. They were not suspected or charged with fakery. Only the *source* of the miraculous powers which were clearly manifested was called into question. That was the occasion of the warning of Christ. It seemed to have a sobering effect. The warning against blasphemy of the Holy Spirit was not repeated although miracles which provoked the hierarchy to jealousy continued.

Could it then be that the sin of which we speak cannot be committed today? Don't count on it. If it is a sin so restricted it can only be committed by using some precise phrase, and in a most precise setting, then perhaps not. But if it has to do with the motivation of what is said and done, remember: God knows our inmost thoughts. Beware!

229

4. Attributing to Satan the Manifest Works of the Holy Spirit

Another view is that the blasphemy against the Holy Spirit is attributing to Satan the manifest works of the Holy Spirit. This view has somewhat to commend it in that such is involved, in part at least, in the context of the key passages which are the occasions for this discussion. Jesus' antagonists openly charged that the miracle they had witnessed was done by the power of Beelzebub, the prince of Demons. But Jesus did not respond by informing them they had actually committed the sin of which he then spoke, hence they were already guilty of an eternal sin, for which they could never be forgiven. Were that so his words would have been words of warning only to those who stood by. As it is he was *warning* his critics, not announcing eternal damnation had now befallen them.

The problem with this fourth conjecture is that it assumes Jesus' antagonists *knew* that the miracle they had witnessed was done by the power of (or "in the name of") the Holy Spirit. Was the power or the presence of the Holy Spirit really that manifest? Did Jesus incant some such phrase as: "By the power of (or in the name of) the Holy Spirit which has been given me, you unclean spirit, I adjure you to come out of this man"(?) At no time, of record, did Jesus ever invoke the Holy Spirit to perform some sign or wonder, nor did he ever ask the Holy Spirit to enable him to perform a miracle. The power of the Holy Spirit was resident in Christ. He did not need to resort to some mode of incantation. But how were mere observers to know that? It was not all that "manifest" even to Jesus' disciples. In fact the currently "orthodox" trinitarian theology of the Holy Spirit was, at best, only in the making.

Note that Jesus did not upbraid his critics. He took pains to reason with them. He even used a non-threatening parable to help them see the crux of the issue. In the vernacular of our time he said to them in effect: 1) Satan "runs a tighter ship" than what you have charged would allow. He is too clever to "tear up his own house." Satan does not cast out Satan! But I have! How? By what power? Not by any help he might give. How then have I done it? 2) A parable may help set this whole thing in context. Hear the story of the strong man whose house was despoiled. He would never have allowed it to happen, except for the fact one came in and bound him — the lord of his house. Only then could his house be despoiled before his very eyes.

With that line of reasoning, parabolically illustrated, should one of them have persisted in the charge they had brought against him they would no longer be excusable. They would be in league with Satan against the Holy Spirit of God.

Attributing to Satan the manifest works of the Holy Spirit would be a step in the direction of the blasphemy against the Holy Spirit, but there is more involved than simply making such an accusation. Jesus' critics had done that. But in answering them Jesus did not write them off as having committed the ultimate sin, and hence moved beyond the realm of reason, entreaty or pardon.

5. It Is Absolute, Utter Apostasy

Another view is that the unpardonable sin grows out of absolute, utter apostasy, hence can only be committed by apostates who, in effect, have exhausted the resources of a just and righteous God. A case can be made for this from warnings in Hebrews, and kindred texts. But one facet of the sin is not covered by this categorical appraisal.

Blasphemy is a sin of the tongue. Etymologically, as we have noted earlier, the verb means "to speak to hurt." Blasphemy against the Holy Spirit involves far more than that, but it definitely includes that. Hear it again from Jesus:

Every sin and blasphemy (hurtful speaking) shall be forgiven unto men; but the blasphemy (hurtful speaking) against the Holy Spirit

231

shall not be forgiven. And whosoever shall speak a word against the Son of man, it shall be forgiven him; but whosoever shall *speak* against the Holy Spirit, it shall not be forgiven, neither in this world nor in the world that is to come (Matt. 12:31,32).

One may apostatize, and be forgiven. Many have. Apostasy is included in the first clause of the above quotation. Lest one might think otherwise by reason of what Jesus went on to say in verse 32, Jesus was careful to note that blasphemy in general is included in the opening phrase of verse 31. "Every sin" subject to forgiveness also includes "blasphemy," except when that hurtful speaking is targeted against the Holy Spirit. The reason we will attempt to explain later. Just now we are concerned that it be noted that blasphemy of itself is not the unpardonable sin. Neither is apostasy.

On the other hand one would surely have to fit into such a description of apostasy as found in Hebrews 6:4-8; 10:26-31; 12:15-17 to be: 1) so depraved a rebel, and 2) so knowledgable of the role of the Holy Spirit as to focus blasphemy upon him. Unregenerates who have never known the way of righteousness know so little of the Holy Spirit that I have yet to hear even one of them revile him, or use his name, title or whatever in their outbursts of profanity, filth and blasphemy.

At what level of apostasy one becomes either unreachable or unpardonable only God knows. The Hebrew letter provides some clues, but it is still true that "man looks upon the outward appearance, but God looks upon the heart" (I Sam. 16:7).

6. What Then Is the Blasphemy Against the Holy Spirit?

Jesus, in his dire warning, focused attention upon the consequences of this sin rather than providing a definitive statement. From the primary texts we have but two clues: 1) the intrinsic meaning of the word he used to identify the act, 2) the setting in which the warning was delivered.

232

The first, the intrinsic meaning of the word, presents no problem. It has to do with a) speaking, b) what is said, and c) the motivation. A simple definition is: "blasphemy is something said with malice aforethought." The blasphemy of the Holy Spirit then would be something said about the Holy Spirit with malice aforethought.

The second clue, the setting, would seem to muddle the issue somewhat — unless one keeps in mind the fact Jesus did not accuse his accusers of having committed the sin. He was warning them that they were on the border of doing so. One thing was lacking that kept them from inadvertently stepping over the line. That was knowledge of the full import of what they were saying and doing. Hence, Jesus took the time to reason with his critics instead of pronouncing a sentence of eternal damnation upon them. From this one may conjecture that blaspheming the Holy Spirit is not something one does inadvertently.

This observation raises a tangential question. Does a very similar setting have to exist before one can commit the sin in question? (Some have so concluded). If not, what variances are included within the scope of the sin? Jesus did not spell them out. Neither have any of the New Testament writers done so. Beyond the episode reported early in the synoptic Gospels the descriptive phrase does not appear again.

My judgment is that the tritheism inherent in the Nicene doctrine of the Divine trinity is the seat of most of our difficulty in understanding Christ's solemn warning concerning blasphemy against the Holy Spirit. Upon reviewing his warning, as recorded in the synoptic gospels, I take due note of the setting. Jesus was being pressed by a great crowd impressed by the miracles they had witnessed. Mark explains it thusly:

> For he had healed many, insomuch that as many as had plagues pressed upon him that they might touch him. And the unclean spirits, whensoever they beheld him, fell down before him, and cried, saying, Thou art the Son of God, And he charged them much that they should not make him known (Mark 3:10,11).

233

Jesus then withdrew into the mountain where he appointed the twelve apostles and commissioned them to preach and have authority to cast out demons (3:13,14).

In the next scene Jesus entered into a house to eat. But the curious throng ganged the place. Eating was impossible. Apparently Jesus was not upset about that but his friends were. They said he was "beside himself" (Gr. *existemi*, cp. II Cor. 5:13). Our modern expression "spaced out" might well be an equivalent expression. Few can understand how a person in his right mind can become so enrapt in our Divine calling that he will forego meals, sleep, pleasure, etc., to meet human need.

It is at this point scribes from Jerusalem entered the picture. They too thought him to be mad, but in a different sense — demented, even demon possessed. Ah, that would account for the powers he displayed. And they said so. Jesus' reply was twofold. First he appealed to their reason. Satan is too smart to fight against himself. Secondly, he warned them, not so much for opposing him. They could be sincere in that; likely some were. But they were on a collision course with eternal damnation. At this point they might be forgiven for speaking against the son of man (an interesting choice of self-designation, one that could be either messianic or an allusion to his mantle of human flesh). But to blaspheme against the Holy Spirit, not merely as a third person of a triune Godhead, but as the fullness or finality of God's self-revelation is the real "madness." That is the ultimate sin. That is unpardonable — everlastingly.

My judgment is that Christ's warning is not passe. There are those who indeed are "past feeling" (Eph. 4:19), "branded in their own conscience as with a hot iron" (I Tim. 4:2). Some are "impossible to renew unto repentance" (Heb. 6:6). Some are so incorrigible they have never been brought to repentance. Many never will be. Which among such have committed the blasphemy against the Holy Spirit is an academic question. Let us not sit in the judgment seat. When Saul of Tarsus was "breathing threatening and slaughter against the disciples of the Lord" (Acts 9:1) it would have been easy to write him off as one who already had passed the point of no return.

THE WARNING STILL NEEDS TO BE SOUNDED

The warning still needs to be sounded, but judgment needs to be withheld. "Judgment is mine and recompense," says the Lord (Deut. 32:35, cp. Heb. 10:30,31). Many have been persuaded by scare tactics and poor exegesis they have already committed the unpardonable sin.

As a working definition for our day and age we submit the following: The sin against the Holy Spirit is a conscious, willful, rejection of Divine revelation (in whatever form), manifested and augmented by speaking blasphemously with *deliberate* intent of hurting Christ's cause.

Since in our generation revelation is not unfolding and ongoing, but historic, and (short of the second coming of Christ) complete in the New Covenant Scriptures, to blaspheme against the Holy Spirit today would require therefore an open vilification of the Scriptures by one who has had occasion to know better than to do so, but who does so anyway as a personal vendetta, not just against the church (though that likely would be involved) but against God in whatever sense the blasphemer conceives of such a being, or beings, to exist.

POSTSCRIPT

By way of postscript something needs to be said concerning the passages in the book of Hebrews which are commonly cited as having reference to the unpardonable sin, paticularly the verses in chapters 6, 10 and 12.

Hebrews 6:4-8 is often misconstrued. The burden of the epistle was the danger of Jewish Christians reverting back to the bondage of the Mosaic law. The opening verses of chapter six list a series of ordinances under which the Hebrews were once bound. The expression: "leaving the first principles" does not have reference to going on beyond the items involved in the proverbial "five finger exercise" — hearing, faith, repentance, confession and baptism. The writer mentions repentance in the context of the dead works of the law. The faith of which he speaks can scarcely be faith in Christ, for to leave that behind would be apostasy. The faith in God mentioned is that faith which the Jews substituted for God, faith in the works of the law which they made to be their god. The repentance they were to abandon was that which related to the dead works of the law, from which exercise they trusted they were scoring points with God. The teaching of "baptisms" (pl.) is the Greek word baptismoi, which has reference to the "divers washings" (ablution ceremonies) of the law. It is the plural form of baptismos, not baptisma. The latter is the word used of Christian baptism. Baptisma is a word unique to the NT, being found only in the NT and later literature contingent upon the NT. It refers to a "once and for all," non-repetitive event. Baptisma is not completed in the physical act commonly brought to mind, but in rising to "walk in newness of life" (Rom. 6:4).

The impossibility of such persons being "renewed unto repentance" is explained in the indictment which follows. Such persons "crucify to themselves the Son of God afresh, and put him to an open shame" (v. 6). That is to say, to return to the repetitive sacrifices of an abrogated law is to count the sacrifice of Christ as but another episode in the annual ritual of the day of atonement. Trust is thereby removed from the finished work of Christ on Calvary to what Paul has called "the weak and beggarly rudiments" and "bondage" of a dead law (Gal. 4:9).

The agricultural allusion is incriminating. God had carefully tilled Israel for a special role in history. (See "the song of the vineyard," Isa. 5:1,2.) God had planted the field (Israel) with the choicest of vine, "herb meet for those (the world) for whose sake it is also tilled." As such they were to "receive blessing from God."

236

But in reverting to Moses and the Law and thus minimizing the efficacy of Christ and the Gospel, they were in effect sowing the field with that which was, comparably, "thorns and thistles." Anything that comes up in a field other than that which the husbandman hopes to harvest is in that context a weed to be hoed down or plowed under. It encumbers the ground prepared for a higher purpose.

Hebrew 10:26-32 is another text in the same vein. The writer is not accusing them of having willfully sinned after having come to the knowledge of the truth, but he is again warning of the jeopardy in which they would place themselves if they should do do. He would have them cease and desist before they have in effect counted the blood of the covenant of Christ "an unholy thing," that is, something that is not really special, "set apart" from all other sacrifice, but just another routine sacrifice in an ongoing ritual.

With Hebrews 12:16,17 we are confronted with a decided change of setting. In this passage "the father" is the one in whom there is found no "change of mind" (Gr. *metanoia*, commonly rendered "repentance"). In this passage we have the sole instance in which the term is actually translated according to its root meaning. The noun, *metanoia*, is used in the NT twenty-five (25) times, and various forms of the verb, *metanoeo*, thirty-four (34) times. The term is formed by combining the term *meta*, (change) and the noun *noia* (mind). Thus it has to do with "a change of mind," of reason, of resolve — not feeling.

Another Greek word, *metamelomai* has to do with a change in one's emotional state. But even when the apostle Paul used both terms in II Corinthians 7:8-11, in the process contrasting the one with the other with a view to distinguishing between them, his efforts have been thwarted by the King James translators. Being heavily dependent upon the Latin Vulgate they adopted an English word formed from a transliteration of the Latin *re-poenitere*. Because of established usage the error persists in subsequent translations, except for the text now before us.

237

Isaac, for good reason, made up his mind and stood firm. He had made a reasoned decision. He was not swayed by Esau's emotional display. Esau found no place for a change of mind (*metanoia*) in his father, though he sought it diligently with tears," (v. 17). With this text we are given an insight into the doctrine of the unpardonable sin from a different perspective. The birthright of the firstborn son was rightly a sacred trust. Esau traded it for a bowl of beans. What "a slap in the face" that was to his father. Actually it was even worse. That would be but a stinging insult of the moment. There is a sin that our heavenly Father has determined for his own good reason never to forgive.

What is that sin? We are told in general terms what it is, but not precisely. Precisely what does one have to say or do to be "guilty of an eternal sin"? God has wisely seen fit not to tell us. It likely is not some one thing said or done, something which stands alone — one inadvertent *faux pas*. God is not that arbitrary, or limited in range of observation.

When the warning is noted in context it would seem to be oral in its modes of expression. Could one then say the same thing in writing and get away with it? Is it tolerable for one to use every resource at one's command to defame and disdain the Holy Spirit, so long as one does not verbalize his blasphemous contempt orally or perhaps in writing? God is not mocked! He is not that easily out maneuvered.

Suppose it were within the understanding and ability of some one of us to state precisely the one thing a reprobate would have to overtly say or do to fall under the condemnation of which we have been warned. Considering the mind set which devises bywords by which means we can almost take God's name in vain, and that of his Son also, and which provides the ingenuity to almost speak vulgarly, but not quite, surely the same ingenuity would devise the means of coming ever so close to speak blasphemously against the Holy Spirit, but yet not quite do so.

My judgment is that God who "tempts no man" (James 1:13), (that role being ably filled by Satan) has purposely left his most solemn warning imprecisely stated lest the ingenuity of the devilish minded make a game of that warning also.

To those who are worried they may have inadvertently committed the unpardonable sin we may confidently assure you that those who are the most concerned are likely those who are the least apt to have done so.

CONCLUSION

My conclusion, as has already been intimated, is that the warning with which we are wrestling has been purposely left something short of precise definition for a reason. If precisely identified one could, and many would, reason within themselves that since only one sin is said to be unpardonable all else is therefore excluded, and therefore forgivable. Why not make the most of it? Be careful not to commit that one sin, and one can, as the saying is: "Have all this (this world, and its pleasures), and heaven too!" One need only take care not to be guilty of the "super no no." God is not so mocked!

A poem, the author of which has been long forgotten, if indeed it was ever known to me, keeps coming to mind as we seek to bring our study of Christ's most solemn warning to a close.

There comes a time, I know not when,
　A place, I know not where,
That marks the destiny of men,
　For glory, or despair.
There is a line, by us unseen
　That crosses every path
It is the hidden boundary between
　God's mercy and God's wrath

How long can men go on in sin?
　How long will God forbear?
Where ends one's hope and where begins
　The confines of despair

239

One answer from the skies is sent
Oh ye who from God depart,
While it is called Today, repent,
And harden not your heart.

POSTLUDE: CONVICTED BUT NOT CONVERTED

Never do my thoughts turn to the blasphemy against the Holy Spirit but that the most traumatic experience in more than fifty years of Christian witnessing comes to mind. In the early '40's I was called to Bell Gardens, California to lead in an evangelistic meeting. Early on the resident evangelist challenged me to take on the community's resident atheist — a man who was often heard to boast: "I just eat up young preachers." He was celebrating his 80th birthday, which fact provided both an urgency and a low-key occasion for a call.

The man who met us at the door could easily have passed for one much younger. He graciously acknowledged our greeting and invited us in. Once inside we were barely seated ere he asked a leading question, and the bout was on. Providentially, I was prepared for the occasion, having majored in apologetics under the tutelage of the then renowned Dr. Claude C. Taylor of Phillips College of the Bible. The greater part of my master's thesis: *Science's Confirmation of the Christian Faith* had been published serially in the Christian Standard. His appeal to "science" was countered at every point by citations from reputable scientists whose published works contradicted his "authorities" and "confirmed" the Christian faith.

After a time he shifted his attack into the field of textual criticism of the Scriptures, focusing on the Gospel narratives and, to my surprise, resorting to a highly specialized form of NT criticism — *Formgeschichte*. "Form criticism" of the synoptic Gospels was at that time the latest brain child of German rationalism. It seemed incredible that he would be conversant in

240

such a recent and specialized assault against the credibility of the synoptic gospels.

He too was in for a surprise. Again providence seemed to be at work. I had just received an advanced degree in the NT department of the aforementioned seminary. My thesis, *The Synoptic Problem in the Light of Recent Criticism* had won the annual Newby Award for the outstanding thesis of the year. The atheist had again unwittingly chosen to attack in an area wherein, providentially, I was well informed.

Suddenly, in the middle of a halting sentence he stiffened. Eyes set in an unseeing stare. He leaned heavily back in his chair, hands gripping the arm rests, and began to shake as though racked by a fever. The preacher who had taken me there, and I, looked at each other with foreboding. We feared he was having a heart attack. Should we call an ambulance? My friend made the first move. Kneeling on one knee beside him he grasped a quivering hand in his own and gazing directly into unseeing eyes he called the man by name. There was no response.

I was just about to look for a phone when the shivering and rigidity began to subside. The unseeing stare gave way to awareness of our presence. He shook his head as one does in awakening from a deep sleep, or recovering from a blow. He regained his composure to a degree but treated us with manifest reserve. We suggested perhaps we should leave and call again when he was feeling better. At that he arose and stepped to the door and politely dismissed us. We called again twice, but were not invited to come in. He was cordial but his demeanor plainly communicated he was not about to engage in any kind of dialogue.

Once I thought I had witnessed a man commit the unpardonable sin. But I learned that from that day to his death he was not known to ever again speak against the Christian faith. Like Felix and Agrippa, he was convicted, but not converted. He did not die a blasphemer, perhaps no longer an unbeliever. But he died a rejector of Christ.

13

THE ROLE OF THE HOLY SPIRIT
IN CONVERSION

The noun "conversion" occurs only once in the Scriptures, Acts 15:3. But the process which is thus denominated is the recurring theme of the book of Acts. When "Judaizers" from Judah provoked dissension in the church at Antioch, teaching: "Except you (gentiles) be circumcised after the custom of Moses, you cannot be saved" (15:1), Paul and Barnabas withstood them. But the Judaizers, apparently representing their position as bearing the endorsement of the apostles and elders of the church in Jerusalem, continued to foster dissension.

At this point in the controversy the issue became a question of authority as well as of custom. The church therefore judiciously determined that Paul and Barnabas, "with certain others, should go up to Jerusalem unto the apostles and elders about this question" (15:2).

Verse three informs us: "They therefore, being brought on their way by the church" (i.e., deputized, and possibly accompanied and even financed by the church) passed through Phoenicia and Samaria, "declaring the conversion (Gr. *epistrophen*) of the Gentiles."

Epistrophen is the noun form of the verb *epistrepho* which literally means "to turn upon," that is "to turn in response to prompting, command, or other incentive." Turning from one course of action or way of life to another in response to entreaty, reason, command, conviction, etc., is the essence of the word translated "conversion."

What was the incentive that resulted in "the conversion of the Gentiles" (among others)? This is the issue that is now before us. The role of the Holy Spirit in conversion is a topic which confronts us with one of the most crucial and hotly contested issues in church doctrine. Note we said "church" doctrine, not Christian doctrine.

The problem now before us began with a seed thought germinated in the fertile mind of Augustina, Bishop of Hippo, North Africa (A.D. 354-430.) Out of it stemmed the dogma of total hereditary depravity, a dogma that was later to go to seed in the *Institutes* of John Calvin (A.D. 1509-1564).

Once the dogma of total hereditary depravity is allowed man becomes the hapless victim of congenital spiritual blindness and impotency from which there is no reprieve — except one is fortunate enough to be among those chosen of God from the foundation of the world to be one of his "elect." In that case the Holy Spirit will operate in one's heart to implant faith by supplying the power and the disposition to truly believe. Otherwise, Satan will give "a working of error" whereby some may even imagine themselves to be devout Christians. Under that delusion the non-elect may do many "works of righteousness" which appear to be "fruit of the Spirit," but such will be only "a form of godliness" without the power thereof.

For a concise critique of this bizarre travesty the reader will do well to read my critique, "The Big Lie," in the appendix sector of this volume. The dogma of total hereditary depravity turns out to be the tap root from which a plethora of devious doctrines have grown. For the present, here it is in the raw: The dogma finds its classic expression in the *Official Confession of the Presbyterian Church, USA* Revised Edition, 1939, pp. 25,26.

> By this sin (eating the forbidden fruit) they (Adam and Eve) fell from their original righteousness, and communion with God, and so became dead in sin, and wholly defiled in all the faculties and parts of body and soul. They being the root of all mankind, the guilt of this sin was imputed and the same death in sin and corrupted nature conveyed to all their posterity descending from them by ordinary generation. (The latter clause was contrived to absolve Christ from such dire depravity of body and soul). From this original corruption whereby we are indisposed, disabled, and made opposite to all good, and wholly inclined to do evil, do proceed all actual transgressions.

One could scarcely say anything worse of the devil himself than is said in the above citation of a newborn babe, though born to parents (both of whom) are of "the elect," duly called and sanctified.

Extremist doctrines have an almost inescapable polarizing effect. This is certainly true of the dogma of total hereditary depravity as it relates (among other things) to the role of the Holy Spirit in the process of conversion.

EXTREMIST POSITIONS

Doctrinarians have polarized at two extremes with regard to this issue, as is the case with most issues. But "the truth, the whole truth, and nothing but the truth" is rarely found at the extremes to which a doctrine or concept can be pushed or carried.

1. *"The Holy Spirit Alone" Dogma*
Those influenced by Calvinism, consciously or otherwise,

have taken the position that the Holy Spirit operates directly (and, if need be, apart from the Scriptures) to turn men to God and Christ, and hence unto salvation. He is said to operate directly upon the mind, the emotions, the conscience and even the will of "the elect." Thus sinners do not "turn" to God. They are said to "be turned" (be converted). The noun "conversion" and its verb forms "convert," "be converted," stem from the Latin Vulgate. They are often used in preference to the more simple manner of speaking in that theological overtones are more readily suggested thereby. The emphasis is thus shifted from the action of man in responding to God. The subtle inference is that conversion is something that happens to man.

The King James translators have aided and abetted this dogma by translating *epistrepho* as though it were in the passive voice wherever it appears in the context of salvation. The New King James also, for all its careful weeding of archaic expressions and other long overdue emendations, continues to mistranslate such a crucial text as Acts 3:19. To their credit they have rectified the reading of Matthew 18:3 and the four NT texts in which the prophecy of Isaiah 6:10 is said to be fulfilled, (Matt. 13:15; Mark 4:12; John 12:40; Acts 28:27). Isaiah 6:10 also has been correctly translated in the NKJV. Why this was not done in the case of Acts 3:19 is hard to explain. It is inexcusable.

2. *"The Word of God Alone" Dogma*

Reactionaries to Calvinism often take a diametrically opposite stance. Some affirm that the Scriptures alone are sufficient to accomplish the work of conversion. Those who outright deny the existence of the Holy Spirit as a third person in a triune Godhead affirm the Scriptures, as epitomized in the Gospel proclamation, are "*the* power of God unto salvation unto everyone that believes, to the Jew first and also to the Greek," that is, the Gentiles (Rom. 1:16). Those so persuaded note that Jesus, having said: "It is the spirit that gives life," went on to explain, "the words that I have spoken unto you are spirit, and are life" (John

246

6:63).

Others, though believing the Holy Spirit to be a third person in the sphere of the Godhead, cite the same proof-texts (among others), and affirm that the denial of the all-sufficiency of the Scriptures to bring men to a saving knowledge of Christ is to deny what the Holy Spirit himself has affirmed concerning the role of the Scriptures.

In short, reactionaries to Calvinism either hold that a) The Holy Spirit does not exist as a third person in a triune Godhead, and therefore cannot and does not operate independently of the Scriptures to bring us to salvation, or b) if the Holy Spirit does so exist, he does not overtly involve himself in the conversion process, generally.

The qualifying adverb which closes the preceding sentence is by way of acknowledging that in the two classic conversion episodes, Acts 2 and Acts 10, the Holy Spirit occupied an initiatory role. In the case of the latter, the Holy Spirit "fell on" Cornelius and his household, interrupting Peter's sermon to bring the conversion episode to a dramatic climax. But these were, as noted, initiatory, non-repetitive episodes, not the prevailing pattern which ensued thereafter.

3. A Mediating Position

A mediating position, replete with variant forms of expression, normally views the Holy Spirit within the sphere of the Godhead, and participating to some degree in the process of conversion. At the same time it is duly noted that in the conversion accounts chronicled in Acts, the preaching of the Gospel preceded every recorded conversion. Even when the Holy Spirit operated in an extraordinary manner to "set the stage" the pattern prevails: a) preaching of the Gospel, and b) an overt (and quite uniform) response on the part of those converted signalize every conversion recorded in Acts.

REVIEW OF CONVERSION EPISODES
FOUND IN ACTS, CHAPTERS 1-11

A review of the conversion episodes recorded in Acts demonstrates the fact that the preaching of the Gospel figured prominently in every case. While there are cases in which the Holy Spirit receives no mention whatsoever, there is no record of anyone being "converted by the Holy Spirit alone." Conversion is uniformly recorded as occurring in direct response to the preaching of the Gospel.

1. On the day of Pentecost it was Peter's sermon, not the manifestations of the Holy Spirit, that convinced, convicted and converted the multitude. It is of Peter's sermon that it is written: "Now when they *heard this* they were pricked in their hearts and cried, 'Men and brethren what shall we do?' " (2:37). And it was in response to what Peter told them to do that it is written, "They then that received the word were baptized" (v. 41). If even on the day the Holy Spirit's most dramatic manifestation of his presence and power was augmented by the preaching of the Gospel, and the recorded response is attributed to what was preached, surely that pace-setting day has something to say to us.

2. In Samaria, according to record, it was "when they believed good tidings concerning the kingdom of God and the name of Jesus Christ" that "they were baptized, both men and women" (8:12). Simon the sorcerer was undoubtedly attracted by the miracles he witnessed but his conversion is not attributed to any direct intervention of the Holy Spirit. The record would indicate otherwise. Note verse 13, "Simon also himself believed, and being baptized, continued with Philip, and beholding signs and great wonders, was amazed."

3. The Spirit directed Philip to the Ethiopian eunuch. But it was not until "Philip opened his mouth and preached unto him Jesus" that he understood the prophecy he was reading (Isa. 53) and asked to be baptized (8:26-40). There is no mention of the Holy Spirit operating upon the heart of the eunuch apart from the

word of God. If the Holy Spirit could give precise travel instructions to Philip, (and did), he surely could have given spiritual instructions to the eunuch, (were that his appointed *modus operandi*). But he chose to operate through the Word.

4. The case of Saul of Tarsus has much to say to us. We are not told what part the Holy Spirit had, if any, in Saul's vision of Christ on the Damascus road. Christ is represented as speaking to Saul directly. But even He did not tell Saul what he needed to do to have his sins washed away. Christ answered Paul's "Who are you?" question by identifying himself (9:5), but in answer to his "What will you have me do?" question (9:6, cp. 22:10), Jesus said: "Go into Damascus and it will be told you what to do." So Saul did the best he could under the circumstances but three days of fasting and prayer did not absolve his sins. Not until a fellow man, Ananias, came and said: "Arise and be baptized, and wash away your sins, calling on the name of the Lord" (22:16) was Saul's conversion consummated.

While Saul's conversion was precipitated by his Damascus road experience, it was not solely accomplished by miraculous intervention of the Holy Spirit. The preaching of Stephen did not have immediate salutary effect but neither can it be dismissed as a factor in Saul's conversion. Recall that when Jesus confronted him on the Damascus road he appealed to Saul's conscience by saying: "Saul, why do you persecute me? It is hard for you to kick against the goads" (26:14). What goaded or "pricked" (KJV) him? We may reasonably infer that Saul was included among those of whom it is said that Stephen's words "cut to the heart" (7:54). Saul's first sermon of record (Acts 13:16-41) is strikingly akin to the message he heard Stephen proclaim.

5. On the surface it would appear that the conversion of Cornelius and his household might prove to be an exception to the rule. But when the facts are noted it turns out that their conversion also was effectuated through the preaching of the Gospel, and their obedience thereto. As previously noted the Holy Spirit served as "chairman of the arrangements," so to speak, the case

being a very special one. Through careful timing and instruction the Holy Spirit directed the flow of events which brought Peter to the house of Cornelius. The Holy Spirit also conditioned Peter to respond to the situation confronting him in a manner quite out of keeping with his deeply rooted mind-set. (See Gal. 2:11-13 for a telling illustration of how Peter was more accustomed to behave towards the Gentiles). But as active as the Holy Spirit was in bringing Peter and Cornelius together, it is instructive to note it was Peter, not the Holy Spirit, who "spoke . . . the words whereby (they) might be saved" (11:4).

As in the case of the conversion of Saul there were some special ministrations of the Spirit manifested in the episode. This was in keeping with the fact the event was Divinely arranged to signalize that "to the Gentiles also God had granted repentance unto life" (11:18). Peter would never have laid hands on them to baptize them in water if God had not put his endorsement upon them by baptizing them in the Holy Spirit, no less. But not even Divinely credentialized baptism in the Holy Spirit was reckoned as absolving them of the need of water baptism, the normative response to the Gospel throughout the apostolic age (10:47,48). The format for evangelism ordained by Jesus in the Great Commission was never abrogated by the Holy Spirit or Jesus — not even amid extra-ordinary circumstances.

The role of the Holy Spirit in the Caesarean episode was supportive, not supplantive. His ministry was directed as much to Peter and his companions as it was to Cornelius and his household. Peter apparently needed more prodding than Cornelius. Peter had some deep rooted prejudice to overcome. Both Peter and Cornelius needed precise instruction designed to bring them together. That accomplished, the Holy Spirit's next move was designed to convince Peter and his associates, and afterwards those to whom Peter had to give account, that "to the Gentiles also God has granted repentance unto life" (11:18). That it did.

The converts did not need the demonstration. Perhaps by

250

that time this was true of Peter also. His opening remarks (10:27,28) indicate the vision he had received in Joppa, reinforced by the timing of the messengers from Cornelius and their report of his vision, combined to get God's message across to him. The men he had judiciously brought with him likely needed the demonstration (10:45). In turn they provided the "two or three witnesses by which a thing shall be established" (Num. 35:30; Deut. 17:6; Matt. 18:16; etc.).

THE MISSIONARY EXPANSION OF THE CHURCH

Following the conversion of Cornelius and his household the record in Acts shifts to the missionary expansion of the church, stemming from Antioch and spearheaded by the Apostle Paul. This is in keeping with the plot plan which structures the narrative. The book of Acts is the story of a three-fold movement: 1) Religiously, the movement is from the law to the Gospel, 2) Racially, from the Jews to the Gentiles and 3) Regionally, from Jerusalem "to the uttermost parts of the earth." The key verse is found in Acts 1:8, a verse which provides the basic outline of the narrative. Chapters 1-7 record the beginnings of the church in Jerusalem and Judea. Chapters 8-12 record the extension of the Gospel to Samaria. Chapters 13 ff. record the onset of the third stage of development, the extension of the Christian witness to the uttermost parts of the earth.

CONVERSIONS STEMMING FROM THE
MISSIONARY LABORS OF PAUL, CHAPTERS 13-20

Every conversion recorded in chapters after the conversion of Cornelius have one thing in common. They came in response to the preaching and teaching of Paul. The Holy Spirit was sometimes instrumental in directing Paul from one place to

251

another, but not necessarily from one person to another.

1) Paul's first recorded sermon is found in Acts 13:16-42. He seems to have taken his cue from Stephen's defense. The sermon, an historical sketch of God's providence at work through Israel, was delivered in the synagogue of Antioch of Pisidia. "Many of the Jews and devout proselytes" were responsive and asked to hear him again (v. 43). "And the next Sabbath almost the whole city was gathered together to hear the word of God" (v. 44).

Jealousy reared its ugly head when the local Jewish leaders found themselves upstaged by the apostle. They "contradicted" him and "blasphemed" (v. 45). But the Gentiles, presumably "the devout proselytes" mentioned in v. 43, are said to have glorified the word of God: "and as many as were *ordained* to eternal life believed" (v. 48).

The final clause of the verse just cited, as commonly translated, would appear to support the Calvinist doctrine of conversion. The word translated "ordained" (Gr. *tasso*, lit. "set in array") appears nine times in the New Testament. Only twice is it translated "ordain" — here, and in Romans 13:1 where it is said of civil rulers that "the powers that be are ordained of God." Note that it is not said they are "fore-ordained" (Gr. *proorizo*, lit. "determine beforehand"), only that they are set in array. *Tasso* is elsewhere translated "appointed," "determined" and even "addicted" (I Cor. 16:15, KJV; "set," ASV). Acts 13:48 affirms that the devout Gentile proselytes and whoever else "glorified the Word of God" by their response to Paul's preaching were arrayed with the heirs of eternal life, and became numbered with the faithful, in that they too believed.

2. Chapter 14 reports Paul's further labors in the province of Galatia. Iconium was a near repeat of Antioch, except the Greeks also turned on Paul at the prompting of hostile Jews. Other than mere mention that he preached in certain other cities there is no report as to what may have occurred, except for the city of Lystra. There he enjoyed a measure of initial success upon heal-

ing a congenital cripple. But a posse of Jews came from Antioch and Iconium and staged a riot in which Paul was stoned, dragged out of town, and left for dead. But he rose up, went on to Derbe, then returned to Lystra, Iconium and Antioch, confirming the disciples, and exhorting them to keep the faith.

3. Chapter 15 reports an interruption of Paul's missionary journeys that he might participate in the Jerusalem conference. There the apostles and elders hammered out a decision calculated to settle the issue relative to the circumcision of the Gentiles. Verses 7-9 are pertinent to the issue now before us. Peter had something to say about the process of conversion which extends beyond the issue of that day.

> Brethren, you know that a good while ago God made choice among you that *by my mouth* the Gentiles should hear the word of the Gospel, and believe. And God, who knows the heart, bore them witness, *giving them the Holy Spirit*, even as he did unto us: and he made no distinction between us and them, *cleansing their hearts by faith*.

Note: a) The conversion of Cornelius (and his household) is the immediate frame of reference in Peter's testimony. That episode served as a Divine endorsement of the evangelization of the Gentiles. b) The faith of the believing Gentiles is said to have been attained by "hearing the word of the Gospel." It was not zapped into them by some mysterious working of the Holy Spirit. c) The Holy Spirit did not come upon them to impart faith. A major step of faith had already been taken long before Peter arrived. Cornelius is described as "a devout man, and one that reverenced God with all his house" (10:2). That step of faith was attained through the knowledge of God communicated by the Old Testament scriptures. d) The gift of the Holy Spirit that was given at Caesarea bore witness to the fact that God had "cleansed their hearts through faith." Peter did not need that witness, but it likely helped him to understand more fully what God had already said to him three times in the housetop vision which precipitated his trip to Caesarea — "What God has cleansed, make thou not common, or unclean" (10:14-16). But the men whom Peter took with him to Caesarea were not with Peter when the vision came. It was on behalf of their needful supporting testimony that the Holy Spirit was so dramatically given. (See Acts 10:44-47; 11:12.)

e) Peter used the term "faith" senecdochally when he stated that God "cleansed their hearts by faith." That should be obvious. Those who use the text to set aside the plain teaching of Acts 2:38; 22:16; etc., attempt to back treadle when their attention is called to the fact their specious reasoning would also eliminate the "blood of Christ" (I John 1:7), and the "Word" (Eph. 5:26). Peter was not detailing to his hearers the process of salvation. He was bearing witness to the scope of that process now that the "word of the Gospel" has superseded the "works of the Law."

4. Chapter 16 is highlighted by Paul's Macedonian call. The Holy Spirit interceded on behalf of the European theater, else Paul would have followed his own leanings (see 16:6,7). Except for the intervention of the Holy Spirit, Paul likely would have prolonged his ministry in Asia Minor where his time would have been largely occupied by his concern for his own people.

Upon arrival in Macedonia "the man" seen in his vision initially turned out to be a woman, in fact a company of them. Generically speaking, "man" embraces "woman." (Romantically speaking this is true also, else the human race would be thinned out considerably.) A phrase in verse 14, lifted out of context, is used to support the tenets of Calvinsim. Lydia, already "a worshipper of God," (a term used to denote a proselyte to Judaism), is said to be "one whose heart the Lord opened to give heed to the things which were spoken by Paul." Unless one is inclined to "buy the whole package" of Calvinism, of which we shall later speak directly, the text presents no problem. She was already a "worshipper of God" and had led her companions to a place of prayer when her encounter with Paul ensued. That could have been interpreted by Luke as an act of providence, hence the phrasing of verse 8.

The conversion of the Philippian jailor and his household was no doubt enhanced by the unusual circumstances which ensued that night, but the account of it states plainly that Paul "spoke the word of the Lord unto him, with all that were in his house" (v. 32). Contingent upon that instruction the jailor washed the stripes of his prisoners, (a viable demonstration of repentance) and was baptized, he, and all his, immediately (v. 33).

5. Chapter 17 relates the founding of the church at Thessalonica and Berea, and Paul's unscheduled visit to Athens. Though the Thessalonian church began in the synagogue it included a preponderance of Greeks (v. 5). As usual the upstaged Jewish leaders were provoked to jealousy. They incited a riot that precipitated Paul's departure.

6. Paul's next stop was at Berea. There he found the Jews "more noble than those in Thessalonica, in that they received the word with readiness of mind, examining the Scriptures daily, whether these things (Paul's teachings) were so" (v. 11). Thus it is written: "Many of them believed." Note their belief is attributed to two things: a) they were good listeners, b) they researched the Scriptures to check out what was taught. "Many of them therefore believed: also of the Greek women of high estate, and of the men (of high estate?), not a few" (v. 12).

Paul's stay in Berea was cut short by the arrival of the fanatics who had precipitated the riot at Thessalonica. Friends spirited him out of town to the relative safety of Athens. There he preached in the synagogue and the marketplace to any who would listen. In time he was accosted by the resident "intelligentsia" who set up the Mars Hill encounter. He made converts even in that setting. Among those who "believed" were Dionysius the Areopagite (the chief magistrate), a woman named Damaris, and others with them" (v. 34).

7. Chapter 18 reports the founding of the church at Corinth. There Paul resorted to his synagogue strategy. It had its risks, as we have seen. Twice (at Lystra and Thessalonica) it had precipitated a riot. On two other occasions the diehard Judaizers

hastened his departure. But in every case he gained at least a foothold for the Gospel.

At Corinth the pattern was repeated. Initially at Corinth, his "reasoning" in the synagogue "persuaded" both Jews and Greeks (v. 4). But with the coming of Silas and Timothy (v. 5) opposition flared to such a degree that his opponents are said to have "blasphemed" (v. 6). It was at this juncture that Paul shook out his raiment, and said: "Your blood be upon your own heads; I am clean: from henceforth I will go unto the Gentiles" (v. 6). With that he moved to the house of a proselyte, Titius Justus.

It turns out that Paul's synagogue strategy paid off after all. Crispus, the ruler of the synagogue, his household, and "many of the Corinthians," hearing, believed and were baptized. Note the source of their faith, and what they did as a result of believing. The dictum of Romans 10:17 is underscored throughout the book of Acts: "Faith comes by hearing the Word of God."

8. The latter half of the chapter and chapter 19 shifts the scene to Ephesus. Verses 21-28 report an interlude in that ministry. Priscilla and Aquilla had joined him at Corinth. Since they had proven themselves as able students and teachers, Paul left them in Ephesus that he might return to his home base in Antioch, (v. 22). "And having spent some time there, he departed, and went through the region of Galatia and Phrygia, in order, establishing all the disciples" in the churches he had founded (v. 23).

9. Chapter 19 records Paul's return to Ephesus where his longest ministry of record ensued. Upon arrival he found "certain disciples" with a problem very familiar to our time. They had been imperfectly taught about baptism (vv. 1-7). The Holy Spirit was not to blame. They did not even know the Holy Spirit exists (v. 3). In probing the reason for their problem Paul inquired concerning their baptism. Obviously, if they had received the baptism Christ ordained (Cp. Matt. 28:18-20), they would have known the Holy Spirit exists. (See also Acts 2:38,39; 5:32.) Note Paul did not question the validity of their faith. If faith is a gift of the

Holy Spirit, bestowed arbitrarily upon whomsoever he enlightens, something went awry in their case.

Following that episode Paul again resorted to his synagogue strategy, with the usual mixed bag of results. For three months results were reasonably positive. But a hard core of resistance surfaced. At that juncture Paul moved to the school of Tyrannus where he could teach daily. That he did for the space of two years (vv. 8-10).

Opposition from a different quarter then set in. A silversmith who made shrines of Diana, the city goddess, noted an alarming downturn in sales, and readily assessed the cause of it. Rallying others of his guild he incited a riot, shrewdly disguising their motives, making it out to be a religious issue. Thus he incited the idolaters Paul had not yet converted. Were it not for the wise counsel of the town clerk Paul would likely have suffered dire consequences.

10. Chapter 20 notes that Paul removed himself from the scene, reckoning it time he revisited the Macedonian churches, and Greece. His stay in Greece went well for three months. He then learned of a Jewish plot against him. At that he determined to return to Jerusalem, to share once again in the celebration of Pentecost (v. 16).

THE TWILIGHT OF A TUMULTUOUS CAREER
CHAPTERS 21-28

11. Chapters 21ff. chronicle the twilight years of a tumultuous career. The tumult did not cease, however, with the end of Paul's missionary journeys which ended, at least of record, with his return to Jerusalem to celebrate the day of Pentecost.

En route to Jerusalem he experienced a tearful farewell with the elders of Ephesus who met with him at a brief lay over at Miletus (20:13-38). Verse 38 states of the elders: "What grieved them most was his statement that they would never see his face again" (NIV).

His arrival at Caesarea was soon clouded by the dire prediction of the prophet Agabus who had journeyed from Judea to warn him the Jews of Jerusalem would bind him and turn him over to the Gentiles (21:11). At that his friends begged him, but in vain, not to go to Jerusalem.

At Jerusalem Paul was warmly greeted by the brethren. He extended special greetings to James, and the rest of the elders, and related in detail what God had done through him unto the Gentiles (21:17-19). But a week later when the ceremonial "days of purification" ended, some Jews from Asia saw him in the temple, and precipitated a riot. He was dragged from the temple and would have been killed were it not for the intervention of the Roman troops stationed adjacent to the temple to quell such situations (21:27ff.)

12. Chapters 22-28 detail the story of Paul, the prisoner. Thrice he was given opportunity to tell of his conversion, and apostolic call. But no conversion episodes were reported beyond Chapter 19. The point of this extended rehearsal is that Acts relates the "high tide" of the work of the Holy Spirit, in conversion, and equipping for service. But the record simply does not support the Calvinist position.

REFLECTIONS

The reference data in Acts provides no basis for the Calvinistic dogma that the Holy Spirit alone accomplishes the work of conversion. While allowing that the Word of God is sometimes an accessory to the public (visible) manifestation of conversion, only the Holy Spirit Himself is said to convert sinners, for only he is said to know the elect, and it would seem that he would not waste his time pleading with those foreordained to eternal damnation.

But that supposition has its problems. Recall for example that Stephen indicted the intransigent Jews who were gearing up to murder him, saying: "You stiff necked and uncircumcised of hearts and ears. You always resist the Holy Spirit, as your fathers did, so also do you" (Acts 7:51). The indictment of the epistle to the Hebrews speaks in the same vein:

> Wherefore, the Holy Spirit says: Today, if you shall hear his voice, harden not your hearts, as in the provocation.

(Heb. 3:7, and repeated in 3:15, and yet again in 4:7) Isaiah quotes God as pleading to Israel, saying: "I have spread out my hands all the day long unto a rebellious people that walk in a way that is not good, after their own thoughts, a people that provoke me to my face continually, (Isa. 65:2). Why should he waste his time doing that? Did not he (of all persons) know they were born depraved, opposite to all good, and could do nothing that could be pleasing in his sight unless his Spirit would quicken them? But his Spirit couldn't possibly do that because they were foreordained to be damned of body and soul from before the foundations of the world were laid, and He, Jehovah God, "changes not." Such is the essence and the utter absurdity of Calvinism.

CONVERSION EPISODES IN ACTS

Episode   Supernatural Manifestations Mentioned

Collective Conversions

1. Pentecost (2:36-41) Audible visual HS phenomena attracted the crowd
2. Samaritans (8:12) Philip performed miracles in their presence
3. Pisidian Antioch (13:14-52) Converts "filled with HS" (v. 32)
4. Iconium (14:1)

5. Lystra (14:8-22)   Paul healed congenital cripple, survived stoning
6. Derbe (14:21)
7. Thessalonica (17:1-4)
8. Berea (17:10-16)
9. Athens (17:16-34)
10. Corinth (18:8)
11. Ephesus (18:19-20:1)   Paul performed miracles (cp. 19:11,12)

Household Conversions

*1. Cornelius & H. (Ch. 10)   Visions set up the meeting, Baptism in HS
*2. Lydia & H. (16:13-15)   Vision to Paul brought him to Macedonia
3. Jailor & H. (16:25-34)   Earthquake, prison opened, set up meeting
4. Crispus & H. (18:8).

Individualized Conversions

1. Simon Magus (8:13)   (cp. v. 11,13b Philip performed miracles)
2. Ethiopian (8:26-39)   An angel directed Philip to him.
*3. Saul/Paul (9:1-18)   Christ appeared to him enroute to Damascus
4. Sergius Paulus (13:6-12)   Paul exorcizes a demon in his presence

Summary: Of the 19 reported episodes, only in *three (see above) is the HS said to have been involved in the conversion process. However, in eight episodes miracles peformed in their presence doubtless influenced them favorably. In three others Divine direction sent the messengers on their way.

SUBJECTIVE QUESTIONS STATED AND MET

Two subjective questions arise in connection with the fatalistic mold in which the Calvinistic doctrine of conversion is cast. One of my esteemed mentors, the late Dr. Claude Carson Taylor, was wont to quote a bit of satirical verse to express the dilemma into which the non elect lost are cast, even though they may long to be saved and though they throw themselves on the mercy of God.

You shall! (But you can't!)
You will! (But you won't!)
You will be damned if you do!
And you'll be damned if you don't!

Question Number One

What is the incentive for missions and evangelism if the saved are predestined to be saved, and will be saved "no matter what," and the lost are predestined to be everlastingly damned "no matter what"? If such will happen in either case to each and everyone according to the foreordination of God's sovereign will, why suffer hardship for the Gospel, or become involved in any way?

For example, if Paul knew that, (and supposedly he did, for his writings are cited as the basis of the dogma), what was his incentive to suffer stoning, shipwreck, flogging, imprisonment, etc.? If Calvin was right, not one person who believed his message would be lost whether or not he ever opened his mouth to preach or took up his pen to write. Why? Because, "it was foreordained" that he do so. He had no choice. Did he not say? "I have been laid hold on," and again, "Woe is me if I preach not the Gospel"?

But how so? Could Paul have undergone any more severe hardship or suffering by not going forth than he suffered because he did? The Calvinists answer: "That's beside the point. Paul

261

couldn't help but go. It was foreordained that he would — eventually. As a gambler would say: 'The deck was stacked. He played the hand that was dealt him.' "

Question Number Two

How do the elect know they are of the elect? Herein is the tap root of the experience-centered dogma which follows in the wake of the faith only, eternal security syndrome. On the premise one is not saved, and cannot be saved, by conscientiously and trustingly doing the things God has commanded that we do — on the promise (His promise, no less) that in so doing he will give us "the gracious gift" (Gr. *charisma*, Rom. 6:23) of "eternal life in Christ Jesus" — then how are we saved, and how do we know that we are?

Obedience "from the heart to that form of doctrine delivered us" (Rom. 6:17,18) is supposedly not enough to provide us the "blessed assurance" of popular song. Doing things like believing the Gospel, repenting of sin, confessing Christ openly before men, surrendering the body to burial with Christ in baptism unto the death of sin, rising to walk in newness of life — all this according to the popular evangelism is but "dead works" — akin to the ceremonial observance of the abrograted law of Moses. God is said to be offended thereby. Our salvation is to be all of Him. Only after we are saved, *and know it*, and do such things as "witness" to what He has done, is God pleased with such doings — particularly so with baptism, except for the revisionary substitute of the sprinkling of helpless, hapless infants.

How then can we be saved, and know we are saved? If we can't take God's word for it, how can we be sure? According to the dogma, we must have a subjective experience — a vision, a voice, or at least a feeling must come over us. Until fairly recently a person had to relate an "experience" that would pass muster with the denomination of one's choice to become a candidate for baptism and/or membership in a Calvinistic oriented denomination.

BACKLASH

Ultimately a backlash resulted, at two levels. 1) Some, perceptive enough to see through the deception, "threw the baby out with the bath water," so to speak. Many were driven to infidelity thereby. 2) Others, torn within by hypocrisy, but hopeful that in time a "sign" would be given them, made up a whopper in the genre currently in vogue and were welcomed into the company of "the elect." For many of these the backlash came upon reflection, on this wise:

> I told the church the truth (I believed that Jesus is the Christ the son of the living God, that he died for our sins and was raised from the dead, and now sits at the right hand of God as our intercessor) but the church voted me down, denying me the right to become numbered among them. In despair I told a lie and they voted me in. The whole system must be a lie. I want no more of it.

Of course the "whole system" is not a lie. But the Calvinistic model of conversion is one of the many fruits growing out of one common tap root of error — the big lie — the dogma of total hereditary depravity. (See Appendix: *The Big Lie*, for further comment and exposition.)

THE CALVINIST'S DEFENSE STATED AND MET

Calvinism has perhaps a no more eloquent spokesman than the renowned Floyd B. Hamilton. His work: *The Basis of the Christian Faith*, Harper & Row, has been systematically revised and updated, and widely used as a text in Apologetics for two generations. Recent editions have included a chapter (XVI) entitled, *Doctrinal Difficulties in the Bible*. The chapter is prefaced with an introductory paragraph which reads:

I. *If the Bible is True it is Our Duty to Accept its Doctrines*
As has been pointed out in a previous chapter, if the Bible is the

Word of God, it is not for us to say whether the doctrines taught therein are reasonable or not. If God has given them to us, they must be true. It is our place to study them, and accept them as true, whether our finite minds can reconcile them or not.

That having been said, he attempts to respond to a number of objections his Calvinistic presuppositions raise in "our finite minds." The fifth in the series is germaine to the topic now before us. It reads:

E. *The Doctrine of Predestination*
One of the greatest stumbling blocks for unbelievers and even for some Christians is the doctrine of predestination. The Bible teaches that God has not only *foreknown* all things but actually foreordained *whatsoever* comes to pass. This includes all the events in nature, not merely the beautiful opening of a rose, and the songs of birds, but the catastrophes of nature in all their terror and horror. But it also includes all the free actions of man, both good and bad. It includes the predestination of some to everlasting life and the predestination of some to everlasting punishment for their sins. "He holds the whole world in his hands."

Among the problems connected with predestination none is more difficult than the relation between predestination and the free agency of man. How can man be free to act and at the same time have every action predestined by God? How can man have any responsibility for his sinful actions if God predestines everything? One thing is certain, and that is that whether we can explain it satisfactorily or not, the Bible teaches that man is free to act according to his nature, and that God does hold him responsible for all his actions.

Perhaps a little relief for this problem is as follows: man is *free* to act *when he can do what he wants to do*! God's control and predestination enter into the reasons *why* man does what he wants to do. God controls the *springs* of man's desires and the external circumstances and the material atoms and molecules that constitute his body. The man who has been regenerated by the Holy Spirit naturally wants to obey God, so of course God controls his life. The man who is spiritually dead in sin naturally wants to do only evil things, so God limits and circumscribes all his evil desires and activities, causing everything to work together for the

264

plan of God.

Another difficult problem is that of sin. How can a good God predestine sinful actions of man? Does not that make God the author of sin? The Bible teaches that God is not the author of sin and that man is responsible for all his sinful action. This is hard to understand, but the Bible teaches that the most wicked act in history, the betrayal and crucifixion of our Lord, was nevertheless predestined by God for the salvation of His people. If that greatest of sins was predestined for a great purpose then the lesser sins of mankind can be fitted into the plan of God! Though God has a reason, usually unknown to us, for permitting every sinful act, that does not make the act less sinful or take away the responsibility of man for his sin. Man is commanded not to sin; he is warned of the results of his sin; he is told of the punishment for sin; but he is permitted to sin for unknown reasons, though the effects are all overruled according to the plan of God.

Whether we like it or not, and whether we can understand it or not, the Bible clearly teaches predestination, and we had better understand and accept that fact and shape our lives accordingly. Nevertheless we could not accept the doctrine were we not convinced that God has revealed it in the Bible and foreordains whatsoever comes to pass for His own glory. We should never equate this doctrine with the pagan doctrine of fate. Fate teaches that man is in the cogwheels of a blind, implacable doom, while predestination teaches that we are in the hands of a warm, loving heavenly Father, who so loved us that He gave His only begotten Son to die on the cross to redeem us from eternal damnation (pp. 290-292).

RESPONSE

Isn't that comforting! Suppose you have been elected from the foundation the world to be damned to hell — to the hell of Calvinist dogma, no less — to be tortured throughout all eternity. Bear in mind it is from the Calvinists that the fundamentalist dogma of hell became full blown, whereby it is to be understood that the non elect will be provided with asbesticized bodies, with nerves (also asbestocized) in order that they may glow red hot, like the elements of a space heater, and where (apparently) asbestocized worms bore deep within to carry the torture to the very core of one's being.

On the supposition you are one so condemned, would you really find it comforting to know that you are not the hapless "victim of fate," caught "in the cogwheels of a blind, implacable doom"? No, "predestination teaches that we are in the hands of a warm, loving (but nonetheless implacable) heavenly Father," who elected before times eternal to decree you to hell. There the fires will be so much warmer than God's hands you will not be able to feel how warm and loving he is, especially toward those he predestined to be saved — loving them enough that he gave his only begotten Son to die on the cross (for the elect alone) to redeem them, and only them, from eternal damnation.

Note: According to the Calvinist "Tulip Tree" matrix: 1) Total hereditary depravity. 2) Unconditional predestination to salvation or damnation. 3) Limited atonement — Christ died only for the elect. 4) Irresistable grace — if elected you couldn't fail to become a Christian, no matter how hard you tried. 5) Perseverance of the saints — if you have it you can't lose it, "no matter what"! How absurd! Note No. 3: Limited atonement. So He died only for the elect? Paul, whose teaching in Romans is supposedly the basis of predestination dogma, said in Romans 5:6, "Christ died for the ungodly." That means the elect are "the ungodly"! The Godly would therefore be the non-elect! "Consistency, thou art a jewel" indeed!

THIRTEEN PROPOSITIONS SET FORTH
BY ALEXANDER CAMPBELL

In the year 1843, at Lexington, Kentucky, Alexander Campbell and N.L. Rice engaged in a protracted formal debate on the subject we have taken occasion to evaluate. Rice championed the Calvinist position, the dominant position of the American clergy at that point in our national history. Campbell, in his refutation, represented the minority position. As usual, the supporting constituency on either side claimed the victory, but it is significant that experience-centered evangelism noticeably waned in the aftermath of that widely publicized debate, and has had a low profile ever since.

Mr. Campbell set forth thirteen propositions. In substance, somewhat paraphrased or condensed, they may set forth as follows:

Argument from . . .

1. The constitution of the human mind. It has a specific constitution, as does the body. God does not violate it. He works through it. Everything we know comes to our knowledge through the mind.

2. The fact no one can be found possessed of a single propositional truth of the Gospel where the Bible or the teaching thereof has not preceded.

3. The great law of organic existence, whether animal or vegetable, whatever is essential to the production of any specimen is found to be necessary to the begetting of all of like kind.

4. The Holy Spirit's demonstrated method of addressing unconverted men: a) by signs addressed to the one or another of the five senses, and b) propositionally, through words addressed to their understanding.

5. Advocate, the Holy Spirit's official designation in the work of conversion, implies he is to use words in pleading his case.

6. The Commission given to the Advocate. He was sent to convince men in three respects — all based on appeals to recorded facts of Gospel history, John 16:8.

7. The very significant and sublime fact that the first gift of the Spirit bestowed in the Gospel age which was signally inaugurated by his descent on the day of Pentecost, was the gift of *intelligible* tongues, addressed to the understanding of those who heard, and *that* through the Apostles from whom we have received His duly certified Word. What better symbol of his office, and of the fact that he would address us through their words.

8. The direct and explicit testimony of the apostles, a) affirming regeneration and conversion through the Word of God as the seed (life principle) thereof (James 1:18; I Pet. 1:23-25) and b)

the record of the book of Acts, demonstrating that it was so both from the beginning of the church and throughout the *inspired* record of church history.

9. The commission a) to the Messiah, as reported in Isaiah 42:6,7 and 61:1,2, and b) to Paul, with respect to the Gentiles, Acts 13:46,47. In each case His purpose is said to be accomplished through preaching.

10. The fact that whatever is ascribed to the Holy Spirit in the work of conversion is ascribed also to the Scripture, and conversely. There is never any hint of contradiction in the testimony given, or the requirements enjoined.

11. The fact that those who resisted the Word of God and/or the persons who proclaimed it, are said to have resisted the Holy Spirit.

12. The fact that the strivings of the prophets through their words are represented as the strivings of the Holy Spirit. (This argument is the same in principle as No. 11. Campbell apparently was not hung up on the number thirteen).

13. The most sublime and impressive fact that nowhere, and at no time has God operated apart from his word, either in creation or in redemption. The *naked* Spirit of God has never operated on the *naked* spirit of man.

Mr. Campbell applied this argument extensively, and effectively also. He drove home the point that even in the creation of the physical universe God operated through his Word. He spoke things into existence and established them in their order. (See Gen. 1:1,3,6,9,11,14,20,22,24,26,28. Cp. John 1:1-4,14; Heb. 11:3.) He thus reasoned:

1) God operated on vacuity, bringing forth entity out of nothingness through his Word. 2) He then operated upon entity, bringing order out of chaos. Mass and motion became a "cosmos" (order), a "universe" (that which turns as a unit, a unified system) by his Word. 3) He then brought forth life forms out of inorganic matter by his Word. 4) Now that he has in man a being capable of receiving, understanding and responding to His Word, how illogical it would be to by-pass the use of his Word and address man apart therefrom. It is written, "Come let us reason together, saith Jehovah" (Isa. 1:18).

14

INSPIRATION OF THE SCRIPTURES

PART ONE

My basic and unwavering conviction as to the inspiration of the Holy Scriptures is well summed up by two familiar passages of Scripture, II Timothy 3:16,17 and II Peter 1:20,21, to wit:

> All scripture is "God-breathed" (Gr. *theo-pneustos*), and is profitable for doctrine, for reproof, for correction, for instruction in righteousness, that the man of God may be "fitted," "completed," (Gr. *artios*), for every good work having been "outfitted" (Gr. *ex-artizo*).

for:

> Knowing this first, that no prophecy of Scripture is of private interpretation, for no prophecy ever came by the will of man: but holy men spoke from God, being borne (Gr. *pheromenoi*) by the Holy Spirit.

Obviously no one of us can lay claim to having originated that definition of inspiration. For if we are jointly indebted to the apostles, Paul and Peter. They were no doubt speaking primarily of the Scriptures we know as the Old Testament. But it is inconceivable that the revelation which has come to us through Jesus Christ and his Spirit-filled apostles would be given to us through less authoritative channels or with less safeguards than the Scriptures of the "prophets" (spokesmen) who spoke (and wrote) for God before them.

In all sincerity I can attest I have never been inclined to question what is stated in the texts cited above. Hence, it has long been my confidence that when I have taken the pains to research every passage of Scripture which touches upon a topic of Divine revelation, and have come to a conclusion in harmony with "the whole counsel of God" (to borrow a phrase from Paul, Acts 20:28), I, (even I!) have the mind of the Spirit concerning the truth God has seen fit to reveal unto us — "upon whom the ends of the ages are come" (I Cor. 10:11).

DEFINITION OF TERMS

1. Inspiration

Imagine yourself holding a Bible in one hand and a brown paper bag in the other. How might you describe them? You might say the Bible is "inspired." The brown bag is a rather flat mundane utility item. Now pucker the opening of the bag so that you can blow your breath into it, filling it out. Now the bag is "inspired," that is, it has been "breathed into." That is precisely what our English word "inspired" means. Obviously, however, we are not talking about the same thing when we speak of the Bible as "inspired," and a paper bag we have breathed into as "inspired."

Is "inspiration" the best word to describe the Divine quality that distinguishes the Bible from all other literature? I think not.

270

Even when we qualify the statement by enjoining the expression "the inspiration of the Scriptures by the Holy Spirit" we are still not saying of the Scriptures what Paul said of them in II Timothy 3:16.

Our English words "inspired," and "inspiration" have come into our language via the Latin Vulgate. What they denote, when taken literally, is not what Paul was communicating to Timothy. The Scriptures are not something to which God has simply added dimension by infusing them with an invisible entity. Paul said of the Scriptures that they are *theopneustos* — "God-breathed." *Theopneustos* is a verbal adjective. The word describes the unique essence of the Scriptures. The "breath of God," speaking anthropomorphically (as is often done within the Scripture text), or, perhaps even more succinctly stated, the "Spirit" (*pneuma*) of God, is the Divine causative agent that brought the Scriptures into being. They are not merely infused with a Divine "in-breathing." They are a Divine product emanating from the Spirit of God.

Technically, the Scriptures are not inspired. The writers were! The Scriptures were "given by inspiration," or, to be more exact, (as Peter has stated it), "No prophecy (pronouncement in behalf of God) is of private interpretation, but holy men spake from God, moved (borne along) by the Holy Spirit" (II Pet. 1:20). The NIV comes still closer to saying what Peter and Paul have stated. The NIV translates II Peter 1:20,21 as follows:

> Above all, you must understand that no prophecy of Scripture came about by the prophet's own interpretation. For prophecy never had its origin in the will of man, but men spoke from God as they were carried along by the Holy Spirit.

So too with I Timothy 3:16,17, the NIV reads:

> All Scripture is God-breathed, and is useful for teaching, rebuking, correcting, and training in righteousness, so that the man of God may be thoroughly equipped for every good work.

2. Revelation

The term "revelation" also needs to be properly defined if we are to grasp clearly the Divine essence of the Scriptures. This word also came into our language via the Latin Vulgate. The Greek word so translated, (*apocalupsis*), is derived from the preposition *apo*, meaning "from, out of" (as in such words as apostle, apostate) and the verb *kalupto*, meaning "to cover." Hence *apocalupto* means to "uncover, unveil." If we think of a painting, or a piece of sculpture that is shrouded from view until the propitious moment it is to be shown, the apocalypse, the revelation, the unveiling takes place when the shroud is swept away.

For the purpose of this study we shall deal with the terms inspiration and revelation as the two sides of the same coin. By way of a working distinction, in the NT our word revelation pertains primarily to the content of the Scriptures, that is, the message, the truths "revealed" therein. Inspiration applies primarily to the process by which the things God has seen fit to reveal to us came to be written. Other distinctions are possible, but for practical purposes we shall limit our discussion of inspiration and its corollary, revelation, to the intrinsic nature of the Scriptures and the manner in which they came to be written.

Generally speaking, inspiration is a term that may be applied to the total scope of revelation. For example, all the apostles were inspired — even those whose words are not recorded in the book of Acts and who did not write any of our New Testament documents. They certainly were inspired on the day of Pentecost. We are told that "they all spoke as the Spirit gave them utterance" (Acts 2:4). But only what Peter said that day has been preserved for us in writing. Elijah and Elisha are counted among the greatest of the Old Testament prophets. But for reasons unknown to us they were not "moved by the Holy Spirit" to record their preaching for posterity. Our attention therefore will be focused on the phenomena of inspiration and revelation as these relate to

272

what we have received as the written "word of God."

3. Inerrant, Verbal, Plenary Inspiration

Of late it seems not to be enough to simply believe in the inspiration of the Scriptures. The guardians of orthodoxy must now shore up the apostolic pronouncements with a growing list of adjectival incrustations. "Whereunto will this thing grow?"

First it was verbal, then plenary, and now inerrant has been added to the apostles' doctrine of inspiration. The problem is not so much with the growing array of new terms which confront us, but the controversy over the precise sense in which each of the terms is to be understood.

a) Generally speaking, the doctrine of *verbal* inspiration implies that the very *words* of the original manuscripts were chosen by the Holy Spirit. To some verbalists, "implies" is not enough. Their doctrine of verbal inspiration demands that the Holy Spirit did more than prompt the minds of the writers to choose the proper words. They insist the Holy Spirit himself supplied the words — all of them.

b) *Plenary* is a term which denotes fullness. Thus plenary inspiration affirms the Scriptures, at every point, are fully and wholly inspired. Plenary is a term that is applied to the scope, the total compass of the Biblical revelation. All Scripture, from Genesis 1:1 through Revelation 22:21 has been given through the inspiration of the Holy Spirit who supplied the information and guided the penman even in the selection of the words used. Such is the implication of the term plenary inspiration.

c) *Inerrant* is a term which denotes free from error. Whatever a chosen penman touched upon in the course of writing is vouchsafed to be free from any form of error — *in the original manuscripts*. The last clause covers for the fact there are errors, even contradictions in the text of the Scriptures as they have come down to us. But these errors can be blamed on copyists, not the original writers.

In researching the subject of the inspiration of Scriptures there came to mind the words of the late Robert A. Millikan, a renowned scientist of a generation ago. Millikan maintained a strong theistic stance in the American Association for the Advancement of Science. For that he drew censure from some of his colleagues, and from some of the liberal theologians of his day also. In that context Millikan was once asked: "If you had to choose between conservatism and liberalism, which would you choose?" His reply was to the effect that if those were his only options, if he had to choose one instead of the other, and had "no way to take to the woods," he would choose conservatism over liberalism as being more rational.

Through the years I have had occasion to recall those words of Robert Millikan. Often I have found myself in the cross fire between liberalism and conservatism, or fundamentalism (the latter being the term preferred by the right-wing segment of the religious spectrum). As I have intimated, this is one of those occasions.

Why should I want to take to the woods, so to speak? Is that trip necessary? Do I have reservations about the inspiration of the Scriptures? No. I have none. What then is the problem? Permit me to declare myself without equivocation. My view of the Bible is somewhat akin to the old country preacher who, when asked if he really believed all the things the Bible says, answered: "I believe it from cover to cover." And added a moment later: "And I believe the cover also! It says here, 'The Holy Bible.' To that appraisal of this blessed book I say, Amen." I too say, "Amen."

What then is the problem? Simply this: There are those who insist on equating a creedal theory of inspiration with the Bible *per se*. For example, Edward J. Young (*Thy Word is Truth*, p. 49) has declared: "Only one doctrine of inspiration is taught in the Bible, namely that of plenary and verbal inspiration, to which the modern mind is hostile." Note how he seeks to box in and dispose of those who do not assent to his view of inspiration. Any one who thinks otherwise not only is 1) written off as not holding

274

to "the only doctrine of inspiration taught in the Bible," all such persons are 2) branded as "hostile." Despite his name, Dr. Young is resorting to an *old* ruse, and to a theory that finds its authority not in the language of the Scriptures but in creedal dogmatics.

If the only choice open to us is verbal, plenary inspiration as defined by Young, or the rejection of the Scriptures as the inspired Word of God, I will accept (with fingers crossed) Young's creedal dogma. But with respect to the choice before us we are not as hemmed in as Robert Millikan may have felt himself to be. Why take to the woods when we have a better option? We can take the words of Peter and Paul at face value, and maintain intellectual honesty and commitment to Biblical phraseology in the process.

ALTERNATE THEORIES OF INSPIRATION

A variety of theories of inspiration have been promoted through the years, with variants within the compass of most of them. Since there are clues within the Biblical literature to the effect that all the documents were not prompted nor produced in the selfsame manner, likely no theory of inspiration explains the actual penning of each and every book of the Bible. Luke, for example, candidly states he engaged in extensive research before penning the Gospel which bears his name. Such epistles as II and III John appear to be quite impromptu in origin.

1. Natural Inspiration

Modern theological liberalism has advanced what is called the theory of natural inspiration. No, what you have just read is not a misprint. Liberals also speak of the Scriptures as "inspired." But theirs is a doctrine of natural as distinguished from supernatural origin for the documents which make up our Bible. The theory is that some people are by nature more perceptive, more observant and intuitive than others. And they are more gifted in expressing themselves.

According to this matrix the Bible is simply a collection of some of the more sublime writings of sensitive and creative minds of bygone days. The Scriptures may well be read for their exalted insights and rhetoric, but are not to be regarded as authoritative, as though in some way they are communicating to us the will of God. Other writings, we are told, are equally deserving of our attention. (Whenever someone states that, you may well surmise that the person saying so considers his (or her) insights to be in the same exalted category.)

The papists hold to a doctrine of Scripture which has some affinity to the foregoing. The papists would have us believe that the Bible is but a "paper pope," exalted by the heretic reformers to replace the Vatican pope whose true and on going authority they had rejected. But the truth is, men looked to the Scriptures for authority and enlightenment long before the first pope made his appearance.

Jesus and his apostles, in no uncertain terms, made it clear they regarded the Old Testament Scriptures as the Word of God. The New Testament writers wrote in the same vein. They were not just writing *of* God and His Christ, but *for* Him, being moved by the Holy Spirit.

2. Verbal, Plenary Inspiration

At the other extreme is the traditional orthodox position, commonly called verbal, plenary inspiration — a rather rigid, inflexible matrix to which of late a third qualifying term, "inerrant," has been added. The primary definition of such terms, is as follows.

Plenary is a term derived from the Latin *plenus*, from which stems such words as plenty, plentiful, plenitude. The root denotes that which is full or complete. When applied to the doctrine of inspiration the main thrust of the term is that the Scriptures in their entirety, Genesis through Revelation, are the written word of God, and all sufficient for faith and conduct. In theory, creeds may be employed to condense, highlight and systemize the truth of the Scripture but not to add thereto or take away therefrom.

Verbal is a shortened form of the Latin, *verbalis*, derived from the root, *verbum*. Verbal is defined as: "of, or pertaining to, words." Applied to the doctrine of inspiration the term is used to teach that "the superintendency of the Holy Spirit extended even to the choice of words used by the original writer." This assumption has caused the verbal, plenary inspiration theory to be called the robot, mechanical dictation theory of inspiration. Advocates chafe at that suggestion. Nonetheless they insist that unless the superintendency of the Holy Spirit included the choice of words it would not have been plenary. We will have occasion to return to this juggling exercise in semantics.

Inerrant has been added of late to the affirmative statement. The Scriptures are said to be without error in all that they teach and report. I find no fault with that affirmation. But I do find fault with what proponents often thereby insist the Scriptures "teach and report."

3. Neo-Orthodox Mediating(?) Matrix

At this juncture the Neo-Orthodox have stepped in to offer what they consider a mediating position. Since "the truth, the whole truth and nothing but the truth" is rarely found on any subject at the extremes to which divergent human thought extends, the Neo-orthodox attempt to provide a viable option should at least be noted.

The Neo-orthodox propose that the Bible *per se* is not the Word of God, but it does contain the Word of God. This solution(?) presents more problems than it solves. Such a conjecture makes every scripture a matter of private interpretation. If the Bible is not in its entirety the Word of God, if it only contains the word of God, (as the proverbial woman's purse may contain a sum of money along with an encyclopedic array of other things), then it is left to each of us to decide what is and what is not the Word of God. Of course the scholars who have brought that insight to light would be pleased to have us accept their own enlightening criteria. But they are not always around when a troublesome doctrine claims one's attention. And there is no agreement from one to another as to what is or what is not the kernel of Divine revelation amid the seed pods of wisdom which man's wisdom teaches.

Neo-orthodoxy may seem to offer the best of both worlds, but they have yet to come forth with a set of viable guidelines whereby we can objectively determine which book, and/or which chapters, and which verses are the Word of God scattered here and there amid the word of man. If that is the only option offered to those caught in the cross fire between liberalism and fundamentalism one is again tempted to head for the tall timber in the hope of getting away from it all. But there is another option.

4. The Doctrine of Noematical Inspiration

For some years my study of the Scriptures has led me to set forth the doctrine of noematical inspiration. The key word stems from the Greek *noema*, "thought," hence noematical means: "pertaining to thought." In that words are "vehicles of thought," the means by which thoughts best travel intact from one mind to another is through oral or written communication. We speak therefore of thought not abstractly; of thought in its ethereal form. We speak of thought in its communicable form whereby one mind devises a means of communicating and inter-relating with another. Noematical inspiration, as God's *modus operandi* for the writing of the Scriptures, implies that:

> The office and work of the Holy Spirit, operating in the context of the inspiration of the Scriptures, may be described as a super-natural influence exerted upon the minds of the divinely chosen writers, whereby their writings may be unequivocably called the Word of God.

Such a matrix is 180° removed from the leftist liberal doctrine of natural inspiration. At the same time it is at some distance removed to the right from the neo-orthodox position. But it is somewhat to the left of the fundamentalist dogma of verbal, mechanical inspiration. One never needs to apologize for being somewhat to the left of fundamentalism. As a people we stand somewhat to the left of the so-called fundamentalists with regard to many things — the dogma of inherited Adamic guilt, salvation by faith only, eternal security, the ultimate and utter rout of the church to be superseded by a physical, premillennial, Jewish oriented earthly kingdom — these are only a part of the nefarious package.

FUNDAMENTALISTS' DENIALS STATED AND MET

Leading fundamentalist theologians hotly deny that they, "or any other reputable evangelical scholar teaches, or has ever taught a doctrine of mechanical dictation." That disturbs me. Not only was I so taught, in turn I taught the same to others. That makes the two instructors who had the greatest influence on my life during my college and seminary days "disreputable scholars." And by the same token I was then "disreputable" also. But in whose sight? Not in the sight of those who championed the inspiration and credibility of the Scriptures. Here, word for word, is an illustration I copied from the lecture notes of a highly respected professor during my college days:

> While awaiting a train in the cavernous waiting room of the Union Station at St. Louis, Missouri, I saw a pen writing upon a scroll, though there was no hand to guide it. My curiosity aroused, I inquired about the purpose and the mechanics of what I was seeing. I learned that the Trainmaster, in an office above, was receiving information concerning the vast network of rails converging at that place. He was using the device I was seeing to dispatch instructions to the trainmen below. Aware that were his instructions blared over a public address system they might be garbled or even unheard amid the rumble of the crowd, and the noise of the frequent arriving and departing trains, he took up a special pen and wrote his instructions word for word. Through wizardy of electronics and engineering the very words he wrote were duplicated by other pens on scrolls below. There, what he wrote above could be read and reread, understood and obeyed. Moreover, they were preserved as a record against any one who might misread and disobey.

That, my instructor explained, is somewhat the way we got the Bible. God, in heaven, took up (as it were) his pen and wrote. Through the power of the Holy Spirit controlling chosen penmen, what God wills for us to know and do came to be written on earth below.

If that is the way we got the Bible inspiration might then be defined as:

> A supernatural influence exerted upon the fingers of chosen penmen, by means of which their writings are no more to be attributed to their authorship than a letter I compose and give to a secretary to type and mail could rightly be called her letter.

As a young preacher I was intrigued by the illustration, and so were those who heard me speak of it. Consequently the first time I visited St. Louis, although travelling by car, a visit to the union station was given high priority. It was true. In fact, not just one but several such pens were to be seen in operation. Every one hun-

280

dred feet or so in that vast waiting room there were stands with slanted glass panels through which one could observe the phenomenon of a pen writing, in long hand no less, just as though a man were doing it. In a sense one was. "The man upstairs" (pardon the expression), the train master, was actually writing the words which were appearing below.

But is that really the way we got our Bible? Was it first written above and then transmitted to earth as the Holy Spirit dictated verbatim the words which were first formed in the mind of God and then transmitted by penmen to scrolls here below? In a manner of speaking, one might say that. But would that be literally, actually so? One should never confuse an illustration of a thing with the thing itself.

One cannot but wonder how and why fundamentalist writers of commentaries and books in the area of Biblical Introduction see no inconsistency in the fact they settle the question of the authorship of anonymous Biblical documents by noting that certain words, or expressions or ideas are typically "Pauline," or "Johannine," etc. If "the superintendency of the Holy Spirit extends even to the words that are chosen," how and why may we make a case for one writer over and above another on the basis of vocabulary, style or emphases?

Are we misreading the fundamentalists and hard-line plenary verbal inspirationists? James A. Packer, *Fundamentalism and the Word of God*, seems to say so, in so many words. Note the following citation (p. 79),

> Because evangelicals hold that the Biblical writers were *completely* controlled by the Spirit, it is often supposed that they maintain what is called the "dictation theory" of inspiration . . . but it is not so. The dictation theory is a man of straw. It is safe to say that no Protestant theologian from the reformation until now has ever held to it.

Packer goes on to cite fourteen well known evangelicals (including Benjamin Warfield, Frank Gaebelein, Louis Gaussen, and

Eric Sauer) all protesting they "do not hold to any such theory." So too with Rene Pache. In his widely touted work, *The Inspiration and the Authority of the Scriptures*, Pache refers to the protestation cited above, and adds (in effect) his name to the list. That should close the case. But in the very next chapter (Ch. 7, "Plenary and Verbal Inspiration") Pache asks: "What do we mean by plenary and verbal inspiration?" Suppose we allow him to tell us, lest we be suspected of misrepresenting him.

> The church has held from the beginning that the Bible is the Word of God in the sense that its words, though written by men and bearing indelibly impressed upon them the marks of their human origin, nevertheless were written under such influence of the Holy Ghost as to be the Word of God.

That is a rather standard definition of inspiration. Aside from his usage of the medieval term, Holy Ghost, I have no quarrel with it. But now hear the rest of the quotation. Pache continues as follows:

> It has also been recognized that this conception of co-authorship implies that the Spirit's superintendency extends to the choice of the words by the human authors, (verbal inspiration, but not mechanical dictation). (The brackets are Pache's.)

He lost me. With a concession to the proverbial "amen corner" he found himself affirming what he seems to have quickly sensed to be inconsistent with what he had written in the paragraph cited above. His bracketed disclaimer does not bail him out. Perhaps "mechanical dictation" is not the best term. Even under hypnosis a person is not a mechanical instrument. But the semantic problem is Pache's, not mine.

A DISTINCTION WITHOUT A DIFFERENCE

It seems to me some of the fundamentalists are making a

distinction without a difference. If the superintendency of the Holy Spirit "extended even to the choice of words" (which is what *verbal* inspiration is all about, that is the very essence of verbal inspiration. That is why it is called "verbal" inspiration. How then, we beg to ask, do the various books "bear indelibly impressed upon them the marks of their human writers"?

Suppose I order you to sit down at a desk with a loaded revolver pressed against the base of your skull. And suppose I order you to write a ransom note. And suppose my superintendency over you, via the gun barrel pressed against the back of your head, extends even to the choice of the very words you are "moved" to write. When you have finished how much of your personality, your mind, your feelings will be "indelibly impressed" upon your literary producton?

If God wanted to convey to us the idea that he chose even the words that were penned by the forty or more Biblical writers, he could have very easily have done so. All he would have needed to do would be to cause each writer to write in a style and vocabulary distinctly different from his common mode of self-expression.

For example, had the Holy Spirit "moved" Paul to write in a style completely obscurant of his specialized background and normal manner of speaking, God could have demonstrated thereby who was in control of the literary work that was being circulated. But what would God have gained thereby? If Paul's personality, his hopes and dreams, his "gut feelings," his recollections, his *humanness*, if these things were not a part of the letters he penned, then why "move" him to pen letters?

Why did not God just have Paul pen doctrinal and moral essays? Or, except for the fact the recipients might be more inclined to read what was written if it bore Paul's signature, God could just as well have used some unemployed scribe, and left Paul free to preach and teach by word of mouth.

That suggests another possibility. If God had used some illiterate nobody to write in the weighty, logical rhetoric we find in the book of Romans all would be obliged to concede that the Biblical writers contributed little more than the pen, ink, parchment, and the skill to take dictation and reduce it to writing, word for word. That would be verbal, and perhaps inspiration, but would it be "inspirational"?

Consider too the case of Luke. Except for what he may have gained in personal satisfaction, the research of which he makes mention in the prologue to the gospel that bears his name was pretty much wasted, if the superintendency of the Holy Spirit exercised such control over the chosen writers that is extended even to the choice of words.

PART TWO

THE CASE FOR NOEMATICAL THEOPNEUSTOS
INSPIRATION RESTATED

Noematical inspiration much more accurately describes, and hence more correctly defines, the phenomena of our Sacred Scriptures than does the doctrine of word for word dictation, alias verbal inspiration. Granted, when pressed, contenders for verbal inspiration attempt at least to explain they do not actually teach word for word dictation. Why then use terminology which, when taken at face value, suggests that one does so?

In the noematical matrix God is said to have illuminated the minds of his chosen spokesman and penmen. In so doing God so quickened and guided their thought processes that as each of them spoke and/or wrote, while "moved by the Holy Spirit" (II Pet. 1:21), they expressed what God wanted to be said, likely very much in the manner He Himself would have done were He incarnate among them, and shared their tongue and experience. In fact that very thing God's only begotten Son actually did in the days of His earthly ministry.

The Gospels make it very clear that when "the Word became

flesh and dwelt among us" He used the vocabulary common to the people among whom he sojourned, and became in all things like as we are — except for this: "He was full of grace and truth." He was not only without sin, he was the epitome of Truth in all that he said.

Let us now pick up again on a point we touched upon earlier. Every writer, whether in the Old Testament or the New, employs his own distinctive vocabulary and writing style. Moses, schooled in all the wisdom of the Egyptians, was a master of both prose and poetry. His magnificent summation of creation is balanced by his artful ability to narrate the flow of history. The story of Joseph, to which Moses devotes the final one-fourth of the book of Genesis, has been hailed by literary critics as the most perfectly told story in all literature. The scope of subject matter in the Pentateuch reflects both Moses' education and experience. But it also reflects insights which could only come by way of Divine revelation.

Consider the opening sentence of the book of Genesis. What a magnificent and comprehensive opener. In just seven words (the very number is significant) Moses picks upon the four innate ideas which are now seen to be our basic tools of learning — time, space, cause and being. And in seven words Moses employs all four of those comprehensive concepts to the miracle and magnitude of creation, in each case taking the mind back to the origin of all things — and that to the point where human comprehension merges with infinity.

	3.	2.	1.
	ELoHim	BaRa	BeReSHiTH
	God	created	Beginning

7.	6.	5.	4.
Ha-aRets	Ve-eTH	HaSHaMaYiM	eTH
(the) earth	and	heavens	(the)

Note: Hebrew reads from right to left as indicated by numbers.

285

Consider also the writings of the courtly Isaiah, the prince among the prophets of Israel; Saul of Tarsus, the scholarly rabbi; Amos, the country preacher; Mark, the activist, the "get-with-it" writer, the assistant and understudy of impetuous Peter; David, the shepherd king; Luke, the physician turned historian; Solomon, the philosopher; James, the half-brother of Jesus who devoted his whole ministry to the church at Jerusalem — name whom you will, every writer has the distinctive style and vocabulary. And, as has already been noted, even those who insist on word-for-word dictation (or whatever each of them may prefer to call it) backhandedly acknowledge the same when they decide who wrote what by noting that certain words and forms of expression are characteristic of certain writers.

The personality and vocabulary of every Biblical writer is indeed "indelibly impressed upon what they have written." From Genesis to Revelation there is a constantly changing pattern of rhetorical style, imagery, idiom and dialect.

NO NEW PROBLEM

The problem with which we are dealing is no new issue, born of the strife twixt modern theological liberalism and creed-bound fundamentalism. A hundred years ago, Isaac Errett, editor and founder of *The Christian Standard*, and the renowned John W. McGarvey carried on an extended discussion of this very subject. Errett, defining verbal inspiration as the mechanical dictation theory, rejected it. McGarvey, ever mindful of his role as the champion of orthodoxy, and with an ear to the "amen corner," maintained the view in question and rose to its defense. Yet, all the while he did so, he apparently no more believed in mechanical, verbal inspiration than I do.

In his classic work, *Evidences of Christianity*, J.W. McGarvey saw fit to liken the relationship between the Biblical writers and the Holy Spirit to that which exists between a well trained horse and the rider. McGarvey noted that generally such a horse is given a rather free rein. While the reins are constantly in the hands of the rider, they are commonly held loosely. The horse, sensing the mood of the rider, and often even where the rider cares to go, moves at a pace pleasing to the master, and only occasionally needs some overt guidance to quicken or slow the pace, or to veer to the right or the left. So too with the Divinely directed writers whose very thoughts were subject to the control of the Holy Spirit, (p. 273).

That makes sense — horse sense! Applied upwards, the concept illustrated is best defined as *Theopneustos* Noematical Inspiration. If we are speaking of the source of the Biblical revelation the term *Theopneustos* should come to mind. If the emphasis is upon the content of the revelation the term noematical is apropos. The Scriptures were not communicated in the verbage of our modern languages. But God's thoughts, "written for our admonition upon whom the ends of the ages are come," can become our thoughts when words familiar to us in our language are used to communicate the message which were aforetime written in Hebrew and Greek.

THE MOVING OF THE SPIRIT OF GOD

The "moving" of the Spirit of God is mentioned at the very outset of the Biblical revelation. Almost immediately following the sweeping statement with which the Scriptures open (Gen. 1:1), it is written: "and the Spirit of God moved upon the face of the deep" (v. 2b). How so? At every point the operation of the Spirit of God in the work of creation is linked with the "word of God" (cp. John 1:1-3) by the repetition of the phrase: "And God said . . . ." And it was so! Immediately God's mind and/or word materialized in the thing He purposed to come into being, and/or come to pass.

Once the created order was complete, God has since "upheld

all things by the word of his power" (Heb. 1:3). The miracle of creation gave way to the more ordinary activity of God which by reason of its constancy (and observable routine) has come to be called "natural law."

This observation has its parallel in the spiritual realm, as it affects the working of the human will and mind to this day. It is written: "God, having of old time spoken unto the father in the prophets in diverse portions and in diverse manners, has at the end of these days spoken unto us in His Son, whom he appointed heir of all things" (Heb. 1:1,2).

Men *moved* (Gr. *pheromenoi*, "borne") by the Holy Spirit are no longer writing Scriptures. But that is not to say the Holy Spirit is not moving in the hearts and minds of mankind today; only that he is not doing so in the same extraordinary (supernatural) way.

The nearest analogy we can offer from experience to the compulsive influence of the Holy Spirit, particularly in the sense of one being "borne along" by the Spirit (II Pet. 1:21), or "led of the Spirit" (Matt. 4:1; Rom. 8:14; Gal. 5:18), is that compulsion felt in the heart of every true preacher of the Word. Ronald Ward in his *Commentary on First and Second Timothy*, has expressed it in this fashion, (p. 200):

> Try to persuade one who knows himself to be called of God to quit the ministry. Try to silence him. Offer him huge sums of money to quit the proclamation of the Word. Bait him with the assurance he not only can make more money doing something else, but his evenings and weekends will be his to do with as he pleases. You may tempt him, but you will not turn him. He must preach. "Woe is me," his heart will cry out, "if I preach not the gospel of Christ" (cp. I Cor. 9:16).

Paul was neither the first nor the last to thus express himself. Jeremiah felt such compulsion, and the tension that attends it when "the spirit is willing but the flesh is weak." Thus Jeremiah wrote:

> If I say, I will not mention him, or speak any more in his name, his

word is in my heart like a burning fire, shut up in my bones. I am weary with holding it in; Indeed I cannot (Jer. 20:9, NIV).

This does not make of a preacher a mere puppet, a programmed robot. Granted we are being driven, and we know it. But as one who unfurls a sail to the swelling breeze, or as one who gives free rein to a spirited steed, we are being "laid hold upon," but we are also "laying hold on that for which we have been laid hold on by Christ" (Phil. 3:12). We are "bondservants of Christ," but it is not forced labor. It is fellowship in a labor of love.

The difference between the apostles and prophets, and ourselves, is not that they were borne along by the Holy Spirit, and we are not. It is found in the role expressed by a second word needing to be noted in the context of this study — Revelation, particularly what is called "special" revelation.

REVELATION

In its broadest sense, revelation is the sum total of all the ways and means by which God has made himself, his works, and his will, known to man, Categorically, revelation is of two orders: 1) general revelation and 2) special revelation.

1. *General revelation* is God's witness to himself for all to behold. That is, it is such revelation as is not restricted to a specific person or people. When the psalmist wrote, "The heavens declare the glory of God and the firmament shows his handiwork" (Psa. 19:1), he was speaking of God's general revelation. Likewise when Paul wrote in Romans 1:20: "The invisible things of him (God) since the creation of the world are clearly seen, being perceived through the things that are made, even his everlasting power and divinity," he was speaking of general revelation. Nature is God's primary vehicle of general revelation.

Nature has been called "God's Book of *Works*," and the Bible "God's Book of *Words*." Nature tells us *that* God is, whereas the Bible tells us *what* (or *who*) God is. And, because of who he is, the Bible tells us what he has a right to require of us because of what and who we are.

At times, as when God called Moses through the burning bush (Exod. 3:2), and when he drew the multitude together on Pentecost by a sound as of a rushing mighty wind (Acts 2:2), God used objects and forces of nature as vehicles of special revelation. But in all such cases nature was caused to behave in an *unnatural* manner. The revelation which came through some object or force of nature was in the order of a *special* revelation in that it was designed for the attention of a specific person or limited company.

2. The Bible is the record, the resume of God's *special* revelation. From the Bible we would soon learn, even if the epistle to the Hebrews had not mentioned it, that "God, in former times spoke unto the fathers in the prophets, in diverse portions and in diverse manners" (Heb. 1:1). Special revelation indeed took a variety of forms.

a. *Dreams.* Sometimes God spoke through dreams. In a revelatory dream the human mind served as a screen on which the Divine mind was reflected. It was not so much a case of the person being "caught up," but rather a case of the revelation *coming down* to man. For this reason dreams have been called "the lowest form of special revelation." Be that as it may, some of the most significant revelations God has given were communicated through dreams.

b. *Visions.* Special revelations have also been given through visions. The principal difference between dreams and visions is that in a dream the subject is wholly passive, in a sub-conscious state. The message being communicated comes into the conscious mind only after the subject has awakened. In the instance of King Nebuchadnezzar's image dream the delay was even greater. He could remember only that he had a dream of extraordinary nature. Apparently he could recall no part of it until Daniel providentially related to him both the substance of his dream and the interpretation (Dan. 2).

In a vision the subject is fully conscious. Isaiah's compelling call to the prophetic office came to him through an exalted vision of Jehovah while he was worshipping in the temple (Isa. 6). Peter's three-fold vision of a sheet let down from heaven, and the verbal instruction which accompanied it, came to him while he was praying on the housetop of his own dwelling (Acts 10:9-16).

In either case, whether by dream or by vision, both mediums of revelation include elements of both visual and auditory communication. For example, John, in the closing chapter of the Apocalypse writes: "I, John, am he that heard and saw these things, and when I heard and saw I fell down to worship before the feet of him that showed me these things" (Rev. 22:8).

The term vision focuses attention primarily upon what is seen. But unlike the old fashioned silent movies, the characters appearing in revelatory visions occupied speaking roles. This was not always so of dreams. Witness the case of Nebuchadnezzar's image-dream. Apparently nothing audible, either by way of instruction or explanation, accompanied what he "saw."

c. *Theophanies.* A third form of special revelation came through what has come to be called "theophanies." The term itself is not used in the Scriptures. It is one that has been coined to provide a technical name for a variety of unique manifestations of the Divine presence. The term is derived from the Greek words: *theos* (God) and *phaino*, (to appear, to become manifest). Manifestations of God commonly called theophanies were generally in the from of an angel. Moses' viewing of "God's backside" (Exod. 33:20-25) is regarded as a very special theophany.

Many of the visions of God recorded in the Scriptures are sometimes reckoned as theophanies. The primary distinction lies in the fact that visions were generally experienced while the viewer was in a trance, or experiencing a revelatory dream. Since the

291

term is of theological origin, and not found in the Scriptures *per se*, we shall not labor the distinction between theophanies and visions or dreams.

d. *Angels*. God has also revealed his will to men through the visitation of Divine messengers designated as angels. Again, there is some overlapping of terminology. Both the Hebrew word *malak*, translated "angel," and the Greek word *angelos*, transliterated "angel," simply denote generically a "messenger" or "agent." The Scriptures make mention, by name, of several "angels" God sent in person, versus a vision or dream of an angelic manifestation. The angel of the annunciation was Gabriel (Luke 1:19-26). Michael is called in Daniel 12:3 "one of the chief princes," and in Jude 9, "the archangel." The appearance of angels was almost always to bear directives calling for immediate action, and/or to announce matters of prime and imminent concern.

e. *Anthropomorphisms*. This anglicized term is compounded from the Greek word for man (*anthropos*) and the word for form (*morphe*). Hence the term is used of any manifestation of God in the form of a man. It is also used to refer to figures of speech in which human traits, feelings and/or features are attributed to God. Scriptures which speak of God's "out-stretched arm," or his eyes, ears, hands, feet, etc., are anthropomorphic expressions. And when "an angel of the Lord" or, on occasion (as at the birth of Christ) a company of angels, came down to talk with men, this too is called anthropomorphism. They served as channels of Divine revelation.

Appearances of such beings may be designated as anthropomorphisms in that those who appeared to men (in both testaments) came in human form, using human speech (versus some "esoteric heavenly language," cp. I Cor. 13:1). And they appeared always in human form, and, pardon the male chauvinism(?), always as males, and without mention of wings, blue eyes and blond hair.

CHRIST: THE SUPREME REVELATION OF GOD

The supreme example of anthropomorphic revelation, indeed the pinnacle of revelation, is found in the incarnation of God in Christ. Paul has said of him that though he "existed in the form (morphe) of God . . . he emptied himself (of that high estate), taking the form (morphe) of a servant" (Phil. 2:6,7). He speaks also of "the light of the knowledge of the glory (being seen) in the face of Jesus Christ" (II Cor. 4:6). John's phrasing of it is; "The word became flesh and dwelt among us, and we beheld his glory, glory as of the only begotten from the Father, full of grace and truth" (John 1:14).

As has been noted, Hebrew 1:1,2 states categorically that in former times God spoke unto the father through the prophets, in various forms and manners, "But at the end of these days he has spoken unto us in his Son" (Heb. 1:1,2). The implication is that the revelation of God in Christ is God's supreme and final revelation in the sphere of time. Paul picks up on that in II Thessalonians, saying: "at the revelation of the Lord Jesus from heaven, with the angels of his power in flaming fire," his coming shall be in judgment. For he shall then "render vengeance upon them that know not God and obey not the Gospel." Such shall "suffer punishment, even eternal destruction from the face of God and the glory of his might" (II Thess. 1:7-9).

A BASIC PRINCIPLE OF REVELATION

It has well been noted that the perfection of any revelation depends upon the perfection of the medium through which the revelation is given. I have seen a picture, a single tin-type photograph of my paternal grandmother who died long before I was born. From that picture, and the few things my father recalled from his early boyhood, I have formed some conception of what my grandmother was like. But suppose there were a

45-minute reel of 16mm film, in technicolor, complete with sound track, highlighting her life from early childhood to her untimely death, how much better my conception of her would be.

It is said that Paganini was once imprisoned on false charges, and held for an extended time. He plead for his violin to be brought to him, and it was. But before handing it through the bars his jailor stood just out of reach and broke the strings one by one, until only one string was left. But through incessant practice Paganini learned to so improvise upon that one string that he could evoke more beautiful music from that single string than ordinary violinists can produce from a full stringed violin. But for all his genius, the full harmonies for which the violin was designed can only be brought forth from a fully stringed instrument.

And so it was, when God was ready at long last to reveal himself to man in the highest mode of revelation of which the soul of finite man is capable of receiving, God chose not a snow-capped mountain, nor the sun, nor a blazing comet, nor an angel or the seraphim — not even a literary collection to be called the Bible, but in the fullness of time, into a human soul, God sent forth his Son, made flesh that he might dwell as an examplar among us. Thus it is written, "in Him dwelt all the fullness of the Godhead bodily" (Col. 2:9). And thus he could say: "He that has seen me has seen the Father also" (John 14:9).

The Bible is the written revelation of God, the resume of God's special revelation through the prophets and apostles. But Christ is God's supreme revelation of Himself, and of his will and purpose for man, this side of heaven.

CONCLUSION

What has the incarnation of God in Christ to do with the inspiration of the Scriptures? Just about everything. 1) Christ, "the power of God and the wisdom of God" (I Cor. 1:24), expressed implicit trust in the Scriptures which had come down to his generation. Every part of the Old Testament canon — the law, the prophets, the psalms — Christ vouchsafed to be the sure word of God (Luke 24:44). Moreover, 2) he made personal provision for the writing of the New Covenant scriptures. Let us recall once again that significant statement to which we have had occasion to refer over and over again in this study: "God, having of old time spoken unto the fathers in the prophets by diverse portions and in diverse manners, has at the end of these days spoken unto us in his Son" (Heb. 1:1,2).

How so? How could he, when the whole of the NT was written after he departed from this earth? How? Through the apostles whom he had chosen, to whom he showed himself alive after his passion, and to whom he gave the promise:

> I will pray the Father, and he will send you another comforter . . . even the Spirit of truth . . . He will bring to your remembrance all things which I said unto you . . . and shall guide you into all the truth (John 14:16,26; 16:13).

It is a fact of no small consequence that before the apostle John was allowed to write the last lines of the final book of the Bible, Christ intervened to place his seal and endorsement upon the book that was drawing to a close, saying:

> I, Jesus have sent mine angel to testify unto you these things for the churches. I am the root and the offspring of David, the bright and the morning star . . . . I testify unto every man that hears the words of the prophecy of this book, if any man shall add unto them, God shall add unto him the plagues which are written in this book. And if any man take away from the words of this prophecy, God shall take away his part from the tree of life, and out of the holy city, which are written in this book. He that testifies these things, says: Yea, I come quickly (Rev. 22:18-20a).

To that John adds, "Amen: Come, Lord Jesus," and pens this final salutation: "The grace of the Lord Jesus be with the saints. Amen" (vv. 20b,21). Amen, indeed! Come, Lord Jesus!

POSTSCRIPT

From the foregoing it should be obvious that the Biblical doctrine of inspiration cannot be fitted into as rigid a mold as some demand, nor thinned to the degree others would prefer. As concerns the first, Hebrews 1:1 cannot be gainsayed. God indeed "spoke unto the fathers through the prophets in diverse forms and diverse manners." God is not bound. He is free to communicate what, and with whom, and as he wills.

For those who want a simple definitive statement, and for those who would prefer a statement inclusive enough to touch bases all around, we offer the following as a closing expression of personal fatih:

The activity of God commonly called the inspiration of the Scriptures was a Divine influence exerted by the Holy Spirit upon the mind and the will of chosen scribes whereby their writings were endowed with Divine trustworthiness.

I close therefore as I began. My basic and unwavering conviction is summed up by two familiar apostolic affirmations, to wit:

All Scripture is God-breathed (Gr. *Theo-pneustos*) and is profitable for doctrine, for reproof, for correction, and for instruction which is in righteousness, that the man of God may be complete, thoroughly furnished unto *every* good work (II TIm. 3:16,17),

for:

No prophecy of Scripture is of private interpretation (Gr. *epilusis*), for no prophecy ever came by the will of man: but men spoke from God, being moved (Gr. *pheromenoi*, lit., "being borne along") by the Holy Spirit (II Pet. 1:20,21).

Amen.

EPILOGUE

THE HOLY SPIRIT AND YOU

Did you receive the Holy Spirit when you believed? Yes, you, the reader of what we have set forth. The intent of this study was not merely to discuss the subject of the person and work of the Holy Spirit academically, although that needs to be done, but to bear in mind that when we speak of the Holy Spirit in the context of the Scriptures we are contemplating the mission of one sent forth from God to "convict us of sin and of righteousness and of judgment" (John 16:8-11), and to dwell within those who thereupon have been sanctified.

The question before us is one the apostle Paul asked of twelve disciples he encountered upon his arrival in Epheus (Acts 19:2). His question was not accusatory. He did not suggest they were not believers, or that they had not repented and/or had not been baptized. To the contrary he appears to have assumed they had heard the gospel and had responded positively. But he sensed there was something lacking. He therefore asked a second leading question.

Their answer has suffered in translation. Literally, they responded by saying, "we heard not if there is (a) Holy Spirit" (v. 2b.) The phrase "is given" is a translator's gloss. From their response we see that Paul's follow-up question brought to light a lack in their instruction. In response to his second question: "into what then were you baptized?" they answered: "into John's baptism." That explains some things. At least for Paul it did. Fortunately, his response explains some things for us.

There was nothing amiss with John's baptism insofar as its mode and purpose was concerned. It consisted of the immersion in water of a penitent believer "for the remission of sins" (Mark 1:4). But apparently the twelve men had received John's baptism out of dispensation.

In the preceding paragraph of the narrative we learn that Apollos, (whose labors in Ephesus preceded the arrival of Paul) "spake and taught accurately the things concerning Jesus" (Acts 18:25), except for one thing. He was not fully informed concerning baptism. In that he has company. Apollos was a prototype of many to this day.

As soon as Paul learned the twelve men not only had not received the Holy Spirit but were unaware of the fact they could (and should) he was afforded one clue as to their problem. Obviously they had not received the baptism Christ enjoined upon penitent believers in what is aptly called the great commission. Christian baptism, the baptism Christ has commissioned for the whole course of the Christian era, not only inducts believers "into (Gr. *eis*) the name of the Father and of the Son of the Holy Spirit" (Matt. 28:19), it is accompanied with the promise of "the gift of the Holy Spirit" (Acts 2:38).

Note Paul did not ask them if they had been baptized. Why should he? They are spoken of as "disciples" (v. 1), and assumed to be believers (v. 2). The currently popular reconstruction of faith and baptism which divorces those two facets of the gospel is a relatively modern phenomenon. Obviously, Paul not only saw a connection between faith and baptism but between Christian baptism and receiving the gift of the Holy Spirit. He sensed the crux of the problem he had encountered did not root in a prototype "faith only" evangelicalism. But the teaching of Apollos, his predecessor in Ephesus, needed updating — and got it, both at Ephesus and at its source (see Acts 18:24-26).

Apparently those discipled by the teaching of Apollos were disciplined also in his openness to new truth. Apollos was not affronted when Priscilla and Acquila took him aside and updated his teaching on baptism. The twelve brethren at Ephesus were of the same teachable disposition, and were immediately rewarded for it. Baptism "in the name of the Lord Jesus" is accompanied by the divine promise of the gift of the Holy Spirit. However, Paul is recorded as doing for them something that he is nowhere reported as doing for others upon their baptism into Christ. He laid his hands upon them, and used his apostolic office to bestow upon them an immediate confirming gift of the Holy Spirit that had been so long denied them by reason of the defect in the teaching they had previously received.

Generally, to receive the Holy Spirit as an indwelling presence is a gift we must at the outset accept by faith. It is some time after we have been begotten physically, in fact even some time after birth before we become acutely aware of our own spirit indwelling and animating our physical body. And it is much longer still before our own distinctive nature, disposition, personality (call it what one will) becomes fully manifest to ourselves and others. Likewise it is also some time before the presence of the Holy Spirit is discerned, and discernible in us.

Let not the foregoing observation be pressed too far, or too rigidly. The time factor is not to be equated between the two. The time factor between "begetting" (by the Spirit) and "the new birth" is most certainly not subject to a nine month's gestation period. No illustration affords a perfect parallel. Of this we will have more to say as we discuss the two questions: How may we know we have received the Holy Spirit? And how may others know we have received the Holy Spirit?

HOW DO WE RECEIVE THE HOLY SPIRIT, AND KNOW WE HAVE DONE SO?

The example of the twelve disciples at Ephesus is especially helpful at this point. They were of a kindred spirit with Apollos, who probably was the one who had imperfectly taught them. When they too had "the way of God expounded unto them more perfectly" they responded as he did. They obeyed the word of God more perfectly.

Nothing is said to the effect they were called upon to repudiate their former teacher. But neither did they exercise an undue loyalty out of appreciation of the fact it was he who had introduced them to Christ. Apollos likewise did not delay his acceptance of the new truth which he learned from Priscilla and Aquila by such a concern as, "what will those I have taught think of me, if I acknowledge my teaching has been faulty at a crucial point?" The fact it is said of him that he was "fervent in spirit" (Acts 19:25) heightened such a possibility. Apollos was not of the "hum ho, so what" mentality.

How can one be fervent in spirit and not be indwelled by the Holy Spirit Paul's adversaries were. Paul said of his Jewish brethren that they had "a zeal for God" (Rom. 10:2) but they certainly were not indwelled by the Holy Spirit. Religious fervor is not necessarily a sign one is led of the spirit. And it is certainly no guarantee that one's teaching should be received unquestioningly.

HOW DOES ONE RECEIVE THE HOLY SPIRIT?

The New Testament does not provide a set pattern, but it

does provide some principles. God has demonstrated that he is not bound by precept or precedent. Cornelius and his household were signally baptized in the Holy Spirit prior to any recorded confession of faith in Jesus as the Christ the Son of the living God, and with no mention of repentance, and prior to (though not exclusive of) baptism in water. But every facet of the account supports the proposition that this was a special case. It does not set a precedent, except for one thing. That was God's way of signally demonstrating to Peter and those with him (and to the church at Jerusalem when they inquired of the matter) that "to the gentiles also God hath granted repentance unto life" (Acts 11:18). Having so demonstrated God did not choose to repeat the performance as Paul, the apostle to the Gentiles and others with him and like him, "spake to the Gentiles also, preaching the Lord Jesus" (Acts 11:20).

The exceptional demonstraton we have just noted should serve to keep us mindful of who is in charge of the giving of the Holy Spirit. But on the other hand, there are some principles to guide us. Our God is not a god of caprice, but of order. Christ, upon the eve of his crucifixion, and again as he was about to leave this earth, spoke of the eminent coming of the Holy Spirit. To his disciples he said: "When he, the Spirit of truth is come, he shall guide you into all the truth" (John 16:13). It is that promise which makes the book of Acts (which immediately, and rightly follows) especially relevant as a source book of information concerning reception of the Holy Spirit.

Such texts as Acts 2:38 and 5:32 are basic to our present inquiry. There is the "gift" of the Holy Spirit as well as "gifts" (pl.) of, i.e., derived from, the Holy Spirit. At this point we are primarily concerned about the former. How do we receive the Holy Spirit as an indwelling presence? The texts to which we have just alluded link reception of the Holy Spirit (as a gift from God) to obedience. Acts 2:38 specifically predicates receipt upon repentance and baptism. Acts 5:32 is more general: "God gives the Holy Spirit to those who obey him."

Obedience is not a "dirty word." It is not the antithesis of faith. It is not an act by which one slams the door on God's grace or provokes him to close the door of his grace against us. It is written even of Christ:

> Though he was a Son, yet learned he obedience by the thing which he suffered, and being made perfect through suffering he became unto all them that obey him the author of eternal salvation (Heb. 5:8,9).

And again:

> Then said I (Christ, through the voice of prophecy) Lo, I am come. (In the roll of the book it is written of me) to do thy will, O God (Heb. 10:7).

How do we receive the Holy Spirit? According to Acts 5:32, God gives the Holy Spirit to them that obey Him. It is significant that in the book of Acts we are promised the gift of the Holy Spirit on the same basis that we are promised the remission of our sins. The guilt-stricken multitude on pentecost, "pricked in their hearts" by Peter's sermon, cried: "What shall we do?" Peter, speaking "as the Spirit gave (him) utterance," answered him, saying:

> Repent, and in the name of (Gr. en, "by," i.e. "by the authority of") Jesus Christ, be baptized for (Gr. eis, "into, unto") the remission of your sins, and ye shall receive the gift of the Holy Spirit, for to you is the promise, and to your children, and to them that are afar off (gentiles) even to as many as the Lord our God shall call unto him (Acts 2:38,39).

About three thousand did what they were told to do, and the Lord did what he promised. They were "added in that day" to those being saved, (v. 41).

302

HOW MAY WE KNOW
THE HOLY SPIRIT ABIDES WITH US?

This is a valid question. The Holy Spirit is not an intruder, nor a guest who overstays his welcome. John records Jesus as speaking of the Holy Spirit as the paraclete (Gr. *para-kletos*, lit. "one called alongside" John 14:16,26; 15:26; 16:7; cp. I John 2:1). In his gospel the term is traditionally translated "comforter." In his epistle the term "advocate" is usually employed. The NIV substitutes a phrase, making the passage to read, "we have one who speaks to the Father in our defense." Howsoever the term is translated the prevailing idea communicated is that of a helper. In Ephesians 4:30 Paul admonishes: "Do not grieve the Holy Spirit of God in whom ye were sealed unto the day of redemption." In Ephesians 3:16 he prays that "we may be strengthened with power through his Spirit in the inward man." Common to all such texts is the underlying idea of one whose presence is not domineering, interfering or unwanted. He is not quick to take umbrage. He doesn't sulk or pout. But he will not abide where he is not wanted.

DOES THE HOLY SPIRIT COME AND GO?

Does the Holy Spirit come and go? This is a moot question. The possibility might be implied from certain OT references such as I Samuel 16:14 which speaks of "the Spirit of Jehovah departing from King Saul, and David's penitential psalm in which he implores God, saying: "take not thy holy Spirit from me" 51:10. Two observations are in order. 1) the term (name?) the *Holy* Spirit is nowhere found in the whole of the OT — Psalms 51:10 and Isaiah 63:10,11 coming the closest to doing so. But the phrasing in the three verses is adjectival, and not nominative. 2) Under the Old Covenant the Spirit of God was not given "across the board" so to speak. The Spirit of Jehovah was rather sparingly, selectively and at times seemingly even arbitrarily bestowed.

THE "LITMUS TEST" OF THE PRESENCE OF THE HOLY SPIRIT

Paul, twice in I Corinthians 10 (vv. 5,11), states that events recorded in the Old Testament "happened unto them by way of example (Gr. *tupon*, from which we have derived such words as type and typical) and are written for our admonition upon whom the end of the ages are come." We can learn something therefore from Saul and David regarding awareness of the presence and/or absence of the Holy Spirit.

There is a certain logic which also bears on the question at hand. We can know the Holy Spirit dwells in us in somewhat the same way we know our own spirit indwells our mortal body. We are alive. We think. We hunger and thirst. We have emotions. Scientists define life as "correspondence of an organism with its environment." For all these there are spiritual parallels. We are alive unto God. Spiritual thoughts occupy our minds — things that are true, honorable, just, pure, lovely and of good report. We hunger and thirst after righteousness. We feed on his Word. We are aware of his love and our love for him. We have joy and peace. We are concerned for the lost. We maintain a conscious correspondence with that spiritual environment which sustains our spirits — the house of his worship and praise, and of our edification, the fellowship of the saints — things which enable the spirit to subdue the flesh and makes our inmost being a hospitable place for the Spirit of God.

There can be no doubt about it. We received the Holy Spirit when we rendered to our God and his Son the obedience of faith, and the Holy Spirit continues to find a habitable place within us. We live and move and have our being in an atmosphere of God-consciousness. For some this may not be enough. Fleshly Israel sought after signs, yet believed not. The witness within abides. Signs are but for a season.

EPILOGUE

THE OTHER SIDE OF "THE COIN OF THE REALM"

In the spiritual realm, as elsewhere, every coin has two sides. The obverse of the criteria of which we have been speaking deserves some attention also. If we cannot say, like David, "I was glad when they said unto me, let us go into the house of the Lord," (Psa. 122:1); if we "forsake our own assembling together, as the custom of some is," (Heb. 10;25); if we do not exhort one another, but rather tend to lead others astray; if we do not search the Scriptures daily to see what things are so; if we have no testimony for Christ, no ready word of praise for him, no eagerness to bring others to him; if we savor and even share the same smut, and profanity of "this (modern) untoward generation"; if we defile our bodies and befoul our breath with the same enslaving addictions; if we "bring forth no fruits worthy of repentance"; in short, if the "works of the flesh" are more manifest in our lives than "the fruit of the Spirit" we have obviously failed to "call alongside" of us the "paraclete, which is the Holy Spirit," according to the word of Christ (John 14:26).

It is written, "as many as are led by the Spirit of God, these are the sons of God" (Rom. 8:14). James has warned that when we go astray "we are led away by our own lusts, and enticed." God, and the Spirit he has sent to be with us, have had no part in the temptation, nor in the lusts which "conceived, bear sin, and which when fullgrown bring forth death" (see James 1:13-15). We do well to recall an oft repeated warning in the Apocalypse: "He that hath ears to hear, let him hear what the Spirit saith to the churches" (Rev. 2:7,11,17,29; 3:6,13,22). The "heavenly dove," as the Holy Spirit is oft called in song, is in no sense, "a dirty bird." His nesting place is a clean heart, a pure mind, a body that is a temple of the Holy Spirit (I Cor. 6:19).

To further the analogy suggested by Luke's description of the descent of the Holy Spirit upon Jesus at his baptism (Luke 3:22), we do well to return to a question touched upon earlier: "Does the Holy Spirit come and go upon us?" It was not so with

305

Jesus. John said of him: "Upon whom you see the Holy Spirit descending, and abiding upon him, the same is he that baptizes in the Holy Spirit," (John 1:33). The saying obviously had immediate reference to the effective "visual aid" God used at Jesus' baptism, but it was also prophetic of what the testimony of Christ's manner of life and ministry would reveal as well.

With ourselves the case is ofttimes different, though it need not be. The "heavenly dove" was not intended to be like the "bird" (shuttlecock) in a badminton game — in and out of our court (heart). Nor is his presence with us actually that "flighty." He is not that easily driven away.

To change the analogy, God's relationship with fleshly Israel and his Son's relationship with spiritual Israel, Christ's church, are likened to the marriage bond. Those bonds were not easily broken. The case of fleshly Israel is evidence of that. Though Israel repeatedly behaved as a harlot (Jer. 2:20; 3:1; Ezek. 16:15,16, etc.) God bore the indignity for generations, even centuries, before he cast her out. But ultimately he did so. The letters to the seven churches of Asia warn that Christ will not forbear forever like behavior on the part of his elect bride, whether it be at the level of the local church — individual congregations, or individual members of congregations. See Revelation 2:5 (Ephesus), 2:14-16 (Pergamum), 2:20-23 (Thyatira), 3:3,4 (Sardis), 3:16,17 (Laodicea). Confuse not the longsuffering of God as slackness, (II Pet. 3:9-13). From of old it is written: "My spirit will not strive with men for ever" (Gen. 6:3).

HOW MAY OTHERS KNOW
WE HAVE THE HOLY SPIRIT?

One question remains: How may others know we have the Holy Spirit? This is an important question. A part of our Christian duty is to maintain an effective Christian witness. Paul has declared, "If a man has not the Spirit of Christ he is none of his"

(Rom. 8:9). To have "the Spirit of Christ" or "the Spirit of God" (as he phrased it in the fore part of the same verse) is to have the Holy Spirit. Note the verse is set in the context of an extended contrast between the fleshly (carnal) life — a life marked by "the mind of the flesh" (v. 6a) and the spiritual life — a life marked by "the mind of the Spirit" (v. 6b).

One way others may know we have the Holy Spirit is to tell them so. "Let the redeemed of Jehovah say so," exhorted the psalmist (Psa. 107:2). A man whom Jesus had exorcised was told, "Return to thy house and declare how great things *God* has done for you" (Luke 8:39a). That he did. Luke writes: "He went his way, publishing throughout the whole city how great things *Jesus* had done for him" (v. 39b). Perhaps he would have done so apart from Christ's request. Be that as it may, the fact is we are under charge to be Christ's witnesses. We are not all equally ready to share our blessings and joys. As one has so aptly put it, "Alas, lips cry, God be merciful! that never yet cried, God be praised!"

There is a basic truth in the cliche, "The best testimony is the testimony of a good life." But of itself it is not enough. An examplary life can become a source of vanity and false pride unless one is ever mindful, and remindful in conversing with others, of the Christ whose life and teachings has set the pattern for us, and of the Spirit which is at work within us.

To answer directly the question, "How may others know we have the Holy Spirit," Jesus, in the sermon on the mount, stated a principle which can scarcely be gainsayed: "By their fruits ye shall know them" (Mat. 7:16). Paul is applying this principle and speaking in specifics when he writes:

Walk by the Spirit, and ye shall not fulfill the lust of the flesh . . . . Now the works of the flesh are manifest, which are these: fornication, uncleanness, lasciviousness, idolatry, sorcery, enmities, strife, jealousies, wraths, factions, divisions, parties, envyings, drunkenness, revellings, and such like . . . . But the fruit of the

Spirit is love, joy, peace, longsuffering, kindness, goodness, faithfulness, meekness, self-control: against such there is no law (Gal. 5:16-23).

In saying the works of the flesh are manifest he is saying they are readily seen. But he is saying more. Also readily seen is from where they come. But the fruit of the Spirit (note the term "fruit" is singular, not plural) is not as readily discernable. The virtues which stem from the Holy Spirit are quiet, unobtrusive. They do not shout their presence. They maintain the essence of the source which produces them. They are like the qualities of a choice fruit — a choice apple, for example. It is sweet, tangy, savory, delicious, crisp, yet juicy, mellow. Those are not seven different fruits all growing on the same tree like the exotic "cocktail trees" advertised in a nursery catalog. They are qualities of a good apple. All seven qualities do not develop at once, along with shape, color and optimum size, but they are latent in each specimen from the fertilization of each blossom. It is even so with the fruit of the Spirit. The qualities Paul lists, and all "such like" are "growed," not bestowed.

Praise God if "such-like life qualities are yours and abound." It is thus that you "are made to be not idle nor unfruitful" (II Pet. 1:8). Be assured thereby that God's Spirit, even "the Spirit of Holiness" (Rom. 1:4), dwells within you. No life is complete without it.

One may build or buy a mansion, furnish it lavishly, sow a lawn and plant shrubbery, put drapes to the windows, food in the cupboards and refrigerator, clothes in the dresser drawers and closets, hang pictures on the walls, and turn on the lights and the TV, or perhaps the lastest thing in stereo equipment. One may even move in, but until one who is of a kindred spirit comes to share the house and the life of the one who dwells therein, and the two become fruitful, and the laughter of children fills the air — not until then does the house become a home.

Even so, one may have many external accruements which

denote success and achievements, but not until one's body becomes a temple of the Holy Spirit does the house in which our spirit dwells become a home — yea, a temple of the Holy Spirit.

> Know ye not that your body is a temple of the Holy Spirit, which is in you, which you have from God, and you are not your own? You have been bought with a price. Glorify God therefore in your body (I Cor. 6:19,20).

Appendixes

SPIRIT IN THE OLD TESTAMENT:
INSTRUMENT OF GOD'S ACTION
From a compilation by Dr. James Strauss: Used by Permission

1. *Definition*: Etymologically, Spirit/spirit (Hebr., *ruach*) is used of air, wind, breath, and being: the latter at all levels, animals, man, angels, and even the instrinsic nature of God.

2. *Goal of Divine action*, through Spirit, is to create and sustain. His breath (*ruach*), His word went forth and creation was accomplished and sustained. The creation hymn, Genesis, chapter 1, is the grand summation of the beginnings of the created order.

3. The following *listing of variant usages* of *ruach* witness the diversity of meanings to be found in the three hundred and eighty three (383) times the word is found within the scope of the Old Testament Scriptures.

A. Biblical texts using *ruach* as wind.
Genesis 3:8; 8:1; Exodus 10:13,19; 14:21; Numbers 11:31; II Samuel 22:11; I Kings 18:45; 19:11; II Kings 3:17; Isaiah 7:2; 17:13; 26:18; 27:8; 32:2; 40:7; 41:16,29; 57:13; 59:19; 64:5; Jeremiah 2:24; 4:11,12; 5:13; 10:13; 13:24; 14:6; 18:17; 22:22 49:32,36; 51:1,16; 52:23; Ezekiel 1:4; 5:2,10,12; 12:14; 13:11,13; 17:10,21; 19:12; 27:26; 37:9; 42:16,17,18,19,20; Hosea 4:19; 8:7; 12:2; 13:15; Amos 4:13; Jonah 1:4; 4:8; Micah 2:11; Habakkuk 1:11; Zechariah 2:10; 5:9; 5:5; Psalms 1:4; 11:6; 18:11,43; 35:5; 48:8; 55:9; 83:14; 103:16; 104:3,4; 107:25; 135:7; 148:8; Job 1:19; 4:15; 6:26; 8:2; 15:2,30; 16:3; 21:18; 28:25; 30:15,22; 37:21; 41:8; Proverbs 11:29; 25:14,23; 27:16; 30:4; Ecclesiastes 1:6,14,17; 2:11,17,26; 4:4,6,16; 5:15.

B. Biblical texts using *ruach* as the human spirit.
Genesis 6:3,17; 7:15,22; 26:35; 41:8; 45:27; (7:15,22-23 — related to animals?); Exodus 6:9; 35:21; Numbers 5:14,30; 14:24; 16:22; 27:16; Deuteronomy 2:30; Joshua 2:11; 5:1;

Judges 8:3; 15:19; I Samuel 1:15; 30:12; I Kings 10:5; 21:5; II Kings 2:9,15; Isaiah 11:4; 19:3,14; 25:4; 26:9; 28:6; 29:10,24; 33:11; 38:16; 42:5; 54:6; 57:15,16; 61:3; 65:14; 66:2; Jeremiah 10:14; 51:11,17; Ezekiel 3:14; 11:5,19; 13:3; 18:31; 20:32; 21:12; 36:26; 37:5,6,8,9,10; Hosea 4:12; 5:4; Habakkuk 2:19; Haggai 1:14; Zechariah 12:1,10;Malachi 2:15,16; Psalms 31:6; 32:2; 34:19; 51:12,14,19; 76:13; 77:4,7; 78:8,39; 104:29; 106:33; 135:17; 142:4; 143:4,7; 146:4; (104:25-29 — animals?); Job 6:4; 7:7,11; 9:18; 10:12; 12:10; 15:13; 17:1; 19:17; 20:3; 21:4; 27:3; 32:18; Proverbs 1:23; 11:13; 14:29; 15:4,13; 16:2,18,19,32; 17:22,27; 18:14; 25:28; 29:11,23; Ecclesiastes 3:19,21; 7:8,9; 8:8; 10:4; 12:7; (3:21 — animals?); Lamentations 4:20; Daniel 2:1,3; 5:12,20; 6:4; 7:15; Ezra 1:1,5; I Chronicles 5:26; 28:12; II Chronicles 9:4; 21:16; 36:22.

C. Biblical texts using *ruach* as an evil spirit.
Judges 9:23; I Samuel 16:14,15,16; 18:10; 19:9; I Kings 22:21,22,23; II Kings 19:7; Isaiah 37:7; Zechariah 13:2; II Chronicles 18:20,21,22.

D. Biblical texts using *ruach* as the Spirit of God.
Genesis 1:2; 41:38; Exodus 15:8; 15:10; 28:3; 31:3; 35:31; Numbers 11:17; 11:25; 11:26; 11:29; 24:2; 27:18; Deuteronomy 34:9; Judges 3:10; 6:34; 11:29;13:25; 14:6; 14:19; 15:14; I Samuel 10:6; 10:10; 11:6; 16:13; 16:14; 19:20; 19:23; II Samuel 22:16; 23:2; I Kings 18:12; 22:24; II Kings 2:16; Isaiah 4:4; 11:2; 11:15; 27:8; 30:1; 30:28; 31:3; 32:15; 34:16; 40:13; 42:1; 44:3; 48:16; 59:21; 61:1; 63:10; 63:11; 63:14; Ezekiel 1:12; 1:20; 1:21; 2:2; 3:12; 8:3; 10:17; 11:1; 11:5; 11:24; 36:27; 37:1; 37:14; 39:29; 43:5; Hosea 9:7; 13:15; Joel 3:1 (RSV 2:38); 3:2 (RSV 2:29); Micah 2:7; 3:8; Haggai 2:5; Zechariah 4:6; 6:8; 7:12; Psalms 18:16 (RSV 15); 33:6; 51:13 (RSV 11); 104:30; 139:7; 143:10; 147:18; Job 4:9; 26:13; 32:8; 33:4; 34:14; Daniel 4:5; 4:6; 4:15; 5:11;

314

5:14; Nehemiah 9:20; 9:30; I Chronicles 12:19 (RSV 18); II Chronicles 15:1; 18:23; 20:14; 24:20.

SPIRIT IN THE NEW TESTAMENT:
DIVINE POWER AND PRESENCE
Adapted From a Compilation by Dr. James Strauss
Used by Permission

PART ONE

COMPREHENSIVE LISTING OF
NEW TESTAMENT USAGES (392) OF PNEUMA
"Spirit" (prefixed/unprefixed by *Holy);
"life," "wind" (each once)
*Ital denotes prefixed by hagios (Holy)

Matthew 1:*18,20*; 3:*11*,16; 4:1; 5:3; 8:16; 10:1,20;
  12:18,28,31,*32*,43,45; 22:43; 26:41; 27:50; 28:*19*.
Mark 1:*8*,10,12,23,26,27; 2:8; 3:11,*29*,30; 5:2,8,13; 6:7;
  7:25; 8:12; 9:17,20,25; 12:*36*; 13:*11*; 14:38.
Luke 1:*15*,17,*35*,*41*,47,*67*,80; 2:*25*,*26*,27; 3:*16*,*22*;
  4:*1*,14,18,33,36; 6:18; 7:21; 8:2,29,55; 9:39,42,55;
  10:20,21; 11:13,24,26; 12:*10*,*12*; 13:11; 23:46; 24:37,39.
John 1:32,*33*; 3:5,6,8,34; 4:23,24; 6:63; 7:39; 11:33; 13:21;
  14:17,*26*; 15:26; 16:13; 19:30; 20:*22*.
Acts 1:*2*,5,*8*,*16*; 2:4,17,18,*33*,*38*; 4:*8*,25,*31*; 5:*3*,9,*32*;
  6:3,5,10; 7:*51*,*55*,59; 8:7,*15*,*17*,*18*,*19*,19,29,39; 9:*17*,*31*;
  10:19,*38*,44,45,45; 11:12,*15*,*16*,*24*,28; 13:*2*,4,*9*,*52*;
  15:*8*,*28*,29;   16:*6*,7,16,18;   17:16;   18:25;
  19:1,*2*,6,12,13,15,16,21; 20:22,*23*,*28*; 21:4,*11*; 23:8,9;
  28:*25*.
Romans 1:4,9; 2:29; 5:5; 7:6; 8:2,4,5,6,9,10,11,13,14,15,16,
  23,26,27; 9:*1*; 11:8; 12:11; 14:*17*; 15:*13*,*16*,19,30.
I Corinthians 2:4,10,11,12,13,14; 3:16; 4:21; 5:3,4,5;
  6:11,17,*19*; 7:34,40; 12:*3*,4,7,8,9,10,11,13;
  14:2,12,14,15,16,32; 15:45; 16:18.
II Corinthians 1:22; 3:3,6,8,17,18; 4:13; 5:5; 6:*6*; 7:1,13;
  11:4; 12:18; 13:*13*.

316

Galatians 3:2,3,5,14; 4:6,29; 5:5,16,17,18,22,25; 6:1,8,18.
Ephesians 1:13,17; 2:2,18,22; 3:5,16; 4:3,4,23,30; 5:18; 6:17,18.
Philippians 1:19,27; 2:1; 3:3; 4:23.
Colossians 1:8; 2:5.
I Thessalonians 1:5,6; 4:8; 5:19,23.
II Thessalonians 2:2,8,13.
I Timothy 3:16; 4:1.
II Timothy 1:7,14; 4:22.
Titus 3:5.
Philemon 1:25.
Hebrews 1:7,14; 2:4; 3:7; 4:12; 6:4; 9:8,14; 10:15,27; 12:9; 12:23.
James 2:26; 4:5.
I Peter 1:2,11,12; 3:1,18,19; 4:6,14.
II Peter 1:21.
I John 3:24; 4:1,2,3,6,13; 5:6,8.
Jude 1:19,20.
Revelation 1:4,10; 2:7; 3:1; 4:2,5; 5:6; 11:11; 13:15; 14:13; 16:13,14; 17:3; 18:2; 19:10; 21:10; 22:6,17.

Pneumatikos (Adjective)

Romans 1:11; 7:11; 15:27.
I Corinthians 2:13,15; 3:1; 9:11; 10:3,4; 12:1; 14:1,37; 15:44,46.
Galatians 6:1.
Ephesians 1:3; 5:19; 6:12.
Colossians 1:9; 3:16.
I Peter 2:5.

Pneumatikos (Adverb)

I Corinthians 2:13,14.
Revelation 11:8.

HOLY GHOST/SPIRIT

Note: The designation, *hagion pneuma*, appears 83 times in the ancient MSS of the New Testament. It is commonly translated Holy Spirit. However, the classic KJV renders it Holy Ghost. The KJV also amplifies five additional texts (John 7:59; Acts 6:3; 8:18; I Cor. 2:13; II Cor. 13:13) to so read. This has been duly corrected in the New KJV c. 1979.

In the aftermath of the formulation of the Nicene Creed I John 5:7,8 was amplified to include the creedal dictum: "For there are three who bear witness in heaven: the Father, the Word, and the Holy Ghost: and these three are one." See I John 5:7, KJV. The New KJV continues to include the addition but calls attention in a footnote to the fact that: "only four or five very late Greek manuscripts contain these words." All such manuscripts, whether Greek, Latin, etc. are of post-Nicene vintage.

Holy Spirit/Ghost (*hagion pneuma*) References: KJV additions [bracketed]
Matt. 1:18,20; 3:11; 12:32; 28:19; Mark 1:8; 3:29; 12:36; 13:11; Luke 1:15,35,41,67; 2:25,26; 3:16,22; 4:1; 12:10,12; John 1:33; [7:39], 14:26; 20:22. Acts 1:2,5,8,16; 2:4,33,38; 4:8,31; 5:3,32; 6:[3],5; 7:51,55; 8:15,17,[18],19; 9:17,31; 10:38,44,45,47; 11:15,16,24; 13:2,4,9,52; 15:8,28; 16:6,19; 19:2,6; 20:23,28; 21:11; 28:25; Rom. 5:5; 9:1; 14:17; 15:13,16; I Cor. 2:[13]; 6:19; 12:3; II Cor. 6:6; 13:[14]; I Thess. 1:5,6; II Tim. 1:14; Titus 3:5; Heb. 2:4; 3:7; 6:4; 9:8; 10:15; I Pet. 1:12, II Pet. 1:21; [I John 5:7]; Jude 1:20.

PART TWO

CLASSIFICATION OF NEW TESTAMENT REFERENCES

I. Biblical (New Testament) Designations of the Holy Spirit.

318

A. In General
1. The Spirit, Matt. 4:1; Mark 1:10; Luke 4:1; John 1:32, etc.
2. The Holy Spirit, Matt. 1:18; Mark 1:8; Luke 1:15; John 1:33, etc.
3. The Comforter (Gr. *paraclete*) John 14:16,26; 15:26; 16:7
4. The eternal Spirit, Heb. 9:14.
B. In Relation to God, the Father
1. Spirit of God, Matt. 3:16; 12:28; Rom. 8:14; 15:10; I Cor. 1:12; 2:11,14; 7:40; 12:3; I John 4:2.
2. Spirit of the Living God, II Cor. 3:3.
3. Spirit of our God, I Cor. 6:13.
4. Holy Spirit of God, Eph. 4:30.
5. His Holy Spirit, I Thess. 4:8.
6. His Spirit, I Thess. 4:5; Eph. 3:16; I John 4:13.
7. Spirit of the Lord, Luke 4:18; Acts 5:9; 8:39; II Cor. 3:17,18.
8. Spirit of your Father, Matt. 10:20.
C. In Relation to Christ, the Son
1. Spirit of Christ, Rom. 8:9; I Pet. 11.
2. Spirit of His (God's) Son, Gal. 4:6.
3. Spirit of Jesus Christ, Phil. 1:19.
D. In Relation to Believers:
1. Spirit of Adoption, Rom. 8:15.
2. Spirit of Faith, II Cor. 4:13.
3. Spirit of Grace, Heb. 10:29.
4. Spirit of Holiness, Rom. 1:4.
5. Spirit of life, Rom. 8:2; 11:11.
6. Spirit of Promise, Eph. 1:13.
7. Spirit of Truth, John 4:7; 15:26; 16:13; I John 4:6; 5:6.
8. Spirit of Wisdom, Eph. 1:7.

Note: Opinions differ as to when the foregoing designations of the Spirit refer to the Holy Spirit as a third person in the Godhead or simply refer to the Divine nature intrinsic in God and in Christ.

II. The Holy Spirit in Relation to the Father and the Son
  A. As the third person of the Godhead, Matt. 28:19; II
     Cor. 13:14.
  B. As one sent from God, the Father, (see I. B.).
     1. The sending of the Holy Spirit is called "the promise
        of the Father," Acts 1:4; Luke 24:49.
     2. The Holy Spirit is called "the gift of God," John
        14:16; Luke 11:13; cp. I Cor. 2:12. (See IV. B.)
  C. The Holy Spirit proceeds also from the Son, Luke
     24:49, and "in Jesus' name": John 15:26; 16:7.
     Note: Jesus' entire earthly life was empowered by Spirit.
     1. The birth of Christ
        a. The conception of Christ was by the agency of the
           Holy Spirit, Matt. 1:18,20; Luke 1:35.
        b. With regard to others interrelated with the birth of
           Christ.
           1) Elizabeth was filled with the Holy Spirit, Luke
              1:42.
           2) Zacharias was filled with the Holy Spirit, Luke
              1:67.
           3) Simeon was filled with the Holy Spirit, Luke
              2:25-27.
           Note: Joseph is said to have been instructed by an
           angel, Matt. 1:20, and later through dreams, Matt.
           2:12,13,19.
     2. His ministry
        a. John, his forerunner, "filled with the Holy Spirit
           from his mother's womb" (Luke 1:15) predicted
           Jesus would baptize with the Holy Spirit, Matt.
           3:11; Mark 1:28; Luke 3:16; John 1:33.
        b. The Holy Spirit descended upon Jesus at his bap-
           tism, Matt. 3:16; Mark 1:10; Luke 3:22; John
           1:32,33.

    c. He returned "full of the Holy Spirit," Luke 4:1.

    d. The Spirit drove him into the wilderness to be tempted, Matt. 4:1; Mark 1:12; Luke 4:1; and he returned in the power of the Spirit, Luke 4:14.

    e. God anointed him with the Holy Spirit and power, Acts 10:38; Matt. 12:18; cp. Isa. 42:1.

    f. He began and continued his ministry by the power of the Spirit, Luke 4:28ff, Matt. 12:17,18,28.

    g. He offered himself to God through the eternal Spirit, Heb. 9:14.

    h. He promised his disciples he would send the Holy Spirit upon them, John 15:26, cp. Luke 24:49, Acts 2:33.

    i. The Holy Spirit raised Christ from the grave, Rom. 1:4; 8:11; I Pet. 3:18.

III. The Holy Spirit Inspired the Biblical Writers

  A. Old Testament writers: Luke 24:44,45.

    1. The Law. Inferences drawn Jesus' references to the law, and the extended discourse in Hebrews, Chs. 8-10 comparing the two covenants. (Note, Heb. 9:8).

    2. The Prophets were "moved by the Holy Spirit." They so declared and ofttimes confirmed the same by powers displayed and by predictions fulfilled. cp. II Tim. 3:14-16, II Pet. 1:21.

    3. The Psalms: 1) of David: Matt. 22:43-45; Mark 12:36; Acts 1:16; 2:25-28,34,35; 4:25,26; cp. 13:33; Heb. 3:7.

  B. New Testament writers: II Pet. 1:16-18; Rev. 1:19; 2:7,11,17,29; 3:6,13,22; 22:6,16,17,20.

IV. Teaching of the New Testament Concerning the Work of the Holy Spirit

  A. In the Synoptic Gospels.

    1. He is given to them that ask, Luke 11:13; Matt. 7:11.

    2. Prediction: The Spirit would speak through the

apostles.
  a. On their first mission: Matt. 10:19,20; Mark 13:15.
  b. On later missions: Luke 12:10.
  c. In the course of their ministry: Luke 24:45-49.
  3. Warning of blasphemy against the Holy Spirit, Matt. 12:31,32; Mark 3:29,30; Luke 12:10.
  4. Disciples commissioned to baptize in the name of the Father, Son and Holy Spirit, Matt. 28:19.
B. In the Fourth Gospel.
  1. Necessity for regeneration by the Holy Spirit, 3:5-8.
  2. The Holy Spirit "not given by measure," 3:34.
  3. It is the spirit that "quickens," 6:63.
  4. The Spirit not yet given "because Jesus was not yet glorified," 7:39.
  5. The Spirit cannot be received by the world, 14:17.
  6. The Holy Spirit is a gift of God, 14:16.
  7. The Holy Spirit is to indwell believers, 14:7; 16:17.
  8. The Holy Spirit's work in relation to believers:
    a. Bring to remembrance the things of Christ, 14:16,17.
    Note: Primarily, this was Jesus' guarantee of inspiration to the NT writers, especially the Gospel writers.
    b. To testify of Christ, 15:26; 16:14,15.
    c. To receive the things of Christ to show to us, 15:14,15.
    d. To glorify Christ, 16:14.
    e. To extend His teaching ministry, 14:26; 16:13.
    f. To declare (Gr. *anangelei* — announce) the things that are to come, Acts 20:20; I Pet. 1:12; I John 1:5.
    g. To convict (Gr. *elengcho*) the world, 16:8-11. The verb used involves the idea of authoritative examination, and decisive judgment.

C. In Acts: The Holy Spirit in the Church
Note: Acts 1:5,8 set forth two significant statements of Christ about the baptism of the Holy Spirit. See also 11:16.
1. The Descent of the Holy Spirit on Pentecost, 2:1-39.
   a. All filled with the Holy Spirit, 2:4.
   b. Spirit gave them utterance, 2:4.
      (This was a partial fulfillment of Joel 2:28-31.)
   c. Gift of the Holy Spirit promised to those who obeyed, 2:38,39, cp. 5:32.
2. Other groups and individuals "upon" whom the Holy Spirit came.
   a. The Samaritans, 8:15-19.
   b. Cornelius and his household, 10:44,45; 11:15-17; 15:8.
   c. Twelve men at Ephesus, 19:6.
   d. Seven appointed men in the Jerusalem church, 6:3.
   e. Stephen, the first martyr, in particular, 6:5; 7:5,55.
   f. Saul of Tarsus (Paul) 9:1; 13:9.
   g. Barnabas, 11:24.
   h. The disciples of Antioch, 13:52.
   Note: Though the phrase is not used of the Samaritans, Cornelius and his household, and the twelve disciples at Ephesus, such phrases as "the Holy Spirit came (fell) upon them" implies as much, see 8:15-18; 19:44,45; (cp. 11:15-17) and 19:6,7.
4. The Holy Spirit's supervision of the church
   a. The church walked in the comfort of the Holy Spirit, 9:31.
   b. The Holy Spirit led in selecting and appointing the first extended missionary expansion, 13:2,4.
   c. Jerusalem Council acted on counsel of the Holy Spirit, 15:28.

    d. Holy Spirit forbade Paul to go to certain areas, 16:6,7.

    e. The bishops of the church at Ephesus were made so by the Holy Spirit, 20:28.

    f. Paul's forthcoming sufferings were revealed to him and to the church, by the Holy Spirit, 20:23; 21:4,11.

    Note: Paul "purposed in the spirit" (19:21) to go to Jerusalem. (His spirit or the Holy Spirit? Reference is unclear, disputed)

    g. Other individuals to whom the Spirit gave special messages
      1) Philip, 8:29; 20:39.
      2) Peter, 10:19; 11:12.
      3) Agabus, 11:28; 21:11.

    i. The Holy Spirit is said to have witnessed to the church, 5:32.

    j. Sins against the Holy Spirit.
      1) Lying (to), 5:3.
      2) Tempting, 5:9.
      3) Resisting, 7:51.

    Note: 1) Besides the foregoing references in Acts, and Jesus' warnings (in the gospels) of blasphemy against the Holy Spirit, the epistles warn of "grieving, quenching, and doing despite" to the Holy Spirit, (Eph. 4:30; I Thess. 5:9; Heb. 10:29), 2) Section IV details other facets of the interrelation of the Holy Spirit and man in the course of the Christian era.

IV. The Holy Spirit in Relation to Believers, deduced from the Epistles

    A. Pertaining to sundry aspects of our regeneration, we are:

      1. Born again (by the Holy Spirit), II Cor. 3:6; Gal. 4:29.

2. Adopted into God's family, as sons, Gal. 4:6; Rom. 8:5.
3. Sealed unto the day of redemption, Eph. 1:13.
4. Given the earnest (guarantee) of the Spirit, Eph. 1:14; II Cor. 1:22; 5:5.
5. Renewed, Titus 3:5; via faith vs. works of the law, Gal. 3:2-5.
6. Indwelt by the Holy Spirit, Rom. 8:9,11; I Cor. 3:16; 6:19.
7. Enjoy the communion of the Holy Spirit, II Cor. 13:14; Phil. 2:1.
8. Made partakers of the Holy Spirit, Heb. 6:4.
9. Given supply of the Spirit of Jesus Christ, Phil. 1:19.
10. By one spirit we are all baptized into one body, I Cor. 12:13.

B. The Continuing Work of the Holy Spirit
1. Bears witness to our Sonship, Rom. 8:16; Gal. 4:6; I John 5:6,7.
2. Provides access to the Father, Eph. 2:8.
3. Assures us Christ dwells within, I John 3:24; 4:13; Eph. 2:22.
4. Makes intercession for us, Rom. 8:26,27, cp. Eph. 6:18.
5. Frees us from the law of sin and death, Rom. 8:22.
6. Conflict exists between our flesh and the Spirit, Gal. 5:17.
7. The Spirit sanctifies us, Rom. 15:16; II Thess. 2:13; I Pet. 1:2.
8. The Spirit helps our infirmities, Rom. 8:26.
9. We are led by the Spirit, Rom. 8:14; Gal. 5:18.
10. We are kept by the Spirit, II Tim. 1:14.
11. The Spirit strenthens with power our inward man, Eph. 3:16.
12. The spirit quickens our mortal bodies, Rom. 8:11.
13. The Spirit teaches us, I Cor. 2:10-13.

14. The Spirit will change us from glory to glory, II Cor. 3:18.
15. The Spirit sheds the love of God abroad in our hearts, Rom. 5:5; 15:30; Col. 1:18.
16. The Spirit imparts joy, I Thess. 1:16.
17. The fruit of the Spirit has nine manifestations, Gal. 5:22,23.
18. We also enjoy "the first fruits of the Spirit," Rom. 8:23.
19. Our lives are living epistles written by the Spirit, II Cor. 3:3.
20. Thereby we witness to the truth, I Cor. 12:3; I John 4:23.
21. The Kingdom of God in us is defined by Paul as "righteousness and peace and joy in the Holy Spirit, Rom 16:17.

C. Because of our relationship with the Spirit we are exhorted to:
  1. Walk according to the Spirit, Rom 8:1,4,5; Gal. 4:16,25.
  2. Live in the power of the Spirit, Rom. 15:13; cp. 19; Gal. 5:25.
  3. Have the mind of the Spirit, Rom 8:6, cp. v. 27.
  4. Obey the truth through the Spirit, I Pet. 1:22.
  5. Pray in the Spirit, Eph. 6:18; Jude 1:20, cp. Rom. 8:26,27.
  6. Keep the unity of the Spirit in the bond of peace, Eph. 4:3.
  7. Use the sword of the Spirit, Eph. 6:19.
  8. Commend ourselves in the spirit, II Cor. 6:6.
  9. Put to death the deeds of the body through the Spirit, Rom. 8:13.
  10. Sow to the Spirit, and so reap eternal life, Gal. 5:5.
  11. Be filled with the Spirit, Eph. 5:18.
  12. Wait for the "hope of righteousness" through the

Spirit, Gal. 5:5.
D. Spiritual Gifts
1. Chapters 12-14 of I Corinthians "concern" spiritual gifts. Nine service gifts are delineated in chapter 12. Chapter 13 is a Psalm extolling "the greatest" of "the greater gifts (love), the apex of a triad of abiding gifts: faith hope and love. Chapter 14 addresses problems that had arisen from the gift of tongues.
2. Galatians 5:22,23 contrasts the ongoing fruitage gifts of the Spirit to the works of the flesh, cp. 19-21.
E. The Resultant Spiritual Man
Note: Spiritual is a translation of the Greek word, *pneumatikos*. It is used of various aspects of the Spirit filled and led life. Except for Eph. 6:12 it is used only of that which relates to the person and work of the Holy Spirit, especially the work of the Holy Spirit in the lives of believers.
1. General use: "he that is spiritual," I Cor. 2:14,15, 3:1; 14:37; Gal. 6:1.
2. Such a one (ideally, potentially) will:
    a. Possess "every spiritual blessing in Christ Jesus, Eph. 1:3.
    b. Enjoy "spiritual wisdom and understanding," Col. 1:19.
    c. Combine "Spiritual words with Spiritual things," I Cor. 2:13.
3. Those who "sow spiritual things" should "reap eternal things," I Cor. 9:11; Rom. 15:17.
4. Such persons will sing "spiritual songs," Eph. 5:19; Col. 3:16.
5. Believers are "built up a spiritual house," to "offer up spiritual sacrifices," I Pet. 2:5.
6. Resurrection bodies will be "spiritual bodies," I Cor. 15:44,46.
7. Paul longed to see the Roman Christians face to face

that he might thereby "impart some spiritual gifts," Rom. 1:11.
Note: "Fruitage gifts" of the spirit are grown. The specialized "service gifts" were bestowed.

VI. Unclassified References to the Holy Spirit and Spiritual things.

A. Miscellany

1. The self-serving request of Simon, the sorcerer, Acts 8:19.
2. The natural man cannot receive the things of the Spirit, I Cor. 2:14, cp. Jude 1:19.
3. The children of Israel, when passing through the Red Sea, "did all eat the same spiritual food, and all drank the same spiritual drink, for they drank of a spiritual rock which followed them — Christ," I Cor. 10:3,4.
4. The "ministration of the Spirit" results in glory, II Cor. 3:8.
5. Jerusalem is "Spiritually" called Sodom and Egypt, Rev. 11:8.

B. The term "the Holy Spirit" does not appear:

1. In the whole of the Old Testament, (cp. Isa. 63:10,11, "his holy Spirit" — an adjectival phrase. Note use of lower case "h")
2. In the following epistles: Galatians, Ephesians, Philippians, Colossians, Philemon, James, II John, III John.
3. In the whole of the Apocalypse. Note: The phrase, "the seven spirits of God" is often conjectured to be a veiled reference to the Holy Spirit. (If that be so the reason for such obscurant usage is not readily explained. See Rev. 1:4; 3:1; 4:5, cp. 2:17.)

IN SEARCH OF A MIRACLE
by William A. Nolen, M.D.

A noted doctor, skeptical but willing to believe, examines the phenomenon of faith healing as practiced by the country's best known exponent, the late Kathryn Kuhlman.

Anyone who works with sick people, as I do, knows there are many unpredictable, ill-defined factors that affect the healing process. The "will to live," for example. A patient who gives up — refuses to eat or get our of bed or take medicines — will, in all probability die in spite of a doctor's efforts. The will to live isn't anything that can be weighed or measured but it certainly exists: ask any doctor. Faith, too, plays a role in healing. Deliver me from any patient who does not have faith in my ability to help; I may be able to treat that patient successfully, but it will be a more difficult chore.

A couple of years ago I began to wonder how great a role faith plays in the healing process. Is faith in someone, or something, enough by itself to effect a cure? There are hundreds of thousands of patients who claim that faith alone has cured them, often after doctors failed to do so. Sometimes it is faith in a healer, but often it is faith in God. Almost invariably physicians have discounted these reports without bothering to investigate them. I decided to take a closer look at healing that was reportedly being done outside of the traditional Western school of medicine. I knew that (since I had been trained in a traditional medical school) it might be difficult for me to recognize that there could be other methods of healing as effective as those with which I was acquainted — possibly even more so. But because of my Roman Catholic background I was already convinced that faith played some role in healing and so I was certain I could approach the subject with an open mind.

Since Kathryn Kuhlman is certainly the best-known and probably the most highly regarded of the Christian faith-healers, I

329

decided that my investigation should begin with her. Kathryn Kuhlman is an ordained minister. She has been "healing" since 1946. In an average year she holds 125 "healing" services and treats approximately one and a half million patients. Her services are held in the largest auditoriums in the biggest cities of the United States. At each service hundreds of sick people claim to have been cured. Miss Kuhlman has written three books. She herself has been the subject of magazine articles and books. In addition to her radio programs, she has a widely syndicated television show. In June of 1973, Miss Kuhlman and her organization came to Minneapolis, which is near my hometown, to hold a service. Through a friend who knew I was writing a book about paranormal healing, I arranged to be an usher and was assigned to the wheelchair division. After the service, I was able to interview Kathryn Kuhlman. So began my investigation of faith healing.

Even though the service wasn't scheduled to begin for another two hours, there were already long lines outside every entrance to the auditorium when I arrived. At one entrance I'd estimate that there were at least 100 people in wheelchairs.

The group to which I was assigned had the responsibility of guiding the wheelchairs from the elevator into the auditorium. I've seen some sad sights in my life, but few that could match the one that greeted me when the doors of the freight elevator opened and our first group arrived. There were about 30 wheelchair patients and their attendants. Many were elderly "stroke" victims. Others were children, crippled by birth defects. There were several middle-aged men and some who had the pale, wasted appearance that a doctor learns to associate with widespread cancer. Every patient I saw — except, of course, the mentally retarded — had the desperate look of having all but given up hope.

In the crowd was one man in his middle 60's who didn't have a wheelchair and must have gotten into the elevator by mistake. He was limping and I could see him wincing with pain, so I offered to find a wheelchair for him.

"I'd appreciate that," he said. "My back and hips hurt like the devil. I have cancer of the prostate. Had it operated on two years ago. Now it's in my spine and my hip. I'm hoping Kathryn Kuhlman will cure me."

"Did you tell your doctor you were coming here?" I asked him.

"I mentioned it to him. He said that was my business. He didn't recommend her, didn't knock her either."

I asked this question often, and the answers were all essentially the same. Apparently, even if the doctors weren't believers, they weren't anti-Kathryn Kuhlman either.

At 12 o'clock the choir volunteers from churches all over the Minneapolis area began to sing. The singing kept everyone entertained until Miss Kuhlman appeared on stage at one.

She wore a flowing robe and came out waving her hands and smiling. She's not particularly beautiful, but she has that indefinable quality known as "presence." Every eye was on her.

"It's so beautiful to see you all here," she said. "I just know the Holy Spirit is going to work many miracles. Wouldn't it be wonderful if every single one of you was healed today?" Everyone applauded wildly.

Dino, one of her assistants, played the piano. Jimmy MacDonald sang hymns in a strong, full baritone. Both were dressed in tails. She gave them rousing introductions and informed the audience that their albums were for sale in the lobby.

Between their performances she talked. She didn't preach; she talked. She told us how wonderful the Lord is and how grateful she is for the works the Holy Spirit performs. And often she commented on the burden she feels in being His instrument.

"The responsibility — the responsibility!" she cried. "I cry for those who won't be cured today. I ask, 'Am I at fault?' Oh, the burden of it all." At this point she buried her face in her hands, sobbing.

But then she recovered. "Is it worth it, O Lord? Yes, it is! It's worth the price when you see one case of cancer healed, one child made better."

It's hopeless for me to try to convey her charisma. You have to be there to see her stride across the stage, watch her gesture and pose with arms outstretched, listen to the emotion in her voice. Like all great evangelists she is, first and foremost, a wonderful actress.

After the piano playing, the singing and some praying, she said, "Now we're going to take up the offering — the money we need so we can come to you people and help the sick and needy everywhere. I want twenty people out there to write out checks for one hundred dollars. I want fifty people to write checks for fifty dollars. I want one hundred people to write checks for twenty-five dollars. We need that money. But if you can't give a hundred or fifty or twenty-five, give whatever you can." At that point, the ushers hustled baskets into the crowd and the choir broke into the offertory hymn.

The hymn took about ten minutes. When it was over, Kathryn Kuhlman gave her sermon. She talked mostly of the wonders of the Lord and the Holy Spirit, and she began to talk more about healing. Suddenly she paused, eyes shut. It was a tense moment, a dramatic moment, and the audience was silent.

"The Holy Spirit is healing someone right not," she said. 'It's a woman. About halfway back. She had a cancer — a cancer of the lungs. And now — and now — she is being healed. You know who you are. Stand up and come forward to claim your healing."

When no one came forward immediately, she suddenly pointed toward the balcony. "There's a man in the balcony who has had bursitis in his shoulder. Now it's gone. Stand up and wave your arm. You've been healed." There was a note of frenzy in her voice. And up jumped a man, waving his arm. The audience gasped.

Then, magically, healings began to take place all over the auditorium. "Don't come to the stage unless you've been healed," Miss Kuhlman said. "But if you have been healed, come up and give praise to the Holy Spirit."

Once the first few started forward, dozens followed. Soon there were lines of people waiting to get up on the stage. One at a time they were led to her by her assistants.

"And you," Kathryn said to one woman, "what did you have?"

"Lung cancer," the woman answered.

"Oh, good Lord, we thank you," Kathryn said, looking toward the ceiling. "Now," she said to the woman, "take a deep breath." The woman did. "Did that hurt?"

"No, it didn't."

"Do you see her?" Kathryn cried. "Lung cancer. And now she can breathe without pain. The Holy Spirit is surely working here today."

Every few minutes Miss Kuhlman would pause between patients, turn as if she heard a voice and point out into the audience. "Back there," she said on one occasion, "way back on the right. There's a man with cancer in his hip. You're cured. Your pain is gone. Come down and claim your cure." The man slowly worked his way down the aisle as the crowd applauded. Behind him came one of the ushers, pushing his wheelchair. When the man got closer to the stage, I could see that he was the fellow I had talked to earlier, the man with cancer of the prostate.

When he was up on stage, the wheelchair behind him, Kathryn Kuhlman said, "Whose wheelchair is that? Not yours surely?"

"Yes, it is," said the man, bewildered. I understood his problem. Technically the wheelchair wasn't his; I had borrowed it for him.

"You've had cancer in the hip and now your pain is gone. Is that right?"

"Yes," he answered.

"Bend over so everyone can see." He bent over. "Walk around." He walked around. "Isn't the Holy Spirit wonderful?" she cried.

Scenes like this were repeated. Patient and wheelchair delivered to the stage. Patient put through running, bending or breathing paces, depending on the nature of the affliction. Applause for each performance.

Occasionally Miss Kuhlman would turn to the audience and say, "Someone with a brace — a brace on your leg — you don't need that brace any more. Take it off. Come and claim your cure."

The first time she called for a brace, no one came forth. You could sense the audience felt this was almost embarrassing for Miss Kuhlman. Finally, a very pretty young girl came up on the stage. She was waving her leg brace and standing, with her pelvis tilted badly, on one good leg and one short, withered leg.

Kathryn Kuhlman questioned her. "How long have you worn this brace?"

"Thirteen years. Since I had polio at seven."

"And now you're cured. You don't need it any more. You've taken it off."

"Yes," she said. "I believe in the Lord. I've prayed, and he's curing me."

Everyone applauded. The girl cried.

The scene, to my mind, was utterly revolting. The girl's leg was just as withered as it had been ten minutes earlier. Now she stood in front of 10,000 people, giving praise to the Lord — and indirectly to Kathryn Kuhlman — for a cure that hadn't occurred and wasn't going to occur. I could imagine how she would feel when the hysteria of the moment had left her and she again had to put on the brace she had worn for 13 years — and would wear for the rest of her life.

This was the case that first made me skeptical of Kathryn Kuhlman and her organization. When the man with prostatic cancer, for whom I had found a wheelchair that morning, was asked, "Is that your wheelchair?," I had accepted his "yes" as a simple misunderstanding. When the ability to take a deep breath was passed off as evidence of a lung-cancer cure, I'd chalked it up to innocent error, even though I know that most patients with lung cancer can breathe deeply.

But the episode involving the girl with the brace seemed pure, unadulterated nonsense. To believe that the Holy Spirit had worked a miracle on this girl, Kathryn Kuhlman would have to be an imbecile — a blind one. I was making every effort to be objective, but at that point the credibility of the whole organization became very questionable in my mind.

Finally, with a hymn and a final blessing, the show ended. All the desperately ill who had been in wheelchairs were still in wheelchairs. As I watched them leave, seeing the tears of the parents as they pushed their crippled children to the elevators, I wished Miss Kuhlman were with me. I wondered if she really knew how much sadness those disappointed patients and parents suffered. I couldn't believe that she did.

I waited about ten minutes and then went back to Miss Kuhlman's dressing room. I found her standing outside, sobbing. Dino had his arms around her. A couple of minutes later, having led Miss Kuhlman into her dressing room, he came out and told me to wait about five minutes and then go in.

"She's always this way after a service," Dino said, "but, she bounces back."

When she let me into her dressing room a few minutes later, Miss Kuhlman had indeed recovered. She was, in fact, buoyant. "Sit right there," she said, pointing to a chair.

"If it's all right with you, I'll get right to some medical questions," I said. "How do you get along with the medical profession?"

"Wonderfully well," she told me. "I have nothing against doctors, and I hope they have nothing against me. I don't cure people — the Holy Spirit cures through me. Doctors cure people, too. I think doctors are wonderful."

"Do you think any of the patients you cure are simply hysterical?"

"Of course," she answered, laughing. "Aren't any of the patients you treat hysterical?"

I admitted they were.

"But many of our cures are documented," she continued. "All those patients we show on television, for example. I always tell people who say they've been cured to go back to their doctors. I have nothing to hide."

"What about organic diseases? Things like gallstones, for example. Do you cure these, too?"

"Oh, certainly," she said. "Gallstones, cancer, arthritis, everything. But don't say *I* cure them. The Holy Spirit cures them."

"Have you any idea why the Lord chooses to work miracles through you?" I asked her.

"I don't know why I've been chosen," she said. "In fact, I always worry that sometime I may go out on the stage and find that the Holy Spirit had decided not to use me as his instrument any longer. But I do know why miraculous healings are occurring. Let me give you a little lesson."

She picked up her Bible. "In the Bible Christ says, 'If you won't believe Me, believe My miracles.' "

"Miracles — miraculous healings — are Christ's way of telling us to prepare for Him. There are more miraculous healings now, in the nineteen-seventies, than there have been at any other time since the days of the early Church."

It took Miss Kuhlman about 20 minutes to review the Biblical explanation of miracles for me. Outside the dressing room, I could see Dino pacing back and forth.

Even if I hadn't felt obligated to leave, I don't think I would have found much more to ask her. It seemed obvious to me that she was a sincere, honest woman who felt that she had been chosen to perform a mission for Christ. She believed without a doubt that she was helping the sick and the maimed as Christ wished her to help them — not personally, as she pointed out endlessly — but as His instrument.

During the service, as those who had "claimed a cure" came

336

down off the stage, two legal secretaries I had enlisted to help me wrote down the names, addresses, phone numbers and diagnoses of everyone who was willing to cooperate in a follow-up study. We got 82 names — almost everyone who was approached. The only reason we didn't get more was that the flow of the cured was so heavy that the secretaries couldn't get to them all.

A few weeks after the service, letters were sent to the names on the list, inviting them to come to Minneapolis on Sunday, July 14, and tell us about their experiences. Twenty-three people showed up, and I made arrangements to interview them individually over the next few months. I've singled out three particular cases to discuss here because they're typical of so many that I have in my files.

Case Number One. Marilyn Rogers, 18; a tall, pretty, intelligent girl, who told her story fluently.

Eight months before the Kathryn Kuhlman meeting, Marilyn fell ill with multiple sclerosis. For a while she had been confined to a wheelchair, but gradually, with treatment, she was able to get around, first with a walker, later with a cane. Before being released from the hospital, she developed severe headaches. The doctors thought they were caused by pressure on her neck muscles. She was outfitted with a neck brace, which reduced the severity of the headaches but did not eliminate them.

At the time Marilyn attended the Kathryn Kuhlman service, she was using her cane all the time but her neck brace only intermittently. She didn't wear her neck brace to the service, but when she arrived at the auditorium and saw the long line of people, she was afraid that she wouldn't be able to take the strain of standing for a long time, so she borrowed a wheelchair.

During the healing service, when Kathryn Kuhlman said, "Go into the aisle, you people with spine injury, but don't come up on the stage till you know you've been healed," Marilyn felt a burning sensation in her spine. She left her wheelchair, dropped her cane and walked down the aisle. An usher brought the chair up to the stage.

When Kathryn Kuhlman asked, "Is that your wheelchair?," Marilyn didn't want to go into a complex explanation so she simply said "yes." "And now you're walking?" Kathryn Kuhlman had asked her.

"Yes, I am," Marilyn answered.

"Oh, praise the Holy Spirit," Miss Kuhlman said, and the audience had applauded vigorously.

Then she had Marilyn walk back and forth across the stage, demonstrating her "new" ability to walk. Since it was obvious to everyone that Marilyn's gait was not completely normal, Miss Kuhlman had explained, "Of course it will take time for these muscles to get back to normal. But isn't she doing well — isn't God wonderful?"

In the two months after the meeting, though Marilyn still used her cane when she was tired, she felt that her gait had improved steadily and that her headaches had decreased in frequency and intensity. She was sure Kathryn Kuhlman had cured her and that it would only be a matter of time till she was perfectly normal. Her doctor had been unable to measure any real change in her muscle strength, but they agreed that she walked very well and offered no explanation of the improvement in her headaches.

After I thanked Marilyn for telling me about her case, I wished her well and watched her leave my office. She walked with the wide-based waddle to which victims of multiple sclerosis often resort. To my eye there was no discernible improvement in her gait, but I was glad her spirits were so high.

Case Number Two. Sister Marian is a Roman Catholic nun of 53.

She went to the service more to observe than to seek a healing. Her only problem was pain, off and on, in her left shoulder — "a sort of bursitis," the doctor called it.

Sister Marian had been sitting about halfway back on the ground floor when Kathryn Kuhlman had said, "All those having trouble with an arm, stand up." Sister Marian hadn't wanted to

338

stand — she felt conspicuous in her nun's clothing — but when Miss Kuhlman said, "Stand up," for the third time, Sister Marian felt obliged to stand.

Then Kathryn Kuhlman said to those who were standing, "Wave your arms, wave your arms. See if the Holy Spirit hasn't cured you." Sister Marian just had to wave her arm. As she did so, she felt no pain, only a tingling, hot feeling, and she thought she actually might be one of those cured.

She was reluctant to go to the stage, but when an usher said to her, "Have you been cured?" she felt as if she had to nod yes. And when he said, "Then go to the stage and claim your cure," she couldn't hang back.

Walking to the stage, she was still undecided whether she had really been cured, and when Kathryn Kuhlman said, "Sister, have you been cured?," she couldn't bring herself to say a definite yes. Instead, she waved her arm in the air. This, of course, was enough to elicit a loud ovation from the crowd.

Sister Marian still has trouble with her shoulder but not as often as before the healing. She thinks her pains may recur off and on until a deeper spiritual healing occurs. She believes Kathryn Kuhlman has started her on her way to that spiritual healing.

Case Number Three. Rita Swanson is 23 and a longtime fan of Kathryn Kuhlman's.

Rita had severe acne. She had been treated by dermatologists off and on for years. The latest therapy had consisted of vitamins and antibiotics.

At the service, Rita was seated in section six when Miss Kuhlman had said, "Someone in section six is suffering from a skin problem. I rebuke that problem. In three days it will be cured." Rita looked around, saw no one else with obvious skin trouble and knew then that she would be cured.

Three days later, she said, her face was very much improved. Since that time, even though she'd stopped taking antibiotics and vitamins, her skin hadn't gotten any worse. Even her dermatologist agreed that her skin was better, though he wouldn't go so far as to say she was "cured."

Let's discuss these three cases at greater length.

Case Number One. Marilyn Rogers, the girl with multiple sclerosis.

Multiple sclerosis is a terrifying disease. No one knows what causes it or how to cure it. Hundreds of drugs have been used to treat it; so far, none has been consistently helpful. Over the short run, however, almost any treatment will seem to work.

There are two reasons for this. First, the disease is cyclic; its symptoms may come and go. Second, multiple sclerosis is a disease in which the psyche plays a major role.

Marilyn wants so badly to be better that she will interpret anything that happens to her as evidence that she is improving. She may even function better physically if it is suggested to her that she can do so.

Her walk, for example. Marilyn has the gait, a sort of waddle, that multiple-sclerosis patients often develop to compensate for loss of strength in their muscles. Sometimes when she is tired her waddle is very apparent. But put Marilyn up on the stage, with 10,000 people watching her, have a woman in flowing robes with a close relationship to the Holy Spirit say to her, "Walk, Marilyn, walk. I rebuke your multiple sclerosis," and Marilyn will walk. Not perfectly, but better, perhaps, than she has walked in months. And her heart will leap with joy and she'll say to herself, "I'm cured, I'm cured."

Perhaps, for a while, Marilyn will be better; eventually, unfortunately, she'll have trouble again. Multiple sclerosis waxes and wanes, but the cure has so far escaped us.

Case Number Two. Sister Marian, the 53-year-old nun with bursitis.

Bursitis is an inflammation in the bursa of the joint. It is an on-again, off-again thing so the fact that Sister Marian didn't have any pain when she waved her arm wasn't really significant. The pain came back shortly after the meeting and her shoulder continues, intermittently, to trouble her.

What is most interesting about Sister Marian's case is that even though she was reluctant to go up on the stage and claim a cure, she did so. When Kathryn Kuhlman asked her if she was cured, she equivocated by waving her arm in front of the audience.

Sister Marian's reaction was typical of many in the audience; no one wanted to let Kathryn Kuhlman down. The whole scene — the religious fervor, the wheelchairs on the stage — casts a spell over the audience. As with Sister Marian, it becomes more difficult *not* to claim a cure than to claim one.

Case Number Three. Rita Swanson, the girl with bad skin.

Rita wants badly to have a nice complexion. Her desire to be cured makes her highly susceptible to suggestion. If someone tells her, as Kathryn Kuhlman did, that her skin will be better in three days, then in three days, when she looks in the mirror, she will look for evidence that her skin has improved and the chances are excellent that she will find it. After all, judging the appearance of the skin is highly subjective. You look in the mirror and unless things are too shockingly obvious you will see what you want to see.

There are two other points worth mentioning here. Kathryn Kuhlman didn't say, "Someone with a skin disease has just been cured." Though she pronounced instant cures of cancer, bursitis, hearing loss — all things that no one could see — Rita's skin defect, which was obvious, would take three days to cure.

The second point is this: Someone with skin disease that falls into the category known as neurodermatitis *could* find that, after attending a Kathryn Kuhlman service, the disease had disappeared. Neurodermatitis is an inflammation of the skin caused by nerves and is sometimes responsive to hypnosis. Since Kathryn Kuhlman uses certain hypnotic techniques, it would be odd if occasionally a neurodermatitis, or one of the many other diseases susceptible to hypnosis, did not respond to her miracle service. Acne is susceptible to suggestion and hypnosis. Emotional problems make acne worse; dermatologists know, for example, that students who have acne will almost invariably complain that their skin gets worse at examination time. So it is possible that Rita's skin improved as a result of Miss Kuhlman's suggestion. But her acne scars, which are organic, will never respond to a miracle service.

In talking to these people, I tried to be as honest, understanding and objective as possible, but I couldn't dispense with my medical knowledge and my common sense. I listened carefully to everything they told me and followed up every lead that might have led to a confirmation of a miracle.

I was led to an inescapable conclusion: Of the patients who had reported that they had experienced cures claimed at the miracle service, not one had, in fact, been miraculously cured of anything.

And what about the cancer patients who had claimed cures? None of them had returned to Minneapolis. Since I was anxious to find out what had happened to them, I contacted everyone on my list. This is what I learned.

Case Number One. Leona Flores, the woman who had claimed a cure of lung cancer and who, on the stage at Kathryn Kuhlman's suggestion, had "proved" her cure by taking deep breaths without any pain.

When I contacted her, Leona told me that she had not had lung cancer at all. "I have Hodgkin's disease," she said, "and some of the glands in my chest are involved. But since no one else got up when Miss Kuhlman said, 'Someone with lung cancer is being cured,' I figured it had to be me.

"I've been back to my doctor and he says he can't see any change in my X ray. I think I breathe better, but it's hard to tell, since I never had much trouble breathing anyway."

Case Number Two. Gerald Warren, the 63-year-old man with prostatic cancer that had spread to the bone. He is the man for whom I found a wheelchair and who walked to the stage without it as evidence of his cure.

Two months later, when I contacted Mr. Warren's daughter, she told me that for three or four days after the miracle service her father had felt "real good," but then he began to get weak again and since then has gone downhill. "He goes back to the doctor once a week for shots," she told me, "and he needs pain pills now for his back. I guess Dad was wrong when he thought Kathryn Kuhlman had cured him."

Case Number Three. Mrs. Helen Sullivan, a 50-year-old woman with cancer of the stomach that had spread to her liver and to the vertebrae in her back. At Kathryn Kuhlman's suggestion Mrs. Sullivan had taken off her back brace and run back and forth across the stage several times. Two months after the miracle service I talked to Mrs. Sullivan. She was confined to her bed, which had been moved into her living room.

"I knew about Kathryn Kuhlman from watching her television show," she told me, "and when I read that she was coming to Minneapolis I got pretty excited. My husband kept telling me not to get my hopes too high, but when you're awfully sick and someone tells you that you may be cured, it's impossible not to get excited.

"At the service, as soon as she said someone with cancer is being cured, I knew she meant me. I went right up on the stage, and when she asked me about the brace, I just took it right off, though I hadn't had it off for over four months. While I was up on that stage, bending over, touching my toes and running up and down, I felt just wonderful. I was sure I was cured.

"The next morning I woke up with a horrible pain in my back. The doctor put me in the hospital and got some X rays that showed one of my vertebrae had collapsed. He said it was probably from the bending and running I had done. I stayed in the hosptial in traction for a week. When I went home, I was back in my brace.

"Since then I've gotten a lot weaker. I can't make it upstairs any more — that's why we've got the bed down here."

Mrs. Sullivan died of cancer four months after she had been

"cured" at Kathryn Kuhlman's miracle service.

The more I learned of the results of Kathryn Kuhlman's miracle service the more doubtful I became that any good she was doing could possibly outweigh the misery she was causing. I wrote her and asked if she'd send me a list of people she had cured.

Miss Kuhlman was most cooperative. Almost by return mail I received a letter listing a dozen names with addresses, telephone numbers, and diagnoses. Her letter was very friendly, but the line that interested me most was this: "What I tried to do [referring to the list of patients] was give you a variety, and diseases that could not possibly have been psychosomatic." When I studied the list, I found that two thirds of the patients suffered from diseases such as multiple sclerosis, rheumatoid arthritis, paralysis (no cause listed), loss of sight and allergies — all diseases in which the psyche plays an important role. It was apparent from her letter that Miss Kuhlman knew very little — next to nothing — about psychosomatic diseases.

I wrote to all the cancer victims on her list — eight in all — and the only one who offered cooperation was a man who claimed he had been cured of prostatic cancer by Miss Kuhlman. He sent me a complete report of his case. Prostatic cancer is frequently very responsive to hormone therapy. This man had had extensive treatment with surgery radiation and hormones. He had also been "treated" by Kathryn Kuhlman. He chose to attribute his cure or remission, as the case may be — to Miss Kuhlman. But anyone who read his report, layman or doctor, would see immediately that it is impossible to tell which kind of treatment had actually done the most to prolong his life. If Miss Kuhlman had to rely on his case to prove that the Holy Spirit "cured" cancer through her, she would be in very desperate straits.

Kathryn Kuhlman's lack of medical sophistication is a critical point. I don't believe she is a liar or a charlatan or that she is, consciously, dishonest. I think that she believes the Holy Spirit works through her to perform miraculous cures. I think she sincerely believes that the thousands of sick people who come to her services and claim cures are, through her ministrations, being cured of organic diseases. I also think — and my investigations confirm this — that she is wrong.

The problem is — and I'm sorry this has to be so blunt — one of ignorance. Miss Kuhlman doesn't know the difference between psychogenic and organic diseases. Though she uses hypnotic techniques, she doesn't *know* anything about hypnotism and the power of suggestion. She doesn't know anything about the autonomic nervous system. Or, if she does know something about these things, she has certainly learned to hide her knowledge.

There is one other possibility: It may be that Miss Kuhlman doesn't *want* to learn that her work is not as miraculous as it seems. For this reason she has trained herself to deny, emotionally and intellectually, anything that might threaten the validity of her ministry.

I'm inclined to rest my case on the axiom, often used by the defense lawyer in malpractice cases when a sponge has been found in the patient's abdomen after an operation: *Res ispa loquitur* ("The thing speaks for itself"). (Used by permission.)

EXCURSUS ON ORIGINAL SIN

THE BIG LIE

The most noxious seed ever sown in the soil of the Christian faith is the dogma of original sin. Every branch of the Christian doctrine of salvation has subsequently been corrupted. Someone has said, "One of the nicest things about telling the truth is that one doesn't have to remember what has been said." On the other hand, telling a lie is like stepping off onto a ski slide. There is no stopping until one hits the bottom. The bigger the lie the more precipitous the slide. For every lie that is told, another, and another, etc., etc., etc., must be told. Such is the history of the "big lie" in denominational dogma.

The dogma of original sin produced the doctrine of total heredity depravity — the teaching that man is by nature, in consequence of Adam's transgression, dead in sin from the moment of conception. This doctrine is generally attributed to "Saint" Augustine who lived in the latter half of the 4th century. Historians, however, point out that Augustine should only be credited with the particular form of the doctrine attributed to him. He was a compiler, not an originator.

A Jewish sect as early as the Exilic period is known to have taught a doctrine of similar import. This is attested by the vigorous refutation of such contemporary prophets as Jeremiah and Ezekiel (see Jer. 31:29,30 and Ezekiel 18, particularly vv. 1-4 and 19,20). Notwithstanding the thoroughness and finality of the prophets' refutation the teaching persisted, supported by false application of such passages as Exodus 20:5 and Psalm 51:5.

The Jewish form of the doctrine sought only to provide excuse for man's personal wickedness. It was argued he came by it naturally. Father was a sinner, his father was a sinner, his father, also, etc., etc. The phrase that was coined to express this was a cute one — "The fathers have eaten sour grapes and the children's teeth are set on edge" (Ezek. 18:2; cf. Jer. 31:29,30).

The modern behavioristic school of psychology would find in the ancient Jewish sect minds kindred to their own.

The Augustinian doctrine is a perversion of deeper dye. Not the consequences only, not even just a susceptibility or tendency to sin, but the very guilt of Adam's sin — this too is transmitted unto all generations through the process of procreation! This is the big lie in denominational dogma — the most noxious seed ever sown in the soil of the Christian faith. Behold how every branch of the Christian doctrine of salvation has been corrupted by it.

PART ONE

APOSTASIES CULMINATING IN THE DOCTRINE OF SALVATON BY WORKS (ALONE)

Infant Baptism

Out of the doctrine of total hereditary depravity grew the practice of infant "baptism" (Quotation marks may be omitted, insofar as the mode is concerned at the outset, for the Roman Church as well as the Greek branch in Augustine's time immersed, and continued to do so for several centuries afterwards.) If the doctrine of total hereditary depravity be allowed then infant "baptism" becomes mandatory even if it isn't commanded, alluded to or allowance made for it, in the New Testament. As soon as it began to be believed that "there are babes in hell not a span long" (because of the transmission of Adam's guilt) mothers began to clamor for their babies to be admitted to the rite of baptism.

The reason is not hard to understand. If babies are born sinners, then (since baptism is for the remission of sin)[1] obviously babies should be baptized at the earliest time possible.

---

1. The notion that "baptism for remission of sins" violates the principle of justification by faith is of much later origin, being a reaction to the doctrine of sacerdotalism which arose out of the practice of infant baptism.

SACERDOTALISM, BAPTISMAL REGENERATION, ETC.

Out of the practice of infant baptism arose a cluster of closely related perversions of Christian doctrine. Obviously the "baptism" of infants posed a problem. In that infants cannot fulfill the requirement of faith (Mark 16:16) it was necessary to reason around this requirement. This was accomplished (1) by attributing "priestly" powers to the officiating ministers (sacerdotalism, the basic ingredient of the Romanist hierarchial system), or (2) by assuming that the faith of believing parents sanctifies their children, through baptism. The logical outgrowth of such reasoning is the doctrine of baptismal regeneration (water salvation, as it is sometimes scornfully called).

Our brethren, in this heydey of the faith only cult, are often charged with teaching and practicing baptismal regeneration. To make such a charge is to neither understand the terminology employed nor the teaching and practice of our people. Baptismal regeneration is a necessary corollary of infant baptism. In our insistence upon believer's baptism we reject the very conditions that necessitate such a doctrine. No, not the baptism of penitent believers "for the remission of (personal) sins" (Acts 2:38) but the "baptism" of unwitting (and often unwilling) infants for the remission of Adam's sins — this is "baptismal regeneration."

John 3:3-5 clearly informs us we must be spirit begotten (regenerated by the Holy Spirit) as well as be born of the water to enter into the kingdom of heaven. Thus we insist that baptism be reserved for those who have first been evangelized by the Christian gospel, who profess their faith in Christ thereby, and who come repentantly surrendering body and soul to the Lord Jesus Christ.

CONFIRMATION

Another outgrowth of The Big Lie is confirmation, as practiced throughout the Paedo-baptist denominations. In a society where it was customary for the parents to make life's greatest decision for their children, even to their occupations and partners in marriage, it was not at all difficult to develop this corollary to infant baptism also. The child, "baptized" without his (or her) knowledge or consent, upon reaching the age of accountability was required to confirm (personally accept) the decision the parents had made for him.

SALVATION BY WORKS

The "leaven of the pharisees" (Matt. 16:6), the doctrine that salvation is secured by ritual was infused into the "lump" of Christian doctrine by the foregoing development. Two divergent movements have grown out of such a notion — Roman Catholicism and Protestant Liberalism.

ROMAN CATHOLICISM

Roman Catholicism represents one end to which the doctrine of total hereditary depravity has led. Besides the foregoing a number of kindred errors peculiar to the papist system have arisen. The doctrine of the immaculate conception (introduced to spare the Christ child the guilt of Adam's transgression) and more recently the doctrine of the assumption of Mary are contingencies. Purgatory, works of supererogation and a number of other encrustations are other contingencies. The bridge between these and the Augustinian dogma is the sacerdotal system.

PROTESTANT LIBERALISM

Protestant liberalism has avowed to cut itself adrift from all tradition, to seek truth wherever it may be found. But the road to salvation blazed by the papists is the road these would travel also. Only the vehicles in which they would have us travel differ. These too expect to find salvation (whatever that may mean to a liberal protestant) *by works.*

Ethicism and sociology replace the vehicles in which the Romanists expect to ride up to the pearly gates. Liberal protestants may not be too sure the road they are traveling leads to eternal life in that "better country," but to whatever ultimate goal they do expect to arrive, if any, they are sure the way to get there is by "works of righteousness which we do ourselves" to borrow a phrase from Paul, in which he denied the very thing the liberals avow! (Titus 3:5).

PART TWO

APOSTASIES CULMINATING IN THE DOCTRINE OF SALVATION BY FAITH (ALONE)

(Synopsis of Part One)

In Part One we trace the dependency of the papal doctrine of salvation (by works) upon the dogma of original sin. We showed too that modern protestant liberalism is nourished from the same stock. In the instance of the latter the dependency is akin to such a growth as mistletoe, a vegetable parasite which derives its life from the tree upon which it feeds.

The doctrine of salvation by works as developed by the papists is an offshoot of sacerdotalism, which is an offshoot of infant baptism, an offshoot of the doctrine of the total hereditary depravity of man, growing out of The Big Lie — the dogma of original sin.

Modern protestant liberalism is in no sense native to such a system, but like any other parasite it has enough affinity to that

350

upon which it feeds to sustain itself thereby. The affinity in this case is the doctrine we have taken pains to expose. Whether the doctrine be in its papal form (salvation by ritual) or its protestant form (salvation by social progress) it is utterly false to the Christian doctrine of salvation.

In Part Two we wish to examine the tenets of fundamentalism, and to show its dependency likewise upon The Big Lie. It has been truly said, "The old serpent, the Devil, has a forked tongue!"

THE DOGMA DEFINED

The dogma of original sin finds its classic expression in the official confession of the Presbyterian Church in the U.S.A.:

By this sin (eating of the forbidden fruit) they (Adam and Eve) fell from their original righteousness and communion with God, and so became dead in sin, and wholly defiled in all the faculties and parts of body and soul. They being the root of all mankind, the guilt of this sin was imputed and the same death in sin and corrupted nature conveyed to all their posterity descending from them by ordinary generation. From this original corruption whereby we are indisposed, disabled, and made opposite to all good, and wholly inclined to evil, do proceed all actual transgressions. (Revised edition, 1939, pp. 25,26.)

PREDESTINATION

Such a dogma calls for action — strong, immediate action — on the part of God, or man, else all would be lost. No worse thing could be said of the devil himself than the dogma has said of all Adam's race. One branch of theology has man taking the initiative to spare the race the guilt and condemnation of Adam's transgression. By the introduction of the practice of infant baptism the depraved child is supposed to be provided a way of escape. Another branch of theology has God taking the initiative. With this branch we now wish to deal.

Some such doctrine as predestination seems a logical necessity if the major premise of the dogmatists be allowed to stand. If a child is born "dead" in sin, "utterly indisposed, disabled and made opposite to all good," nothing the child could possibly do, or ever hope to do, could count for righteousness. The fact is, these theories would remind us, a dead man can't do anything! He must first be made alive, and that is a Divine prerogative and function. Thus these theorists would have us believe salvation is wholly of God, and not by anything which we may do ourselves. Our fate is wholly in the hands of God who has predestined (foreordained) all things.

How then shall anyone be saved? This is a matter of God's arbitrary election. God, being both just and merciful, elects some to be lost, others to be saved. All deserve to go to hell in consequence of the guilt of Adam. Those whom God elects to go to heaven are just as deserving of hell but God, to show Himself merciful, elects that they be saved. This is the Calvinistic doctrine of salvation. Calvinists would dignify this farce by calling it the doctrine of the Divine Sovereignty of God. He arbitrarily elects some to participate in the "free grace" of Christ's "finished work on Calvary." He elects, equally as arbitrarily, to allow others to be lost, that His justice may also be vindicated.

THE MOURNERS' BENCH

Out of such a theory came the mourners' bench, altar calls, and "praying through" ceremonies so common to the fundamentalist movement. Herein is one of the paradoxes of fundamentalism. While professing to believe in salvation by faith alone rather than in "works of righteousness which we do ourselves," they have devised a system all their own, having no relevance to the New Testament record of conversion.

Instead of an open confession of Jesus as the Christ the Son of the Living God, fundamentalists instruct sinners to "raise your hand" (while every head is bowed and every eye is closed). That the New Testament provides no authority for such a procedure seems to bother them not at all.

When as many as can be persuaded at a given service to raise their hands have indicated they would have the evangelist pray for them the altar call is given. They are now exhorted to show they "mean business" by coming to the mourners' bench to be prayed through. This is generally required as a deliberate alternative to Christian baptism. The latter would be "a work." But praying through is not a work! How deceived and deceiving can these deceivers be? That which is of faith ("faith cometh by hearing and hearing by the word of Christ," Rom. 10:17) is called a work, and that which is altogether a work of righteousness which men do of themselves, being not by commandment of Christ but by order of fundamentalist evangelists, is pawned off as salvation by faith alone!

SALVATION BY FAITH ALONE

There is no such thing as salvation by faith alone, not even in the practice of those who shout such a doctrine from the tallest transmitters towering above our housetops. Fundamentalists have substituted works of their own devising for "the obedience of faith" (Rom. 1:5; 6:16-18; 16:26). "Raise your hands," "come to the altar," "pray through," "say, pray for me . . . (name of the evangelist.)" These "works" are required of every seeker for salvation, after which they are told, "just believe you have received."

Salvation by faith alone is only a catchy phrase to "catch" the ignorant and unsuspecting. The doctrine itself was conceived as a necessary corollary to the doctrine of election whereby it is

353

assumed God "gives faith" to those upon whom His "free grace" has been "elected" to fall. His Divine Sovereignty foreordains who is to be elected, who is to be omitted. We may agonize and plead and pray at the mourners' bench for God to give us faith, but we dare not "confess with our mouth Christ Jesus as Lord" and "be baptized for the remission of sins." That would be to minimize the grace of God. Salvation could not be the "free gift of God" if we would so work for it. Apparently praying through, sweating it out on a mourners' bench, is not work. But simply yielding oneself, body and soul, to the will of God so completely that one can be represented as having died, and been buried, and raised to walk in newness of life — that's work! Can you believe it?

ETERNAL SECURITY

The cap sheath of this strange mode of reasoning is the doctrine of Eternal Security — "once saved, always saved." It is not generally recognized how necessary this doctrine is to the anti-be baptized cult. In order to hold that salvation is by faith alone these theorists have to teach that not only baptism, but "continuing steadfastly in the Apostles' doctrines, fellowship, the breaking of bread and prayers," and other aspects of the Christian life likewise are just "electives." They may determine the extent of reward in heaven, the size and splendor of our mansion, but not our entrance into heaven itself.

FAITH BASED ON EXPERIENCE

That such doctrines are completely at variance with scores of scriptures does not seem to disturb the fundamentalists one whit. Theirs is a "faith" based on "experience." That experience may be, and often is, a form of self-hypnosis, experienced under the emotional strain and suggestion of the "prayer workers" whose wailing and entreating and exhorting destroys all power to reason. This experience, nonetheless, is made a basis for belief that one has been gloriously and everlastingly elected to salvation, brought under the blood of Christ, and glory bound.

CONCLUSION: Astronomers used to believe that the earth was flat, that it stood still, and that the sun, moon and stars revolved about it. Error of such magnitude led to so many difficulties that when King Alphonso of Spain was being instructed by his court astronomers, he shook his head and said, "Even I could have told the Creator of a better plan."

The difficulties were not with the Creator's plan. They were due to man's false reasoning. When Copernicus, some years afterward, demonstrated the true nature of the solar system the difficulties of which King Alphonso complained were solved.

In like manner the myriad of errors growing out of the Big Lie will never be solved by arguing with our religious neighbors about infant baptism, baptism for remission of sins, predestination, election, etc. The Big Lie itself must be exposed, and God's truth be made clear. The axe needs to be laid to the root of this noxious weed that has become as a great tree.

SUPPLEMENT: The foregoing remarks are not intended to be scholarly or exhaustive, but rather to summarize and expose in terms the ordinary person can understand the terrible fruitage of The Big Lie. As a supplement to the foregoing, a critical analysis of the nature and effect of Adam's transgression is hereby appended.

THE DOGMA OF ORIGINAL SIN

We have reviewed the devious doctrines growing out of The Big Lie — the dogma of original sin. In this supplement we wish to examine the dogma directly. This is no great task, provided that we limit ourselves to the teaching of the scriptures on the subject. The sin of Adam, and the direct and immediate consequences are discussed in Romans 5:12-21 and I Cor. 15:21,22.

An incidental allusion to Adam's transgression is found in I Timothy 2:14.

ADAM'S SIN

From Genesis 3 we learn Adam and Eve ate of the forbidden fruit as an act of willful disobedience. The immediate consequence was that "their eyes were opened." Inasmuch as the tree they had eaten of was the tree of knowledge of good and evil, the inference is that they passed from the state of innocency into the state of moral accountability. In this regard they exhibited a sense of shame at their physical nakedness and set about to cover themselves as best they could. They apparently had no evil imaginations prior to their temptation and fall. The second consequence was that they were "afraid" when they heard the voice of God and immediately undertook to hide themselves as best they could.

WAS ADAM ORIGINALLY IMMORTAL?

At this point we need to note man was not created immortal. Were this so, what purpose would have been served by the tree of life? The fact that subsequent to their transgression they were barred from the tree of life is evidence the perpetuity of their lives was conditioned upon access to that tree. By the sweat of his brow Adam might, and did, eke out a living for himself and his bride for a time, but it was a losing battle. He died, as his posterity have done. Thus God had warned: "Of the tree of knowledge of good and evil, thou shalt not eat of it, for in the day thou eatest thereof *dying, thou shalt surely die*" (Gen. 2:7). (Italics indicate the more exact meaning of the Hebrew text.)

Adam and Eve came under the sentence òf death when they sinned. Like a fish thrown into a stagnant pool, gilling laboriously to escape impending death, so Adam and Eve now turned out of the garden into the cursed earth beyond the gates of Eden, by toil, sweat and pain "lived" for some time and even begat chlidren, but death was inevitable. Inasmuch as the garden with the tree of life was subsequently removed from earth all Adam's posterity passed under the sentence of death.

DID ADAM DIE SPIRITUALLY?

Did Adam and Eve die spiritually the day they sinned? This may be allowed, for sin separates from God (Isa. 59:2) and the basic idea in the Biblical usage of the word "death" is that of separation. The separation of the soul from the body is called death. (This is physical, ordinary death.) The ultimate and final separation of the soul from God, after the judgment, is called "the second death" (Rev. 20:14). The New Testament refers to those in this present life who are separated from God by reason of sin as "dead through trespasses" (Eph. 2:2,5). Reasoning from the dogma of original sin, fundamentalists are inclined to interpret the term in its literal sense, that is in the sense of one being without life, feeling, sensibility, consciousness, inclinations, capacity to act, etc. In such case the sinner is thereby rendered wholly dependent upon the "quickening" grace of God to even so much as have the capacity to believe on the Lord Jesus Christ, to know and love God, trust in Christ for salvation, etc. but this is a decided and obvious misuse of the figure of speech. We repeat, the basic idea in the Biblical usage of the term is that of separation. In the sense in which the scriptures use the term we may allow that Adam and Eve entered the state of spiritual death upon becoming transgressors.

ARE WE ALL BORN "DEAD" SPIRITUALLY?

Are all men "born dead" spiritually in consequence of Adam's transgression? This is the paramount issue involved in this discussion. Exponents of the dogma of original sin teach that all are "stillborn" spiritually. This is a strange wresting of the scriptures. Adam and Eve suffered physical death in consequence of their sin but their descendants certainly are not all born dead (physically), *else the race itself would have died at the stem*. On what basis must we assume all are born dead *spiritually*? Neither by analogy nor by any Word of the Lord may we draw such a conclusion. Paul's statement in I Corinthians 15:21,22 cannot rightly be so construed. If spiritual death is the death he is speaking of, then all men will be saved. The text reads: "As in Adam all die, so also in Christ shall all be made alive." The Universalists are no more in error in using the last half of the verse to teach universal redemption through Christ than are the dogmatists in using the first half of the verse to teach universal Adamic guiltiness. They are no more wrong, *but they are also no more right*.

I CORINTHIANS 15:21,22

The context of I Corinthians 15:21,22 makes it unmistakably plain that the death spoken of is physical death, for the resurrection spoken of is certainly the resurrection of the body. Here we do have a parallel. All die (physically) in Adam. And all are made alive (physically) in Christ. Hear ye Him: "The hour cometh, in which all that are in the tombs shall hear His voice, and shall come forth; they that have done good unto the resurrection of life; and they that have done evil unto the resurrection of judgment" (John 5:28,29).

ROMANS 5:12-21

Romans 5:12-21 is not so easily explained, at least not in so few words. But when explained in the light of the doctrine of inherited guilt a far greater difficulty is raised than any that are explained thereby. It is impossible to escape the doctrine of universal redemption if universal guilt is reckoned as passing upon men in consequence of Adam's transgression. Not all parts of Paul's analogy are readily comprehensible but this much is plainly propounded: Everything that has been "passed upon" man by reason of Adam's transgression is canceled by the gracious act of Christ. To the extent Adam's sin is said to affect us, to the same extent Christ's righteousness is said to nullify that effect. The same number of persons affected by the one are said to be affected by the other. If the solitary act of Adam *condemned all men* to spiritual death (apart from any personal accountability) then one solitary act of Christ *redeemed all men*, apart from any personal, individual accountability. Since all men are not "saved" just because Christ is Savior, all men are not guilty because Adam was a sinner. The one state of being or relationship is no more automatic nor universal than is the other. What Paul is actually saying is not that we inherit Adam's guilt, but simply that Adam introduced sin, condemnation and death into the world. Thus Christ came to bring righteousness, justification and eternal life. To say more than this is to say too much. *If the guilt of Adam's sin is the ground of our condemnation then Adam is greater than Christ, for more by far are thereby "made sinners" (if this interpretation be allowed) than are "made righteous" through Christ.*

GUILT VS. CONSEQUENCES

The dogmatists fail to distinguish between the consequences of an act and the guilt of that act. The children of adulterers, drunkards, murderers, thieves and such like suffer many of the consequences *but none of the guilt.* Exodus 20:5 is often cited to support the doctrine that guilt is inherited. The passage reads, "I Jehovah, thy God, am a jealous God, visiting the iniquities of the fathers upon the children, upon the third and upon the fourth generation of them that hate me." But the next verse reads, "and showing loving kindness unto thousands [of generations, *see marginal note*] of them that love me and keep my commandments."

Psalm 51:5 is the classic scripture used to support the doctrine of inherited guilt. "Behold I was brought forth in iniquity, and in sin did my mother conceive me." If every distress wrought cry in the Psalms were to be taken as a basis of Christian doctrine the confusion would be even greater than it now is. Was David stating a truth that is to be interpreted as being universally applicable? The words were spoken after his own great sin of adultery. He undoubtedly was reminded of a point of law recorded in Deuteronomy 23:2, "A bastard shall not enter into the assembly of Jehovah; even to the tenth generation shall none of his enter into the assembly of Jehovah." From Ruth 4:12-22 and Matthew 1:2-6 we find that David was of the tenth generation to arise from the base fornication of Judah (see Genesis 38:24-30). Contemplating his own great sin of like nature David may well have surmised himself to be born and conceived in sin.[2] But the distressed cry wrung from the heart of the guilty king is hardly a basis for Christian doctrine, especially since the only scriptures he could possibly appeal to in support of such excuse for his folly is a part of the law that was nailed to the cross and made of no effect by Christ's redemptive death.

THE PROPHETS' ANSWER

Scriptures such as Exodus 20:5 and Deuteronomy 23:2 ap-. parently were as misconstrued by the Jews as they are by dogmatists of our generation. The Jews found in such scriptures excuse for themslves. "We can't help it. We are born that way."

---

2. The word David used for "conceive" is not *harah*, the common word for human conception, but *yacham* — animal "heat." This is the sole such use of *yacham* in all the Bible. In this context that needs to be noted.

Yea, "The fathers have eaten sour grapes and the children's teeth are set on edge" (Jer. 31:29; Ezek. 18:2). Therefore God, through His prophets, cried out: "As I live, saith the Lord Jehovah, ye shall not have occasion any more to use this proverb in Israel" (Ezek. 18:3, cf. Jer. 31:29). Having thus spoken God announced through Jeremiah the coming of a new convenant (vv. 31-34) which the Hebrew writer declares to be fulfilled in Christ (Heb. 8:8-13), and through Ezekiel God declares:

> The soul that sinneth, it shall die; the son shall not bear the iniquity of the father, neither shall the father bear the iniquity of the son; the righteousness of the righteous shall be upon him, the wickedness of the wicked shall be upon him (Ezek. 18:20).

This should end the matter. Unfortunately it has not done so. Thus one more observation is in order. The practice of infant baptism arose to meet the emergency created by the dogma of original sin. Noting the fact that the scriptures teach baptism for the remission of sins, the baptism of infants was introduced to remit the inherited sin of newborn babes lest they should die in infancy and thus dying (physically) before they were old enough to be evangelized they should go to hell by reason of being spiritually dead also. But note that every consequence of Adam's sin, real and imaginary, Biblical and traditional, continues in force *after baptism*. Male children, "baptized" as well as unbaptized, must battle weeds in every garden, lawn or field they may have to till. They must sweat, toil and die. Female children likewise suffer the same lot imposed upon Eve, "baptized" or not! What kind of remission of sin is this that remits the sin but wreaks out vengeance upon the remisees nonetheless?

Does one say, it is not the physical consequences of Adam's sin but the inherited guilt that baptism remits? The issue is unchanged. If baptism is for the remission of inherited guilt how is it then the offspring of those who have been baptized still inherit Adam's guilt? Is Adam's guilt remitted or isn't it?

This is too much. It is assumed that infants inherit the sin of Adam and therefore must be baptized. Yet they remain cursed with that guilt despite baptism to pass it on to the next generation. Does God thus mock us?

The dogma of original sin is the biggest lie Satan has told since the day he told the first lie to the hapless pair he caused to be driven out of Eden. "He is a liar, and the father thereof" (John 8:44). Only the world's biggest liar could have conceived The Big Lie which has proven to be the most noxious weed ever sown in the soil of the Christian faith — the Dogma of Original Sin.

THE MOURNERS' BENCH

Whence is it? Is it of God, or of man?

Charles G. Finney, celebrated evangelist of the early 19th century and President of Oberlin College, delivered a series of lectures on evangelism in 1838 which, by popular demand, was made available to the general public in book form. Fleming H. Revell & Co. secured publishing rights. A copy of the second edition, entitled *Revivals of Religion* dated October 22, 1868, is before me.

Evangelist Finney, probably more than any other man, popularized the mourners' bench (or anxious seat, as he preferred to call it) as he led the vanguard of revivalists in the Great Religious Awakening that swept Europe and America a century ago. On pages 254-56 of the 1868 edition, Mr. Finney wrote in defense of the anxious seat. The following quotation is taken verbatim from page 254. Speaking of an "awakened sinner," Mr. Finney wrote:

> If you say to him. "There is the anxious seat, come out and avow your determination to be on the Lord's side," if he is not willing to do so small a thing as that, then he is not willing to do

anything, and there he is, brought out before his own conscience. It uncovers the delusion of the human heart, and prevents a great many spurious conversions, by showing those who might otherwise imagine themselves willing to do anything for Christ, that in fact they are willing to do *nothing*.

The church has always felt it necessary to have something of the kind to answer this very purpose. In the days of the apostles *baptism* answered this purpose. The Gospel was preached and those who were willing to be on the side of Christ were called on to be *baptized*. It (baptism) held the precise place that the anxious seat does now, as a public manifestation of their determination to be Christian.

Mr. Finney goes on to state that there were those who opposed the "anxious seats," but countered by saying, "in modern times those who have been violently opposed to the anxious seat have been obliged to adopt some substitute, or they could not get along in promoting a revival." Note, there is no appeal for evangelists to return to the apostolic practice of baptism, only a defense of the premise that some kind of substitute is necessary "in modern times" to the promotion of a revival.

AUTHOR'S NOTE: The tracing of the doctrine of salvation by works is not a difficult task. The lines of dependency, especially in the papal system, are clear; and are generally conceded. That protestant liberals share the concept of salvation by works is a fact of common knowledge, although it may not be as generally recognized that they are indebted to the Romanists for the development of the idea. In Part Two we have shown that 20th century Fundamentalism also, in its teaching of "salvation by faith alone" is likewise an outgrowth of the same basic error.

The doctrine of salvation by faith (alone) stands today as the antithesis of the doctrine of salvation by works (alone, or otherwise), but the roots thereof are the same. Fundamentalists simply represent another offshoot of the same parent stock. Not since Adam and Eve ate of the forbidden tree and introduced sin and death into this world has one act of man had such dire consequences as the introduction into the church of the dogma of original sin. In Part Two we propose to refute this dogma and discuss also the other branch thereof — 20th century Fundamentalism.

Index of Scriptures

Index of Topics

Bibliography

Allen, Roland, *The Ministry of the Spirit*, Eerdmans, 1970
Arthur, Wm., *The Tongues of Fire, Light and Life*, 1972.
Bickersteth, Edw. H., *The Trinity*, Kregels, 1965.
Bierderwolf, Wm. E., *A Helpt to the Study of the Holy Spirit*, Winona, 1903.
Blackwood, Andrew W., *The Holy Spirit in Your Life*, Baker, 1957.
Boles, H. Leo, "The Holy Spirit: His Personality, Nature, Works," *Gospel Advocate*, 1956.
Bowie, Walter R., *Jesus and the Trinity*, Abingdon, 1960.
Bruner, F.D., *A Theology of the Holy Spirit*, Eerdmans, 1970.
Buchanan, James, "The Holy Spirit," *Banner of Truth*, 1843.
Burdick, D.W., *Tongues: To Speak or Not to Speak*, Moody, 1969.
Calkins, R., *The Holy Spirit*, Abingdon, 1930.
Challen, James, *Symposium: Baptism in Spirit and Fire*, College Press, 1968.
Chapman, J. Wilbur, *Received Ye the Holy Ghost?*, Fleming & Revell, 1985.
Come, A.B., *Human Spirit and Holy Spirit*, Westminister, 1952.
Crawford, C.C., *The Eternal Spirit: His Word and Works*, College Press, 1972.
Dewar, L., *The Holy Spirit and Modern Thought*, Harper, 1959.
DeWelt, Don, *The Power of the Holy Spirit*, Vol. I, II, College Press, 1966.
Frost, Dr. Robert, *Aglow with the Spirit*, Voice Christian Publishing, 1956.
Fortman, Edmund, *The Triune God*, Baker, 1987.
Gardiner, C.E., *The Corinthian Catastrophe*, Kregel, 1974.
Garrison, J.H., *The Holy Spirit: His Personality, Mission and Modes of Activity*, Christian Publishing Co., 1905.
Gordon, A.J., *The Holy Spirit in Missions*, (reprint) Fleming & Revell, 1958.
_____, *The Ministry of the Spirit*, Fleming & Revell, 1894.
Gromacki, Robert G., *The Modern Tongues Movement*, Presbyt. & Reformed, 1967.
Guild (Editor), *The Holy Spirit: Fort Worth Christian College Lectureship*, The Manney Co., 1964.
Henry, A.M., *The Holy Spirit*, Hawthorne Books, 1966.
Hillis, Don W., *Tongues, Healing and You*, Baker, 1969.
Hobbs, H.H., *The Holy Spirit: The Believer's Guide*, Broadman, 1967.
Hoekema, Anthony, *The Modern Tongues Movement*, Presbyt. & Reformed, 1967.
_____, *Tongues and Holy Spirit Baptism*, Baker, 1981.
_____, *What About Speaking in Tongues*, Eerdmans, 1966.
Hoyle, R. Birch, *The Holy Spirit in St. Paul*, Doubleday & Doran, 1965.
Johnson, Ashely S., *The Holy Spirit and the Human Mind*.
Jones, J.B., *A Symposium on the Holy Spirit*, (1879 reprint) College Press, 1966.
Keithley, J.W., *The Mission of the Holy Spirit*, St. Louis M.E. Conf., 1904.
Ketcherside, W. Carl, *Heaven Help Us*, Standard, 1974.
_____, *The Holy Spirit in Our Lives Today: Hartford Forum*, published by author, 1966.
Kildahl, John P., *The Psychology of Speaking in Tongues*, Harper Row, 1972.

Klein, Abbe F., *The Doctrine of the Trinity*, Kennedy & Sons, 1940.
Kuyper, Abraham, *The Work of the Holy Spirit*, Eerdmans, 1956.
Lonergan, Bernard, *The Way to the Nicea*, Westminister, 1956.
Lowry, Chas. M., *The Trinity and Christian Devotion*, Harper, 1946.
McKenna, Stephen, "St. Augustine: The Trinity", *Daughters of St. Paul*, 1965.
Moule, N.G., *The Person and Work of the Holy Spirit*, Kregel, 1967.
Nee, Watchman, *The Release of the Spirit*, Sure Foundation, 1965.
Owen, John, *The Holy Spirit: His Gifts and Power*, Kregel, 1967.
Pache, Rene, *The Person and Work of the Holy Spirit*, Moody, 1954.
Palmer, Edw. H., *The Holy Spirit*, Presbyt. & Reformed, 1964.
Phillips, C.H., "A Study Regarding the Holy Spirit", published by author, 1952.
Piault, Bernard, *What is the Trinity?*, Hawthorne Books, 1959.
Pink, Arthur W., *The Holy Spirit*, Baker, 1970.
Ramm, Bernard, *The Witness of the Spirit*, Eerdmans, 1960.
Rees, T., *The Holy Spirit in Thought and Experience*, Scribners, 1913.
Reese, Gareth, *Do All Speak in Tongues?/The Joy of the Holy Spirit*, published
   by the author, Central Christian College of the Bible.
Richardson, Cyril C., *The Doctrine of the Trinity*, Abingdon, 1958.
Roberts, Oral, *The Baptism With the Holy Spirit*, published by author, 1964.
Sherrill, John L., *They Speak in Other Tongues*, Fleming H. Revell, 1965.
Shoemaker, Samuel, *With the Holy Spirit and With Fire*, Harper, 1960.
Sloyan, Gerald S., *The Three Persons in One God*, Prentice Hall, 1964.
Smith, Chas. R., *Tongues in Biblical Perspective*, BMH Books, 1951.
Starkey, L.M., *The Holy Spirit at Work in the Church*, Abingdon, 1965.
Stegell, Carroll, *The Modern Tongues and Healing Movement*, published by
   author, 1951.
Strauss, Richard L., *The Bible Speaks About Tongues*, published by author,
   1970.
Thompson, Fred P., *The Holy Spirit: Comforter, Teacher, Guide*, Victor
   Books, 1973.
Torre, R.A., *The Holy Spirit*, Fleming H. Revell, 1927.
Unger, Merrill, *The Baptizing Work of the Holy Spirit*, Dunham, 1967.
Van Duser, Henry P., *Spirit, Son and Father*, Scibners, 1958.
Wallace, Foy, *The Mission and Medium of the Holy Spirit*, published by author,
   1967.
Wight, Francis, *God's Great Gift of the Holy Spirit*, Evangelical Press, 1967.
Winslow, Octavius, *Work of the Holy Spirit*, Banner of Truth, 1961.
Wood, L.J., *The Holy Spirit in the Old Testament*, Zondervan, 1976.
Zartman, Rufus, *The Holy Spirit*, Central Publishing Co., 1930.
Zuck, Roy B., *The Holy Spirit in Your Teaching*, Scripture Press, 1967.